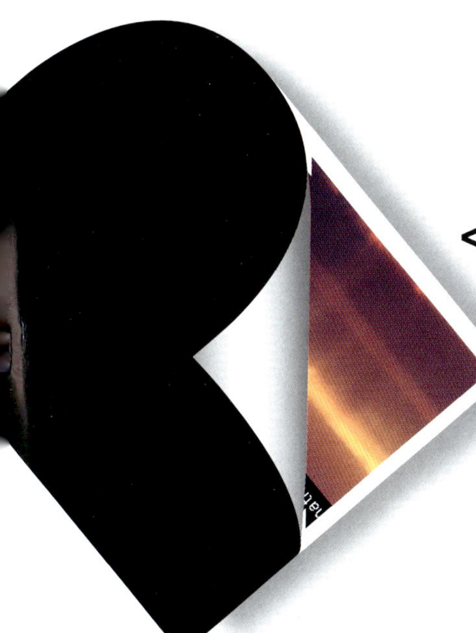

<<< peel back to expose

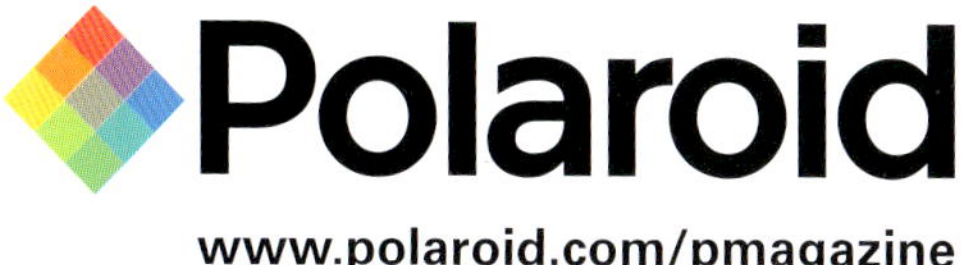

No. 168 / Fall 2002 Aperture

50th Anniversary, Part 1

WORK IN PARTS I AND II BY

Ansel Adams, Robert Adams, Diane Arbus, Richard Avedon, Harry Callahan, Cornell Capa, Robert Capa, Paul Caponigro, Henri Cartier-Bresson, Walter Chappell, Chuck Close, Lois Connor, Gregory Crewdson, Bruce Davidson, Lynn Davis, Mitch Epstein, Barbara Ess, Donna Ferrato, Martine Franck, Masahisa Fukase, Adam Fuss, Gianni Berengo Gardin, Mario Giacomelli, Ralph Gibson, Allen Ginsberg, David Goldblatt, Nan Goldin, Philip Jones Griffiths, Jan Groover, David Hockney, Eikoh Hosoe, Peter Hujar, Graciela Iturbide, Mimmo Jodice, Nicholas K. Kahn and Richard S. Selesnick, Robert Glenn Ketchum, Josef Koudelka, Barbara Kruger, Dorothea Lange, Clarence John Laughlin, Annie Leibovitz, Danny Lyon, Sally Mann, Robert Mapplethorpe, Mary Ellen Mark, Don McCullin, David McDermott and Peter McGough, Ralph Eugene Meatyard, Susan Meiselas, Ray K. Metzker, Duane Michals, Lee Miller, Richard Misrach, Tina Modotti, Inge Morath, Barbara Morgan, Ugo Mulas, Michael Nichols, Nam June Paik, John Pfahl, Pierre et Gilles, Sylvia Plachy, Sigmar Polke, Raghu Rai, Robert Rauschenberg, Eugene Richards, Gerhard Richter, Miguel Rio Branco, Sebastião Salgado, Lise Sarfati, Ferdinando Scianna, Charles Sheeler, Cindy Sherman, Stephen Shore, Raghubir Singh, Clarissa Sligh, W. Eugene Smith, Frederick Sommer, Doug and Mike Starn, Maggie Steber, Chris Steele-Perkins, Joel Sternfeld, Paul Strand, Thomas Struth, Shomei Tomatsu, Larry Towell, Javier Vallhonrat, Nick Waplington, Alex Webb, Brian Weil, Minor White, Garry Winogrand, Joel-Peter Witkin, David Wojnarowicz, Franco Zecchin, and more . . .

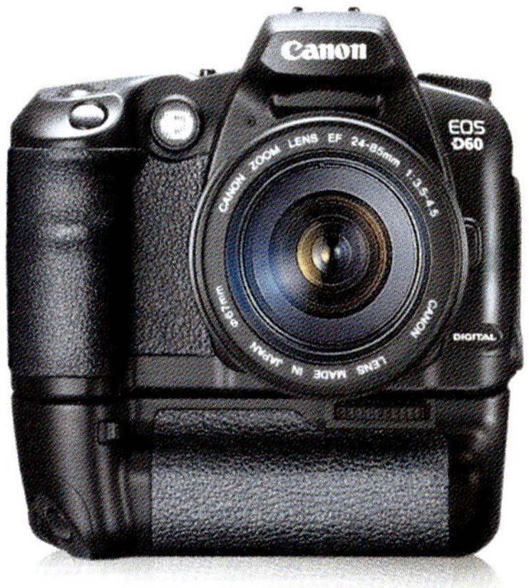

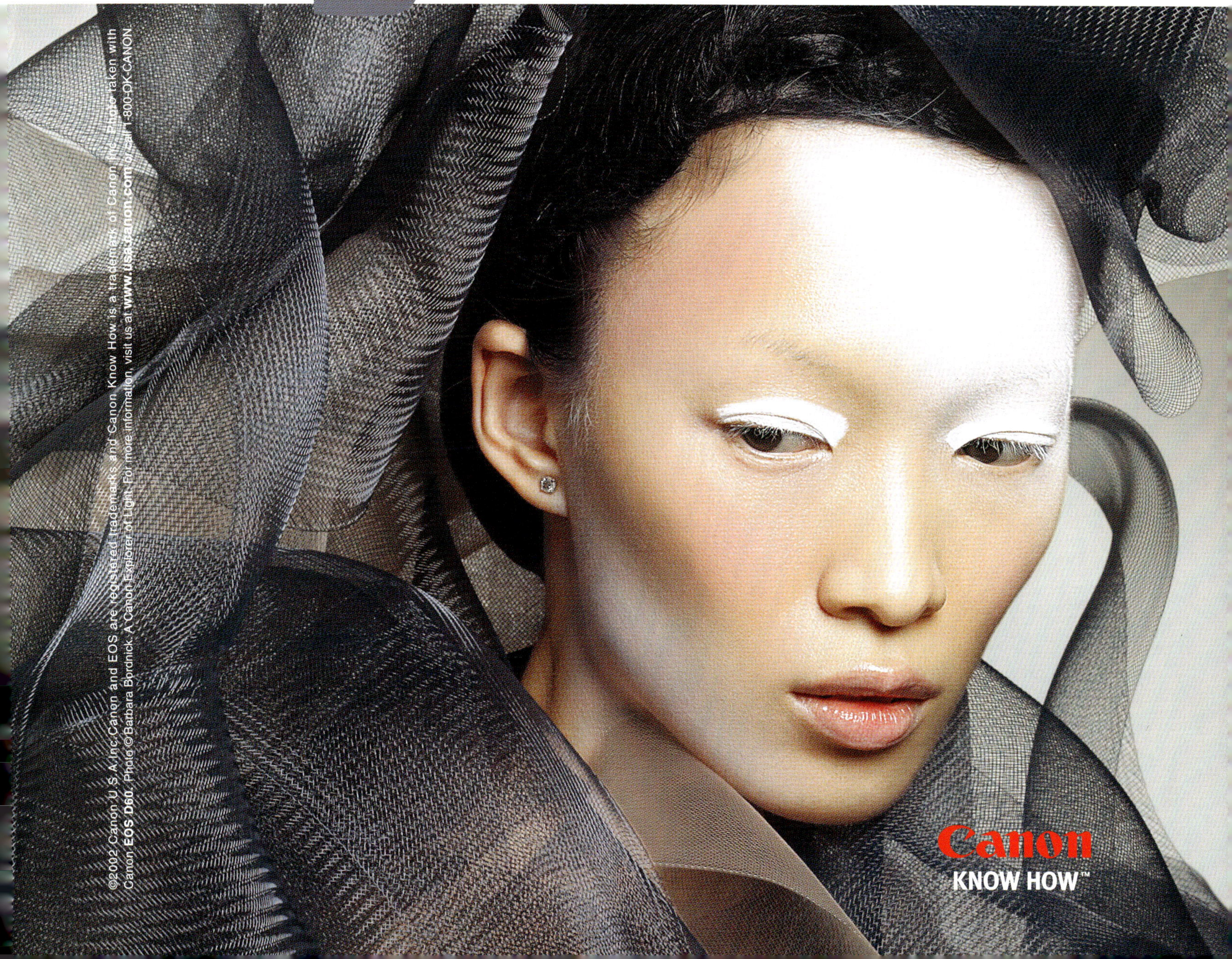

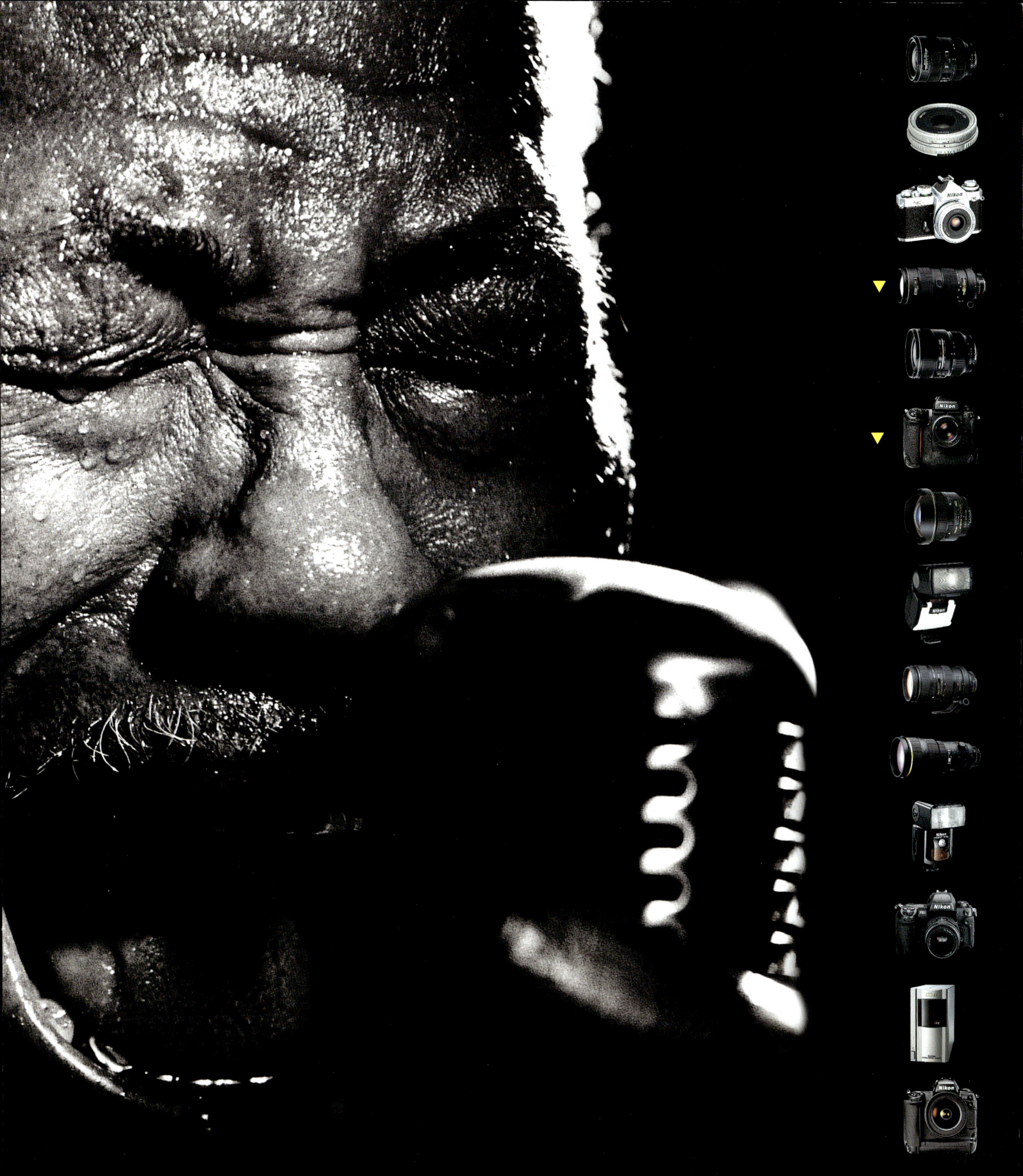

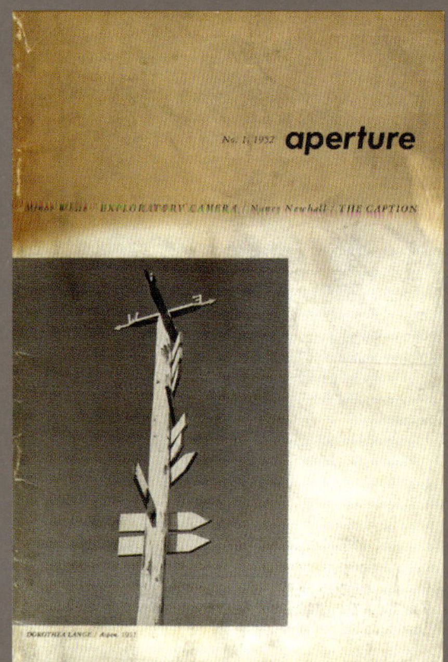

APERTURE has been originated to communicate with serious photographers and creative people everywhere, whether professional, amateur, or student.

Most of the generating ideas in photography now spread through personal contact. Growth can be slow and hard when you are groping alone. It quickens when you meet other photographers who have worked and thought intensively about their medium. You listen, and ask, and a phrase sticks in your memory like a barb. You see a photograph that blazes with significance. Suddenly a way of working, dim till then, comes clear before you.

Every photographer who is a master of his medium has evolved a philosophy from such experiences; and whether we agree or not, his thoughts act like a catalyst on our own—he has contributed to dynamic ideas of our time. Only rarely do such concepts get written down clearly and in a form where photographers scattered all over the earth may see them and look at the photographs that are their ultimate expression.

Aperture is intended to be a mature journal in which photographers can talk straight to each other, discuss the problems that face photography as profession and art, share their experiences, comment on what goes on, descry the new potentials. We, who have founded this journal, invite others to use *Aperture* as a common ground for the advancement of photography.

signed

MINOR WHITE, DOROTHEA LANGE, NANCY NEWHALL, ANSEL ADAMS,
BEAUMONT NEWHALL, BARBARA MORGAN, ERNEST LOUIE, MELTON FERRIS, DODY WARREN

"About *Aperture*," Founders' statement, *Aperture* vol. 1, no. 1, 1952

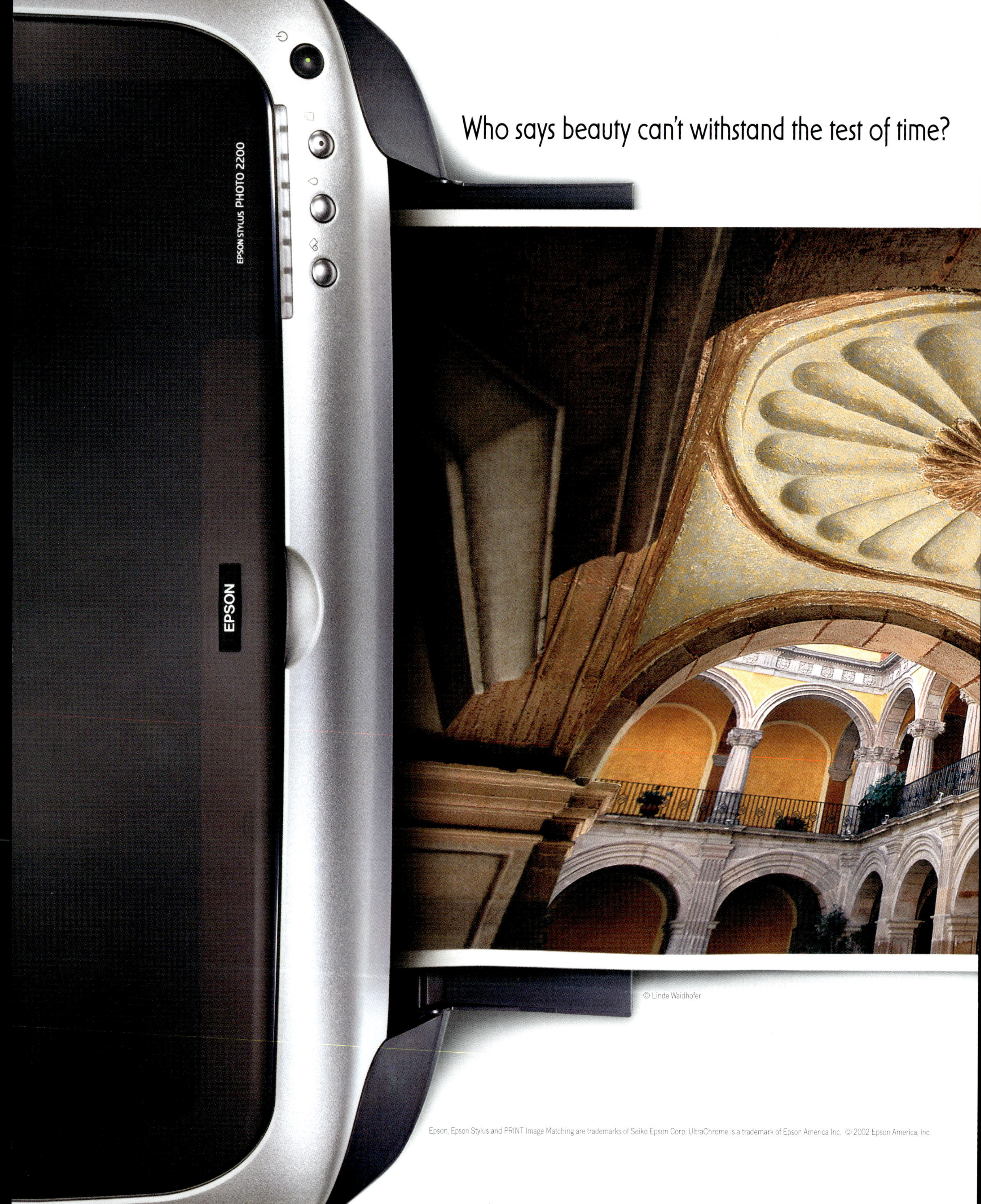

Who says beauty can't withstand the test of time?
EPSON STYLUS PHOTO 2200
EPSON
© Linde Waidhofer
Epson, Epson Stylus and PRINT Image Matching are trademarks of Seiko Epson Corp. UltraChrome is a trademark of Epson America Inc. © 2002 Epson America, Inc.

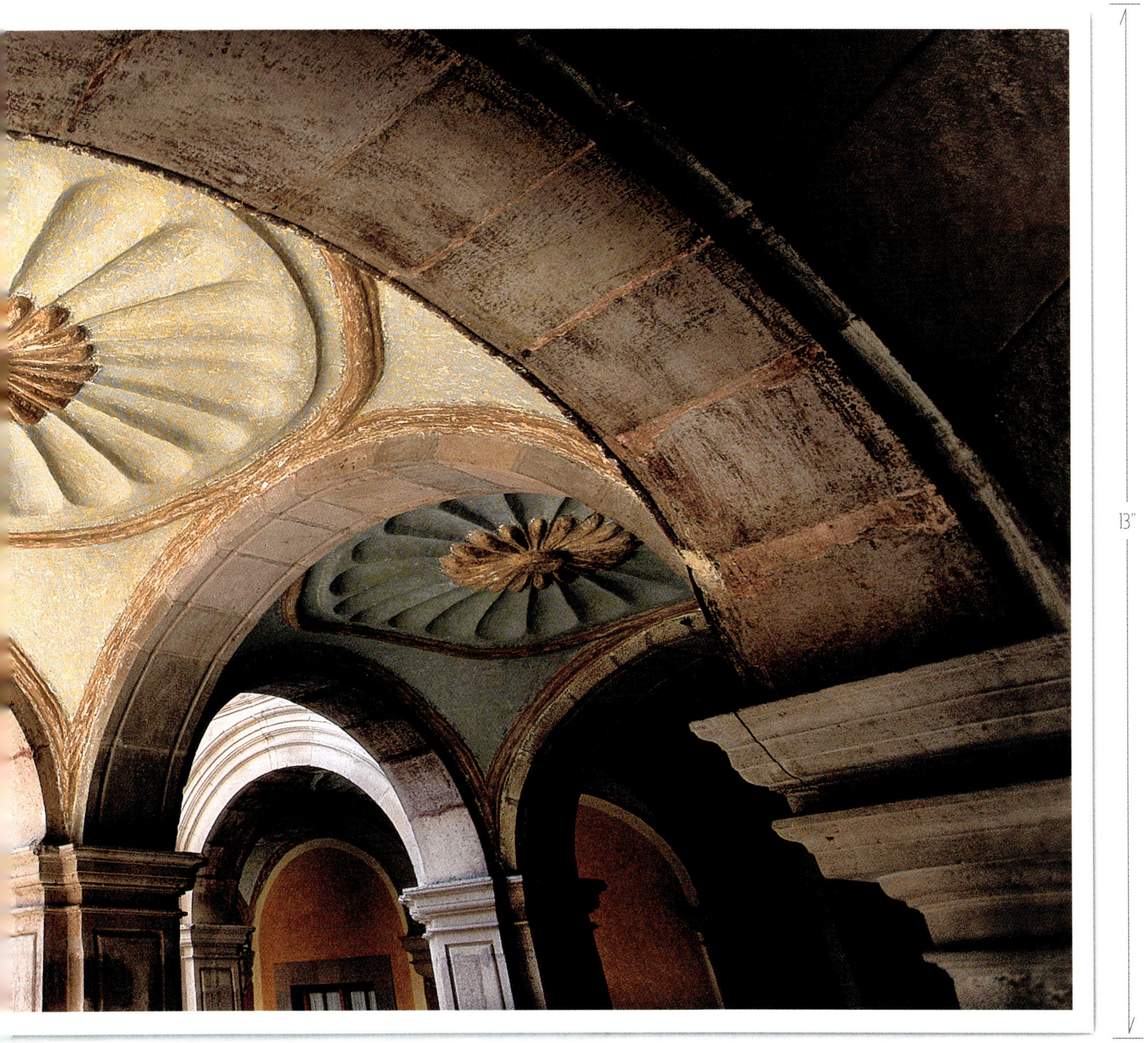

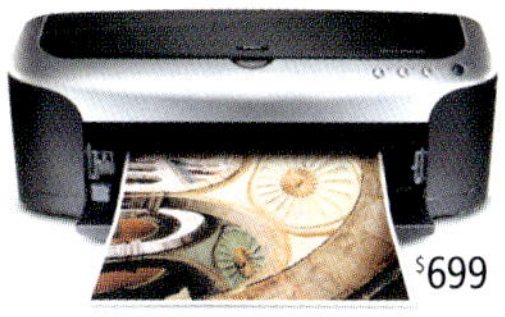

Aperture's 50th Anniversary Founders and Friends Portfolio

The Aperture Founders and Friends Portfolio brings together the seminal work of five masters of photography, linked to Aperture's history, in one portfolio for the first time. Commemorating the convergence of the original visionaries who founded Aperture and fostered it in its earliest incarnations, this deluxe portfolio of unparalleled images from three founders and two dear friends of Aperture — Dorothea Lange, Barbara Morgan, Paul Strand, Edward Weston, and *Aperture*'s first Editor-in-Chief, Minor White — is limited to an edition of 100 and is certain to be a treasured collector's item.

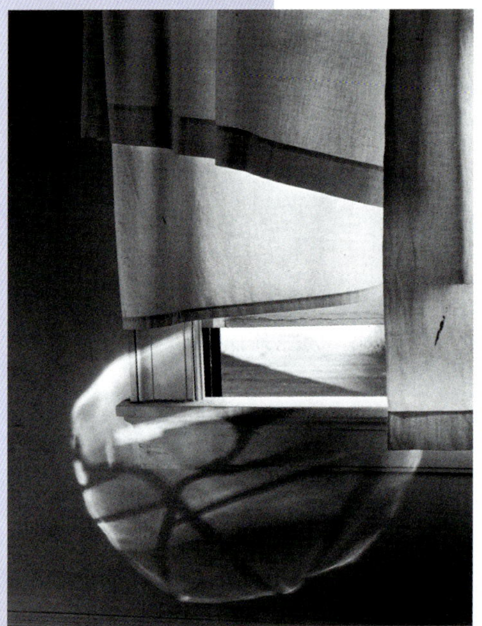

Minor White, Windowsill Daydreaming, Rochester, New York, July, 1958

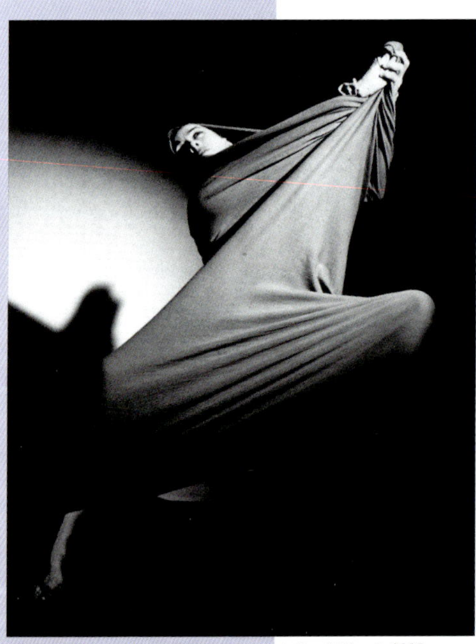

Barbara Morgan, Martha Graham, Lamentation (oblique), 1935

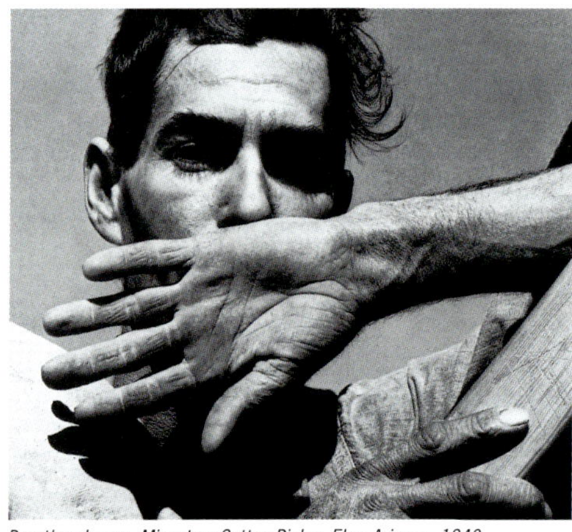

Dorothea Lange, Migratory Cotton Picker, Eloy, Arizona, 1940

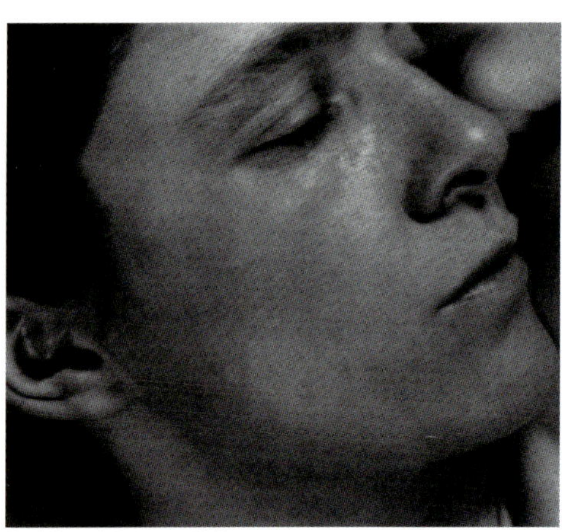

Paul Strand, Rebecca, 1923

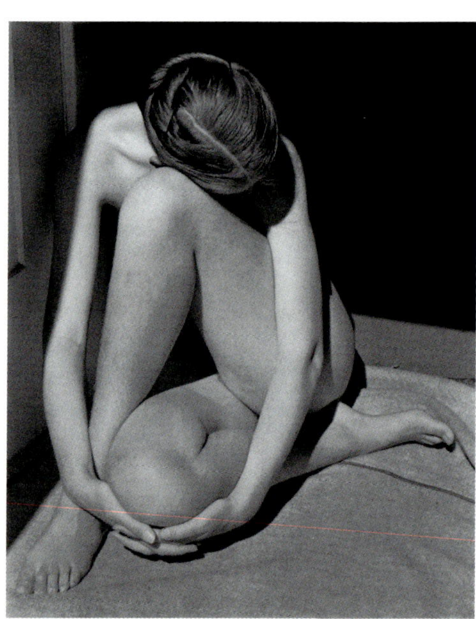

Edward Weston, Charis, 1936

- Each image is printed by premier platinum-palladium printer Sal Lopes
- The edition is limited to 100 portfolios plus 16 atrists' proofs
- Each print bears the official seal of its respective estate
- Packaged in a deluxe clamshell case
- Accompanied by four text panels of the eloquent writing of Beaumont and Nancy Newhall

For inquiries and additional information on *Aperture's Founders and Friends Portfolio*, please call **(800) 929-2323 ext. 414**

To order or receive information on Aperture Foundation's complete list of titles, limited-edition prints and portfolios, or traveling exhibitions, please call toll-free **(800) 929-2323 ext. 414**, fax **(212) 598-4015**, or visit **www.aperture.org**.

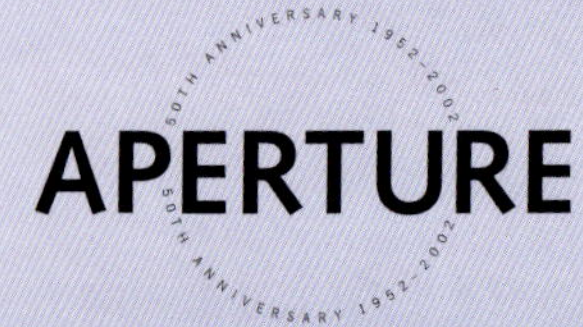

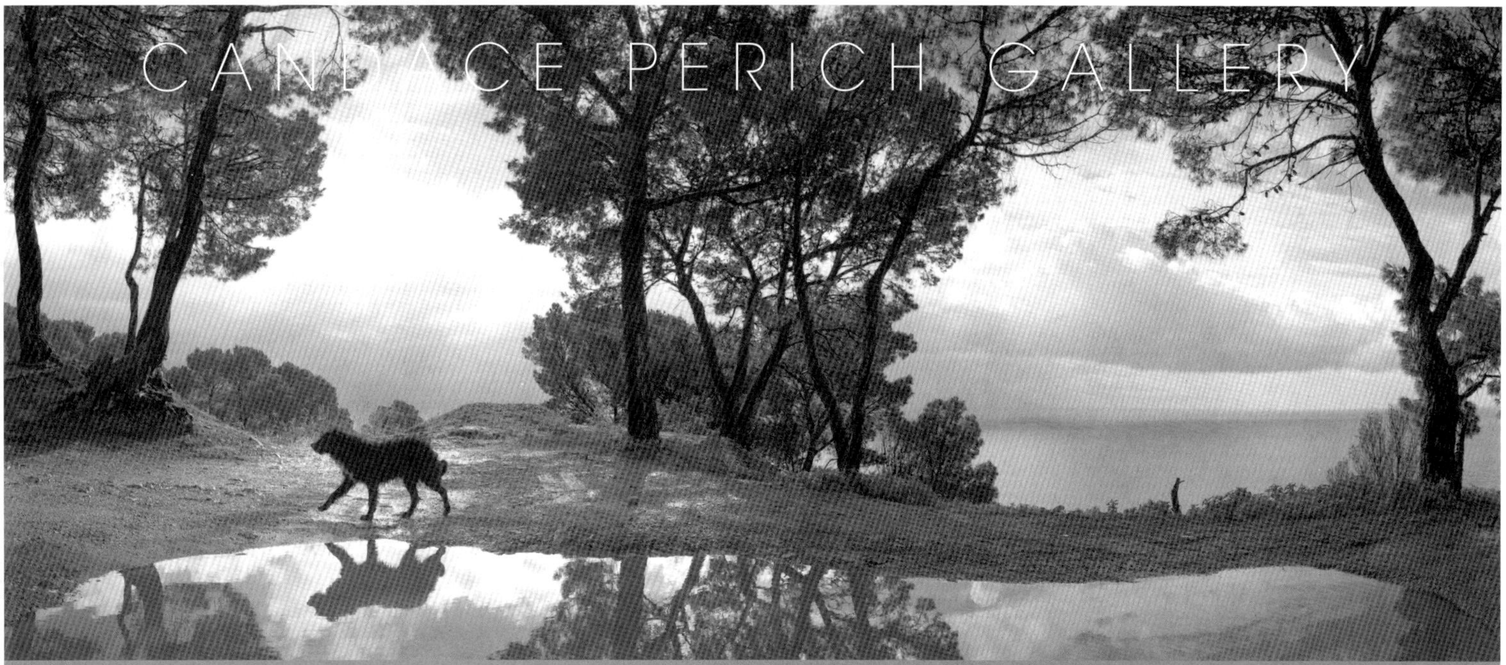

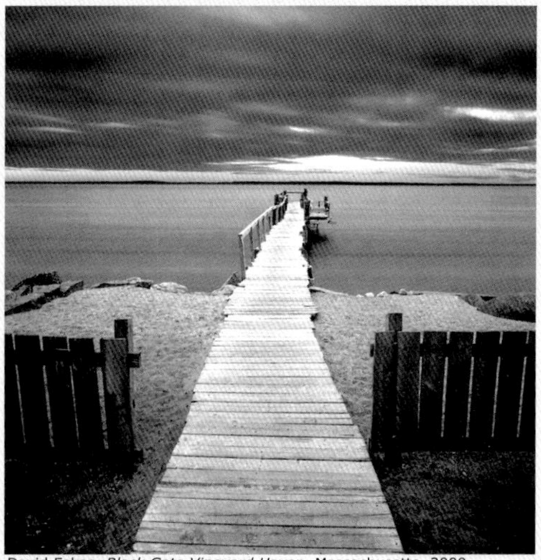

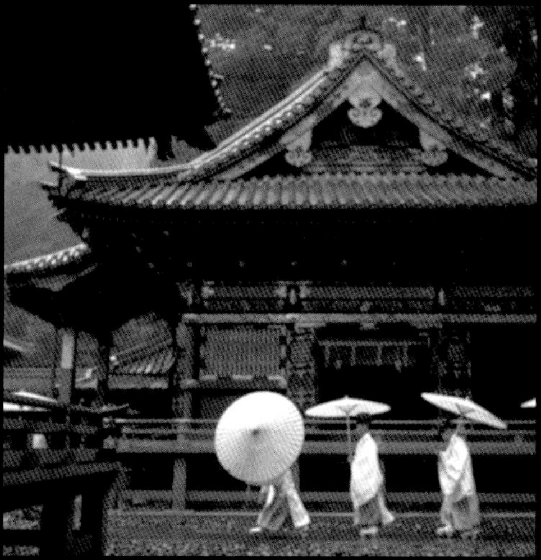

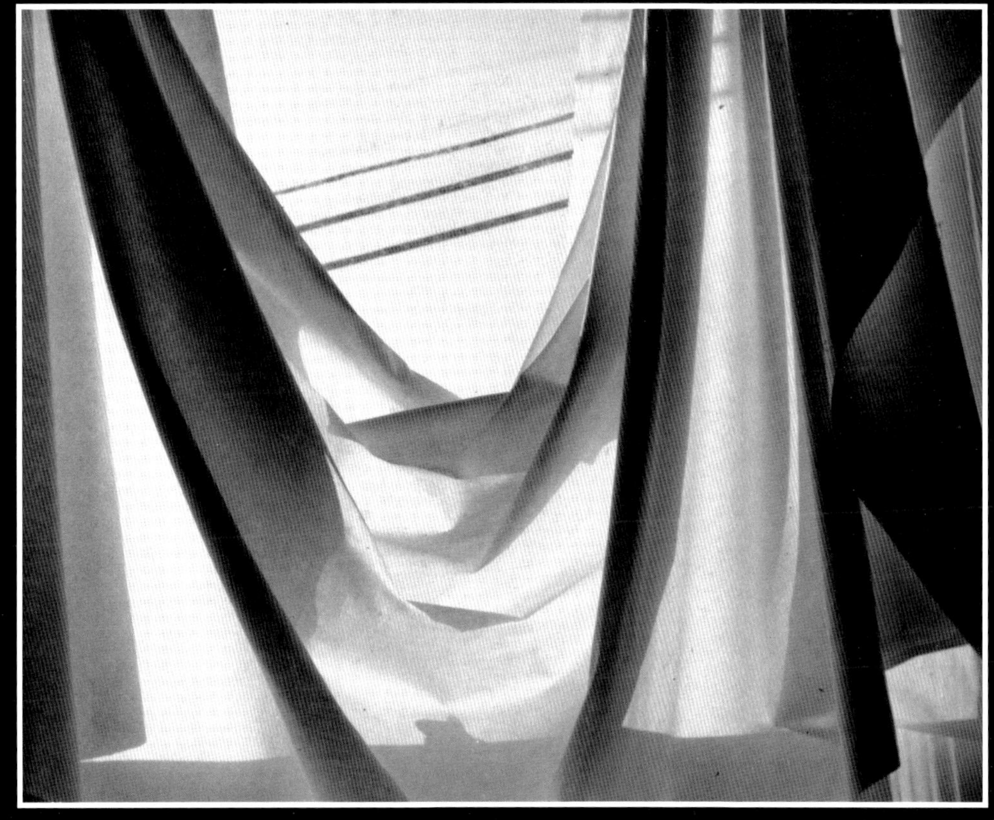

Minor White, *Window, Easter Sunday*, 1963

stepping through the ashes

PHOTOGRAPHS BY Eugene Richards **INTERVIEWS BY Janine Altongy**

"Richards is a great photographer, a sensitive and fearless witness to and commentator on the contemporary plagues of the human condition."

—Cornell Capa

"The fenced-in site of the World Trade Center has been largely dealt with as a crime scene, as a 'marvel' of destruction, or as the tourist attraction it is fast becoming. What I see when I stare downtown is an ever-evolving repository for the missing, a focal point for grieving, for remembering, for reflection, for self-examination."

—Eugene Richards

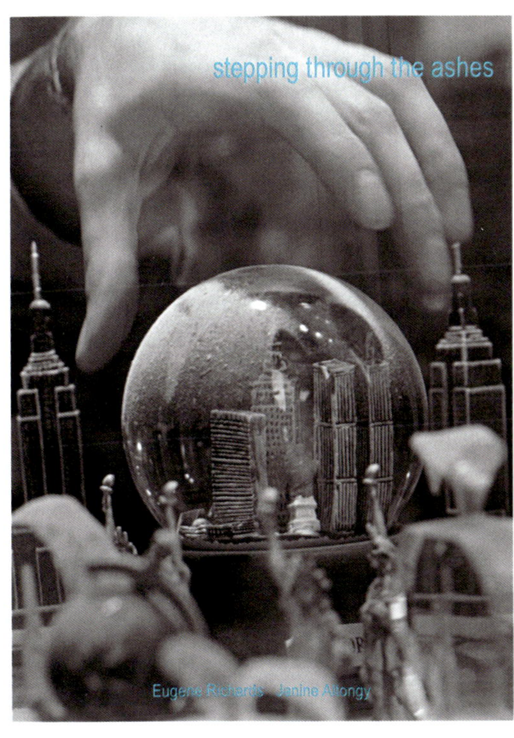

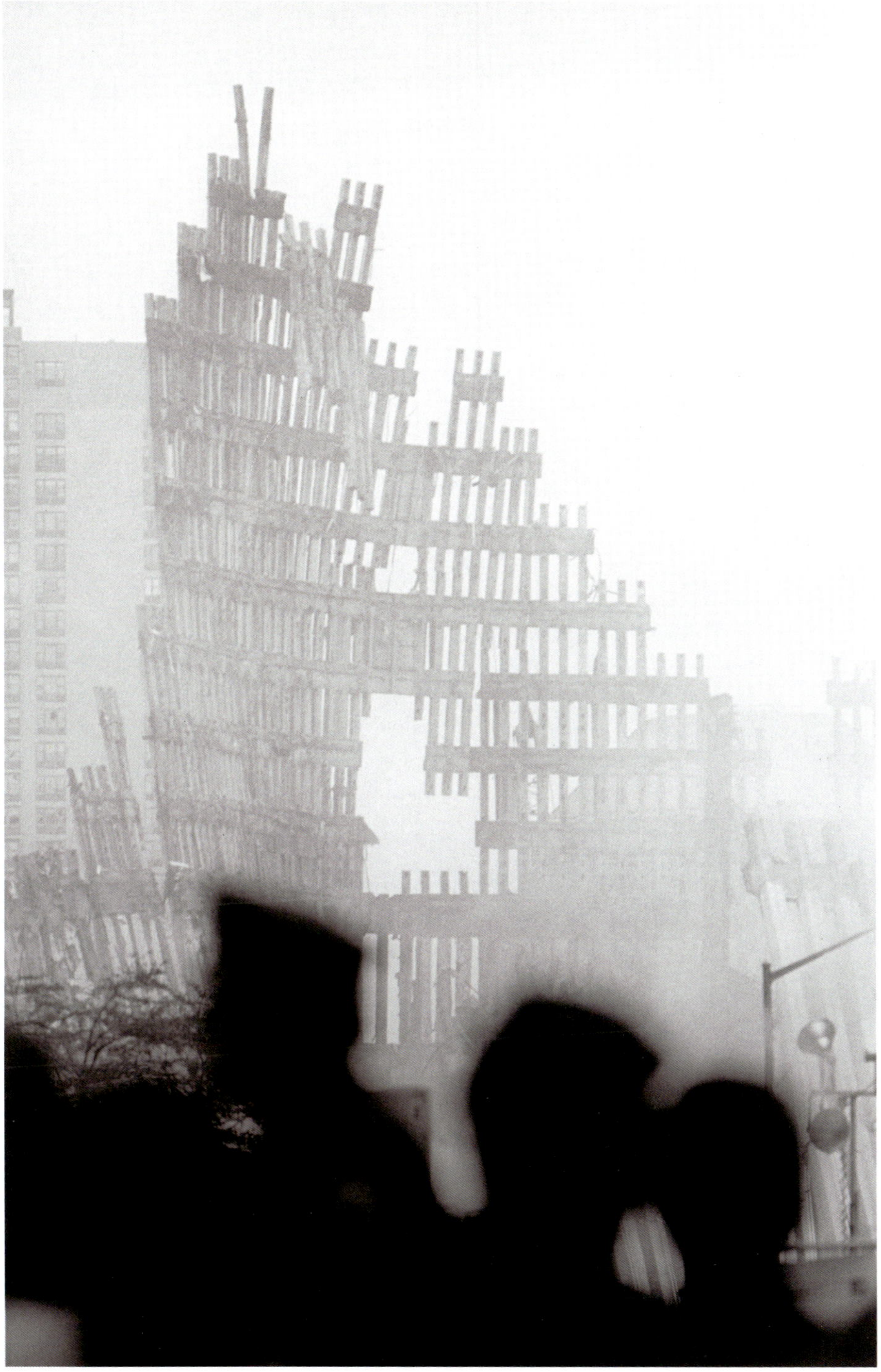

THESE OFTEN METAPHORICAL IMAGES ARE ACCOMPANIED BY INTERVIEWS WITH SOME OF THE FAMILIES WHO LOST SONS, DAUGHTERS, HUSBANDS, WIVES, MOTHERS, AND FATHERS ON SEPTEMBER 11, 2001.

100 duotone images; 9½ x 11½ inches, 192 pages; Hardcover ISBN: 1-931788-01-4, $40.00. Available to order from Aperture, August 1, 2002.

An exhibition of images from *Stepping Through the Ashes* will be presented in Aperture's Burden Gallery from September 4 through October 4, 2002.

Stepping Through the Ashes is made possible in part by the NPPA/Nikon Sabbatical Grant and Many Voices, Inc. Additional support for the Aperture exhibition was provided by The Honickman Foundation.

EDITOR'S NOTE

DEDICATED TO MINOR WHITE (1908–1976) AND MICHAEL E. HOFFMAN (1942–2001)

In 1952, Minor White, Beaumont and Nancy Newhall, Ansel Adams, Dorothea Lange, Barbara Morgan, and others joined forces to create a journal whose impact and longevity they could never have anticipated. Like a force of nature, *Aperture* magazine—having weathered everything from financial difficulties, censorious assaults, attacks from the left and right, every imaginable photographic style, a myriad of spiritual impulses, a group of editors with strong and eclectic sensibilities, three formats, a broad range of themes, ethnic and national focuses, an extraordinary roster of writers, and most recently a complete redesign—is fifty years old. Through sheer will, dedication, and most importantly vision—first Minor White's and then Michael E. Hoffman's—*Aperture* not only survived, it flourished and metamorphosed into a worldwide book-publishing and exhibitions program as well.

So, how to celebrate Aperture at fifty? A "past*forward*" perspective seemed like an inclusive approach. And so, in this issue of the magazine and the next, we cast a look back over our own history—which in many ways has both mirrored and helped to determine the evolution of the medium—in order to understand our present, all the while maintaining an eye toward the future. This is not so much a retrospective as it is a kind of timeless, experiential reunion of photographers and writers, as reflected in the non-chronological sequencing of images and words. Rather than working in a linear mode, we have chosen to offer many entry points, contexts, and, we hope, new ways of looking. You will find excerpts and page spreads from fifty years of issues and books, which reveal how Aperture, in all of its projects, has continuously rethought and reinterpreted the varied aesthetic and social paths set forth by the Founders.

We are celebrating the photographers of Aperture's community in some instances through

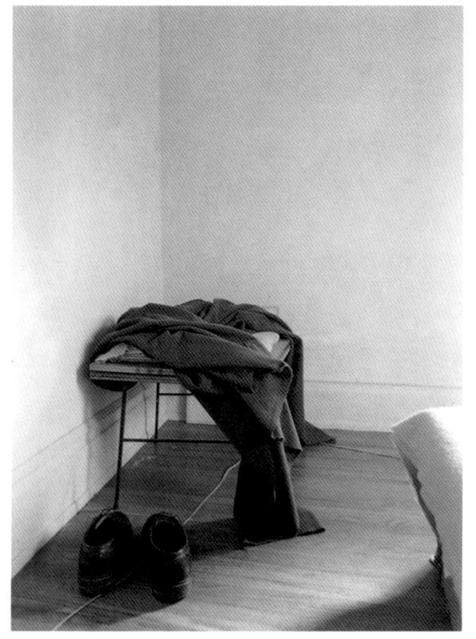

Minor White (below), his bedroom (above), and interior of his apartment (bottom) in Rochester, New York, 1962. Photographs by Stevan A. Baron.

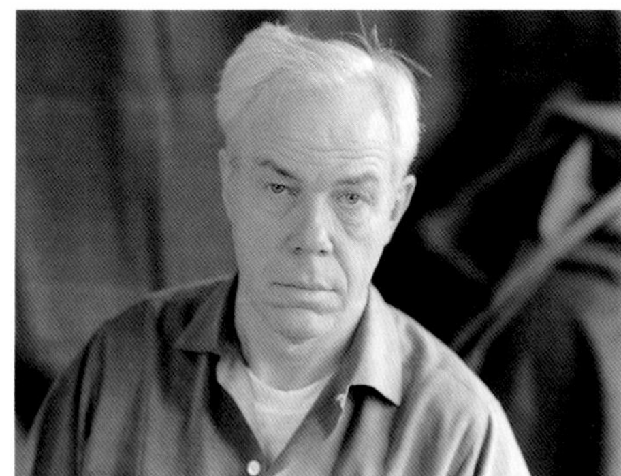

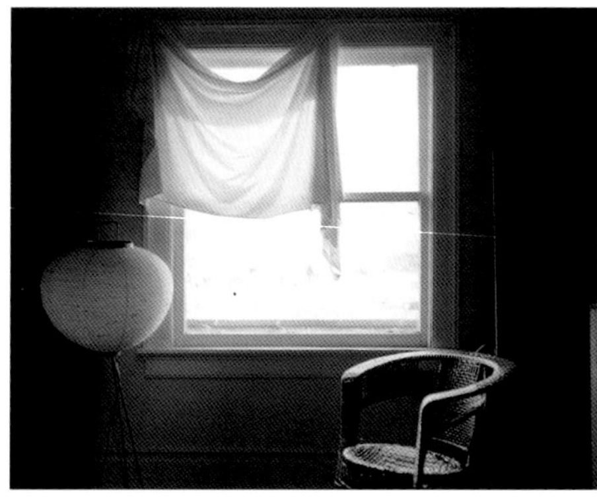

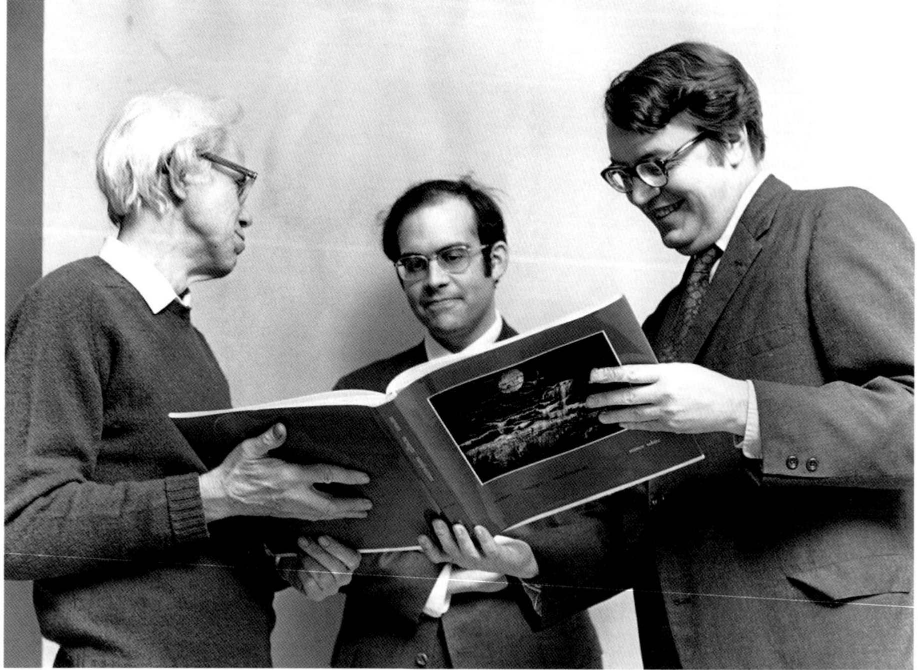

Minor White, Michael E. Hoffman, and Evan Turner, Director of the Philadelphia Museum of Art, during the hanging of "The Circle, Square, and Triangle" at the museum, 1970.

iconic images, and in others with new work that has not been previously published. In all cases, this project has been a collaborative one; many of the photographers themselves selected the work they wished us to feature, others responded enthusiastically to our suggested images. So many have expressed to us their appreciation of Aperture's influence and uniqueness, sharing their "I saw it in *Aperture* first" stories.

The untimely death of Michael E. Hoffman in November 2001, while our work on "the fiftieth" was in process, put a tragic cast on this milestone, as we expected to celebrate together with him. These two issues are dedicated to Michael and to Minor, with love, respect, admiration, and gratitude for the phenomenal devotion, energy, and years they gave to Aperture.

For their extraordinary and ongoing grace under pressure, and strength during a most difficult period, I thank Wendy Byrne, Diana C. Stoll, and Richard H. Cravens—exceptional friends and collaborators—as well as all of the remarkable photographers who have worked so closely with us on this and so many other projects. The staff at Aperture has been wonderful and supportive, as always, and then there is the community at large: past editors, curators, agencies, galleries, estates . . . we have truly harassed everyone with requests for images, fact-checking, picture research and more—thank you all.

Finally, all of us wish to thank our subscribers and readers, our larger "community of interest"—a concept so important to Michael—for your encouragement, good humor, intelligence, tolerance, open-mindedness, and generosity of spirit. Without you and your support, this birthday would have been inconceivable.

—Melissa Harris

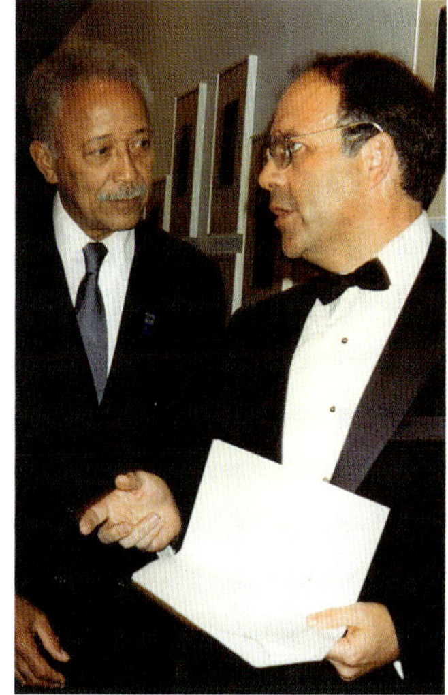

ABOVE: New York's Mayor David Dinkins joins Michael E. Hoffman at Aperture's Annual Appeal dinner, 1990.
BELOW: Michael E. Hoffman with His Holiness the Dalai Lama and Matthieu Ricard in Dharamsala, India, ca. 1995.

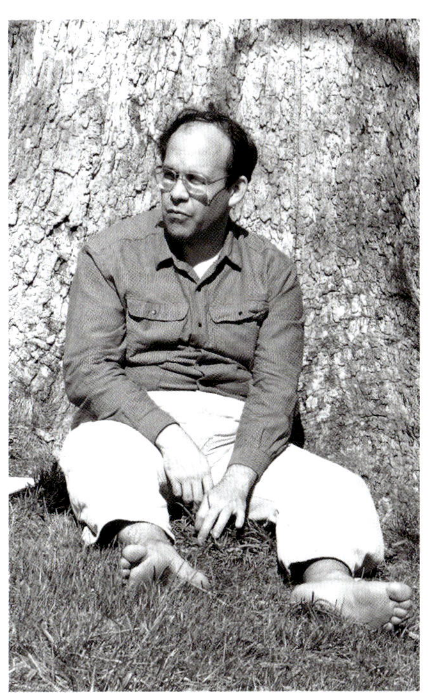

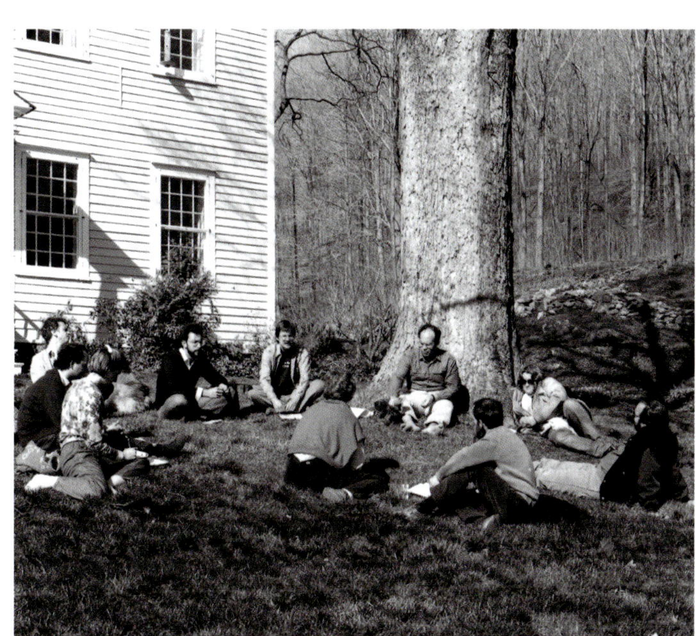

Aperture's senior staff, led by Michael E. Hoffman, meets in Shekomeko, New York, 1985, to work on plans for the future.

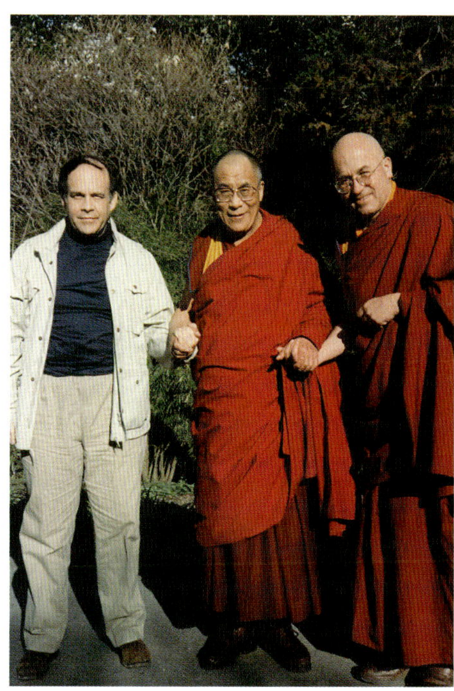

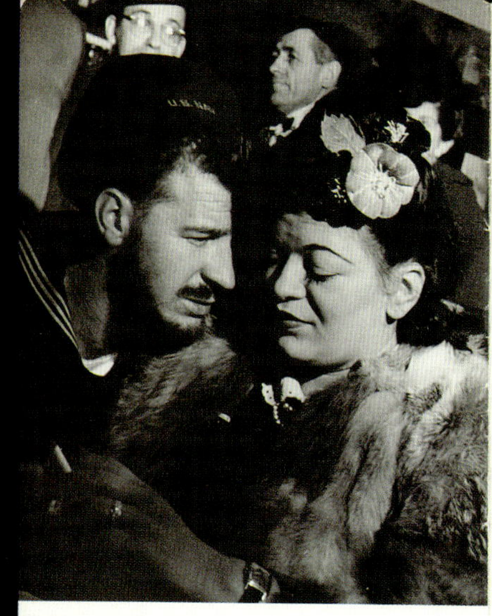

LISETTE MODEL / *Sammy's Bar, New York*

minor white / EXPLORATORY CAMERA

A RATIONALE FOR THE MINIATURE CAMERA

This rationale or working method for the miniature camera is one of discovery. One of using the accidental intelligently; one of treating the camera as an investigating tool to uncover the emotional blind spots of the prejudiced human eye.

To clear the way for discussion two main points need to be made. 1 If photography is to be an extension of vision each type of camera needs to be fully exploited for its unique possibilities, consequently thruout this paper an exaggerated distinction between view and miniature camera technique is kept. 2 The growth of any rationale can be outlined thus:

First, a rationale is firmly grounded in a specific camera, specific film, developers, paper, and so on.

Second, it grows out of technique. "Technique" will be considered a welding of tools and processes and the man into a working unit. During this welding process several things happen to man, tools, and processes. At first the tools temporarily block his expressiveness – just as the conscious phases of any learning process does. Any photographer working out an esthetic for himself is, to start, under the influence, if not the control of the specific instruments and procedures. Such influence is beneficial for during this time the tools, by force of their inanimate limits, powerfully channel or focus the man's ordinarily diffuse seeing. Then, as he masters the equipment and processes, as he absorbs their influence, the channeling is reversed – he gives direction to the medium. Out of this interaction of tools, processes, and man which becomes a technique or working unit, the rationale, or working method, also develops. The rationale is the man's own central and long term direction.

The exploratory rationale presented here is the working method one man developed for the miniature camera. It treats the camera as a research tool for the creative photographer. There are several places in the photographic cycle (or spiral) where tools, processes, and analysis of prints can affect the total rationale, or where the exploratory role of the miniature camera can be put into effect. These are: The *Exposure-Development* phase which is terminated in the negative. The *Printing* phase which ends with a set of fine photographs or reproductions. The *Display* phase which

Visions & Voices

A CELEBRATION OF GENIUS IN PHOTOGRAPH

By R. H. CRAVENS

ARCHIVE

Romancing Edward

Love letters to Edward Weston

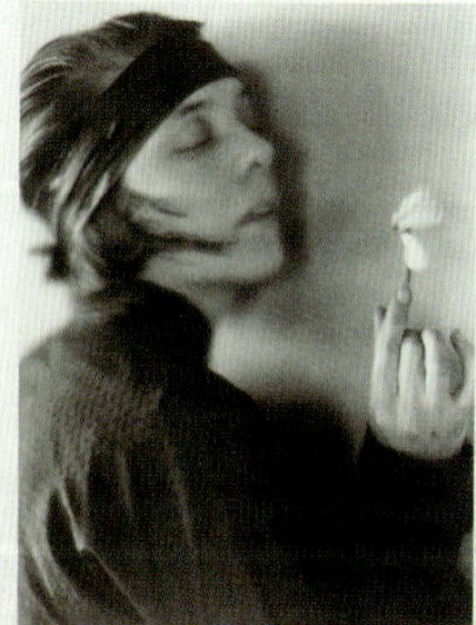

Edward Weston's public self-portrait has nearly always been based on his *Daybooks*—the diaries he kept from 1922 until 1934, writing at 5 A.M. each morning, fueled by a pot of strong coffee. Before the *Daybooks* were published (in two volumes, the first in 1961 and the second in 1966), the originals were brusquely censored by their author's own razorblade; Weston removed entire sections, or sliced out passages leaving windowlike holes in the pages. In these edited journals, a curious, not altogether endearing picture of the artist emerges, one that is sometimes deeply compassionate and other times strident and hyper-declarative. What also becomes clear, though, is that Weston was wonderfully engaged with his work, his love life, and the world at large. In the Weston archive at Tuscon's Center for Creative Photography, however, a more easily alluring Edward Weston surfaces. Along with the Center's vast holdings of his negatives and original prints, there is a carefully preserved collection of Weston's letters, each cataloged along with its own whimsical enclosures: all the romantic ephemera—pressed wisteria blossoms, bamboo leaves, paper wisps of Chinese fortune-cookie predictions—that were once tucked into precious billets-doux are now annotated and painstakingly preserved in museum-quality, acid-free envelopes.

Weston's own writing is rapturous and uninhibited. "Moskowski's Bolero!" he swoons in one of the letters. "I found it just now—I was swept away from the present—carried back in a surge of desire to those moments when you danced to its impassioned rhythms—I heard again the swish of your white kimono—and saw again the gleam of its brilliant textures—gliding—shifting—swirling against the golden gloom of my half lit walls—" Weston was acclaimed as a fabulous dance partner; his words, redolent of ambrosial nights and sensual pleasures, perform a seductive tango all their own. The letters selected here were all written during the years between the World Wars, a time when Los Angeles was considered the newest city in the world; their authors were part of Southern California's first avant-garde. The women observed in Weston's charismatic photographs—the crouching torqued knees, a dreamy profile lost in reverie—were bohemian modernists who openly expressed their political views, artistic and spiritual doubts, and individual freedom. They were variously Weston's studio partners and colleagues, paramours and models: the photographers Margarethe Mather and Tina Modotti, the artists Xenia Kashevaroff and Beatrice Wood, and the dancer Bertha Bruton Wardell. Mather, an ethereal beauty, was a

Introduction by Susan Morgan

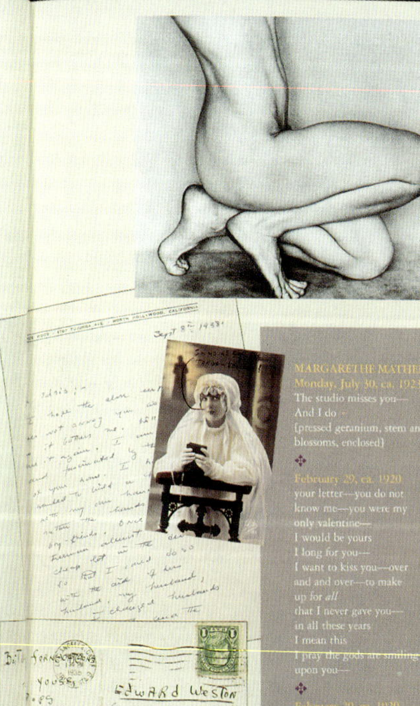

MARGARETHE MATHER
Monday, July 30, ca. 1923
The studio misses you—
And I do –
{pressed geranium, stem and blossoms, enclosed}

✣

February 29, ca. 1920
your letter—you do not
know me—you were my
only valentine—
I would be yours
I long for you—
I want to kiss you—over
and and over—to make
up for *all*
that I never gave you—
in all these years
I mean this
I pray the gods are smiling
upon you—

✣

February 29, ca. 1920
You were in a dream
last night—and now the
day brings only ghosts and I sicken
with fear—and doubt—
this—when in my heart—
a drift of jonquils that I long
to leave at your door—

BERTHA BRUTON WARDELL
My very dear Edward
It makes me so happy to hear from you. And I am not ashamed of my emotions. I quite glory in them as you—pagan yourself, well know. Not seeing you, I must have forgotten how completely trustworthy you are are. So keep the letters or not as you think best—anyway they are yours. If women are changeable perhaps sometimes they can change for the better.

Olga Stack has a book on George Moore which she wishes sent you—to settle an argument which you and she once had in regard to GM's appearance.... Peter Krasnow's exhibit is very moving. The portrait of you has wishfulness which is like you though you also have a slightly Russian Jewish aspect in it which is unfamiliar. The wood carving I would enjoy licking and rubbing my cheek against as well as tucking under my arm to have as my own. How interesting to look from Peter's portraits so elongated to Rivera's painting just out the door so rotund.

Frantie's watercolors are quite astonishing. She is in violent rebellion against the dictates of the art school which she is attending once a week. But as she says—I am learning to use a brush!

✣

July 26, 1923
To Edward Weston
On his way to new lands
Dear, I cannot get it thru my head that you are really going away to another country. My feeling for you has not been a transient whimsy.

TINA MODOTTI
December 26, 1924
Edward—Of all the different emotions which I feel tonight for you not one can be put into words—I have formulated in my mind & then

PART I

Prescient Beginnings

Susceptibility to the highest forces is the highest genius.
—The Education of Henry Adams

PROLOGUE

Aperture began with a few profoundly gifted individuals possessed of lofty ideals, high ambition, and no money, who created a humble photography journal with the life expectancy of a hamster—and not a particularly healthy one.

That its golden anniversary is herewith celebrated is little short of a miracle.

The fifty years accounts for the publication of a quarterly periodical. But it also embraces the subsequent publication of books—nearly five hundred of them; an archive of thousands of original, some near-priceless prints; exquisite reproductions of masterpieces for collectors; an educational program for interns; and Aperture's Burden Gallery in Manhattan, at the 23rd Street headquarters. But thinking merely in terms of a half-century is misleading.

In the pages of Aperture publications appear glimpses of the entire history of the medium, reaching back to its beginnings—the French and English inventors of photography in the late 1830s. From there the image makers represented move through the great Victorians and the twentieth-century masters and innovators right up to photographers at work in the twenty-first century, just before this monograph went to press. The succession of what might be called critical phases advances from Pictorialism, Photo-Secession, "Group 64," Modernism, Postmodernism, and so on, and ranges over descriptive labels such as "purist," "landscape," "surreal," "abstract," "documentary," "mystical," and so on and so on more. Technically, it is a span of imagery from daguerreotype to digital.

Chronologies are mostly irrelevant, however, because photography is the medium that poses conundrums of time. Images as sequenced in the ensuing pages reveal time past and time present, intersecting with hints of time future in chartless rhythms of non-Euclidean history. There is a deeper impulse among these photographs. Each was brought forth by an artist who captured a moment reflective of both inner and outer realities. These are visionary moments that have entered into and altered the psyche of viewers, becoming part of that portfolio of the mind each of us carries about. And each image, through time, contains a history, some essence of its maker.

OPPOSITE TOP: *Aperture* vol. 1, no. 1, 1952, pages 4–5: photograph by Lisette Model. **OPPOSITE BOTTOM:** *Aperture* 159, 2000, pages 20–21: photographs by Edward Weston. **NOTE TO READERS:** *Aperture*'s system of numbering issues underwent a change in 1975, when *Aperture* vol. 19, no. 4 was followed by Aperture 77; all subsequent issues are numbered consecutively, from 77 on.

While thousands of artists, writers, skilled craftsmen, and supporters have sustained Aperture over the years, the improbable fact of its survival is due primarily to one man: Michael E. Hoffman. He kept it going through most of the last four decades: through official closure, the brink of bankruptcy, personal tragedy, and an endless search for the means to continue. In other words, through capacious ability and sheer willpower. And if this not-for-profit foundation has never prospered in a financial sense, Aperture thrives. No one would be more surprised than the people who created it, who are now referred to in rather stately fashion as "The Founders."

Time present and time past
Are both perhaps present in time future
And time future contained in time past
—T. S. Eliot, *Four Quartets*

After an uproarious spring evening in 1952 of talk, music, and drink, nine people gathered in the living room of a frame house with a view of the San Francisco Bay. Their goal was to bring to life an idea—long simmering among several of those present—for a journal devoted to a particular vision of photography. One

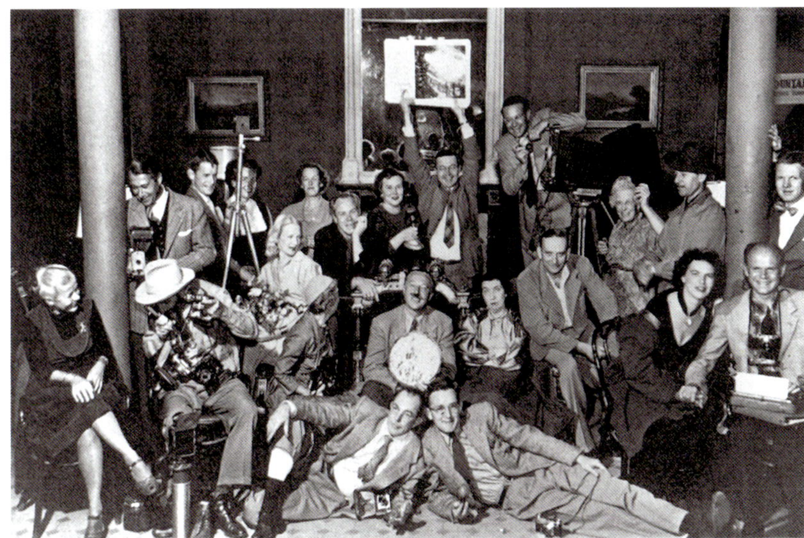

The Aspen Conference at which *Aperture* was first conceived; pictured are the Founders, including Minor White, Ansel Adams, Barbara Morgan, Nancy Newhall, Beaumont Newhall, and others, 1951. Photograph by Ferenc Berko.

wishes the scene might have been recorded, because despite a shared affinity for the subject, those present seldom agreed on much. Chief among them:

ANSEL ADAMS: The host, with his wife, Virginia. Born 1902 in Carson City, Nevada, Adams was America's best-known landscape photographer, an acknowledged master of camera and darkroom technique, and a foremost applied theoretician, whose Zone System of meticulous light-measurement and printing would become a cornerstone of photography education. The son of an avowed Emersonian transcendentalist, Adams had intended to be a concert pianist—a dream he never quite gave up. He subsequently was one of the country's foremost environmentalists and a founder of the Sierra Club.

DOROTHEA LANGE: Her name had become a virtual glyph for the term "documentary photographer." Born 1895 in Hoboken, New Jersey, and struck in childhood by polio that left her with a lifelong limp, Lange had become a fashionable San Francisco portrait photographer by the time she was twenty-five. The Depression called forth her genius. With her second husband, the social scientist Paul Taylor, she traveled tens of thousands of miles for the Farm Security Administration (FSA), recording the plight of farmers, migrants, and breadline unemployed. Her portrait *Migrant Mother*, of a destitute woman with two small children, became one of the most reproduced photographs of the twentieth century. Passionately engaged, Lange was to battle to the end of her life for a photography committed to documenting the enormous changes in the American social landscape.

BARBARA MORGAN: Born 1900 in Buffalo, Kansas, she was raised in Southern California and early in her studies fell under the spell of the concept of "rhythmic vitality" enshrined in the Chinese Six Canons of Painting. Unquestionably the greatest dance photographer in the medium's history—her collaboration with Martha Graham extended over sixty years—Morgan possessed a breadth of philosophical and intellectual interest, as well as being the most protean of photographers. She was self-described as a "kinetic light-sculptor," and her light drawings, double exposures, and photomontages ranged from emotionally charged insight to deft satire—all devoted to her ultimate intent of an "authentic response to life."

BEAUMONT NEWHALL: Scholar and historian, born 1908 in the seacoast village of Lynn, Massachusetts, he was a Harvard-trained art historian and medievalist. Hired as a librarian by Alfred Barr, director of New York's Museum of Modern Art, Newhall went on to create there the first photography department of any American museum, and curated groundbreaking exhibitions in the latter half of the 1930s. Ever anxious about his overly dry, academic approach to the subject, Newhall nonetheless experienced in the most dramatic fashion the power of photography—the selection of human targets and images of the aftermath—when he was assigned to aerial reconnaissance in Europe during World War II. He later created the first American museum of photography at the George Eastman House in Rochester, New York, and among his prolific writings are the classic *History of Photography* and *Focus: Memoirs of a Life in Photography*.

NANCY NEWHALL: Born the same year as Beaumont in Swampscott, a town adjacent to Lynn, she was a painter who later was to say of their marriage in 1936, "When I married Beaumont I married photography." Nancy was among the most gifted writers and undeniably the finest literary editor in the medium in the twentieth century, with accomplishments notably including her landmark edition of the *Daybooks of Edward Weston*. During Beaumont's overseas duty, 1942–45, she was the acting curator of photography at the Museum of Modern Art. Despite tepid support from the museum's trustees, she organized three major shows, including "Art in Progress," spanning the history of photography, as well as monumental retrospectives of Paul Strand and Edward Weston.

MINOR WHITE: Born 1908 in Minneapolis, he received his first camera at age seven, and dated his decision to become a photographer to his twelfth year. After studying botany at the University of Minnesota, he found work in the 1930s with the Works Progress Administration (WPA), photographing civic theater groups and teaching photography workshops. The first national exhibition of White images occurred during the "Image of Freedom" show at the Museum of Modern Art, a patriotic endeavor curated by Beaumont Newhall and Ansel Adams. His World War II service on a destroyer in the Pacific included combat during the Leyte invasion, where, according to his letters, he killed at least one enemy soldier, was wounded, and witnessed the deaths of close friends. These experiences left him too shattered to photograph in the early aftermath of the war. His remarkable story emerges in some detail in the following pages.

Also present at the Aperture Founders' meeting were three individuals who made early and vital contributions: Ernest Louie, Melton Ferris, and Dody Warren. At the outset, the group constituted the Aperture family and as such set the tone for what would become an ever-widening community.

The relationships among the Founders were intense and complex: at times aesthetically and metaphysically exalted, and at others downright melodramatic. Ansel, for example, was rumored to have remarked that he never agreed with anything Minor ever said. Minor, throughout his editing career, was hesitant to publish Ansel's pictures. Dorothea Lange, with her deep social commitment, often felt some of the others—particularly those making "abstractions"—were either wasting their time or betraying the integrity of photography. Ansel and Nancy in due time fell in love, but both remained devoted to their respective spouses. Barbara Morgan healthily bal-

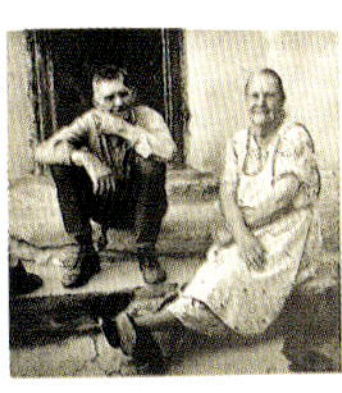

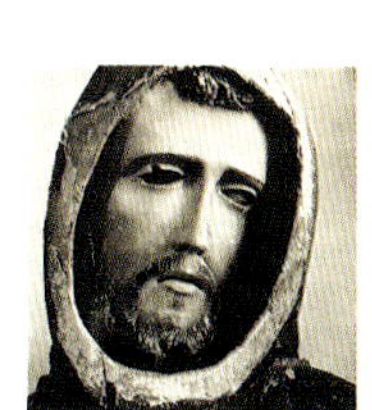

In the pages of Aperture publications appear glimpses of the entire history of the medium . . . Pictorialism, Photo-Secession, "Group 64," Modernism, Postmodernism . . . "purist," "landscape," "surreal," abstract," "documentary," "mystical," and so on and so on more.

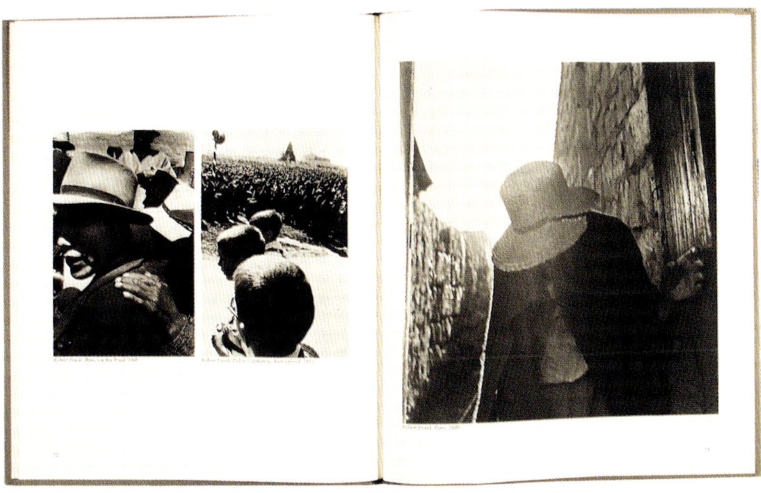

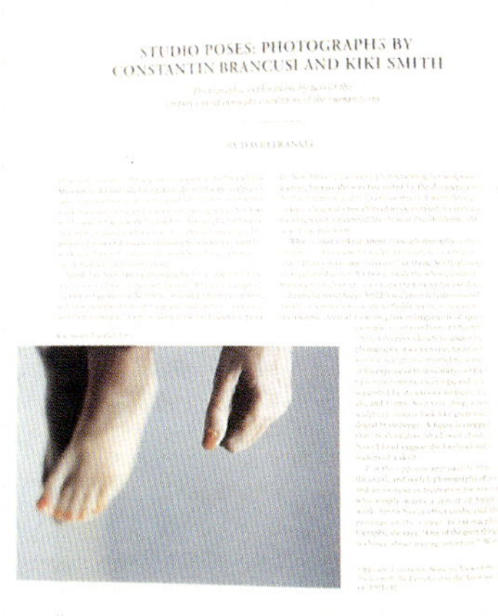

STUDIO POSES: PHOTOGRAPHS BY CONSTANTIN BRANCUSI AND KIKI SMITH

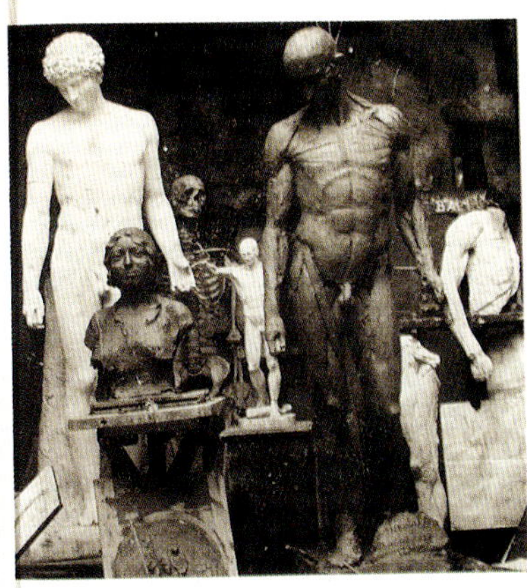

TOP: ***Aperture*** **vol. 2, no. 4, 1953, pages 30–31: (left) photograph by Ansel Adams; (right) photograph by Dorothea Lange. MIDDLE:** ***Aperture*** **81, 1978, pages 72–73: photographs by Robert Frank. BOTTOM:** ***Aperture*** **145, 1996, pages 18–19: (left) photograph by Kiki Smith; (right) photograph by Constantin Brancusi.**

anced family and working life, and carried on a prodigious schedule of photographing, painting, teaching, and designing. Over the years, the only person who seemed able to remain uninterruptedly on speaking terms with everyone else was Nancy Newhall.

Also as in a family, they were fiercely loyal to one another—photographing together, finding jobs for each other, always protective against threats or attacks from outsiders. All the criticisms, carpings, and outright bitchiness to be found in their letters and reminiscences were meant strictly for private consumption: family gossip.

There were other presences at that remarkable meeting in 1952. The need for a serious quarterly devoted to photography had been bruited the previous autumn during a seminar at the first Aspen Photographic Conference. The Newhalls had both attended, as had Ansel, Minor, Lange, Berenice Abbott, Laura Gilpin, Frederick Sommer, and Eliot Porter, among others, and there were representatives from advertising, magazines, and the Library of Congress. Those not present at Ansel and Virginia's house the following year were nonetheless keenly interested in the outcome of the meeting, and several were to become early Aperture contributors and supporters.

Another deeply felt influence was 125 miles down the coast at Carmel: Edward Weston, unable to attend because he was in a long, painful slip from life due to Parkinson's disease. Several of the San Francisco participants were close friends of Weston's and had photographed with him. Each was distressed at the illness that had deprived him of the capacity to use his camera four years earlier. He was now under the care of his sons, including Brett, whose international reputation as a photographer had begun at age seventeen, and Cole, keeper of the Weston legacy and later one of the medium's foremost colorists. Edward represented an ideal for those contemplating the new publication, a singleness of purpose that had underpinned his once-legendary vitality and his incomparable mastery.

And there was a ghost present in San Francisco—no less haunting simply because one does not believe in ghosts. This was the unquenchable spirit of Alfred Stieglitz, dead six years earlier, but deeply imbued in the lives and work of most serious American photographers. Born in 1864, like Lange in Hoboken, and supported by an unusually enlightened, affluent father, Stieglitz traveled extensively in Europe in his youth and had achieved an international reputation in photography salons by his early twenties. He had also begun writing extensively about photography and editing journals devoted to the medium. At the turn of the century, Stieglitz—despite recurring bouts of ill health—unleashed enormous energy on behalf of a new generation of creative photographers breaking free of what he felt were the limp, painterly conventions of the past. He named this movement the Photo-

Secession, and opened a series of galleries to exhibit the work of its proponents, as well as of other groundbreaking artists. The first gallery, called simply "291," and his publication *Camera Work* gave many Americans their initial view of imagery by Edward Steichen and Paul Strand, and also introduced to this audience works by Rodin, Matisse, Picasso, Brancusi, Picabia, and Toulouse-Lautrec, to name only a few. Subsequently, Stieglitz was to devote most of his curatorial efforts to American artists, including Marsden Hartley, John Marin, and Arthur Dove.

Stieglitz's most notable collaboration was with his second wife, the painter Georgia O'Keeffe. He mounted her first one-person show, launching one of the most remarkable careers in twentieth-century art. And she provided him with his perfect model, inspiring hundreds of photographs—nudes, portraits, and hands—which constitute an enormous block of Stieglitz's finest achievements.

The specter of Stieglitz present among the Aperture Founders that day in 1952 was largely the matter of an indelible personality and an elusive ideal. He was old when he came directly into the lives of Adams, White, and the Newhalls, but no American photographer of the time was untouched by Stieglitz's influence. In appearance, he had become a simulacrum of a black-and-white photograph: white hair and thick, well-trimmed moustache; almost unlined, near-albino skin; dark, penetrating eyes; he dressed in the whitest of linen and the blackest of tie, suit, and cape. Stieglitz was an at-once man: at once kaleidoscopically complex and evangelically simple, at once humble in the best sense and arrogant in the worst, at once remarkably patient and unnecessarily abrupt, at once a kind man and cruel.

His final gallery was An American Place, located in an office building on Madison Avenue, just a block from the Museum of Modern Art. Here, he would accept no money for himself but required the purchaser of an artwork to make a "contribution" to the artist. If, however, Stieglitz judged a buyer to be unworthy, he might refuse to sell him a photograph, drawing, or painting at any price. He had a general dislike of museums and the world of art galleries. Beaumont Newhall became his whipping boy for years after a visit in 1935. Representing the Museum of Modern Art, Newhall sought prints for an exhibition (Stieglitz wouldn't consider it), and asked innocently if a certain photograph was taken with panchromatic film. "Young man," Stieglitz snapped, "that has nothing at all to do with the picture"; and he walked off.

Two years earlier, Ansel Adams had made his pilgrimage to An American Place to show his work. After an unfriendly greeting, Stieglitz did go over the portfolio, and then looked at the images again, and described them as "some of the most beautiful photographs I've ever seen." To Ansel he granted the supreme accolade of a solo show—something Stieglitz had not done since his Strand exhibition nearly twenty years earlier. When Minor went to An American Place in 1946, shortly before Stieglitz's death, the old man was kind, encouraging. Looking at Minor's prewar photographs, he asked, "Have you ever been in love?" Minor said yes, and Stieglitz told him, "Then you can photograph." It was the moment, Minor later said, that released him from his wartime traumas and reawakened his desire to photograph. To Nancy Newhall, Stieglitz was affectionate—almost fatherly; he was supportive of her writing and provided her with extensive recollections about his own life.

Stieglitz's deepest relations were with women—O'Keeffe, Nancy Newhall, and for many years the multitalented Dorothy Norman, who became his primary biographer. To his famous remark "Photography is my passion. The search for Truth my obsession," should be added a comment he once made to Nancy: "My medium is Woman." His relationships with the male artists he championed always began hopefully, and were always disappointing. At the turn of the century, Stieglitz had looked to Edward Steichen as the disciple who would carry on his ideals and work. By the late 1930s he had shifted his hopes to Ansel Adams. The problem was, neither Steichen nor Adams—both with families—had any affection for the poverty that Stieglitz ascetically embraced. Both went on to public success and considerable wealth—apostasy to Stieglitz.

And what of the ideals? Stieglitz is usually associated with the struggle to have photography recognized as an art form in itself, carrying on a struggle started in the late nineteenth century by the English polymath P. J. Emerson. This is a somewhat misleading simplification. As Michael Hoffman was to suggest years later, Stieglitz in his photography and writings was trying "to come in contact with a cosmic order, or a harmony." It was an effort manifested in the making of his series of photographs called "Equivalents."

The concept arose from a series of cloud photographs Stieglitz made in 1922, returning to a subject that he felt had defeated him years earlier. In looking at the cloud series, Stieglitz said, his aim was "increasingly to make my photographs look so much like photographs that unless one has eyes and sees, they won't be seen—and still everyone will never forget them having once looked at them . . . of greatest importance is to hold a moment, to record something so completely that those who see it will relive an equivalent of what has been expressed." Later, Stieglitz would come to believe that all art in the truest sense is an equivalent.

For all of his own writings and subsequent commentaries, Stieglitz's "equivalents" remains a slippery idea, and therein lies its enduring power. Once an ideal is nailed down it becomes mere ideology. As an ideal that informs intuition, the feeling for "equivalents" entered into the Aperture ethos from the beginning.

Ansel provided the name *Aperture* for the new journal, which was scheduled to be a quarterly. With Minor White volunteering as editor, the first issue appeared in April 1952. It was a modest affair compared with its inspiration, Stieglitz's *Camera Work*, which he had published from 1902 to 1917. One of the most beautiful journals in any medium of any time, *Camera Work* had been printed on Japanese tissue paper with Stieglitz's own photogravures of the artists represented. Stieglitz had enlisted writers as diverse as Gertrude Stein, John Galsworthy, Lewis Mumford, Hart Crane, and Waldo Frank. That first issue of *Aperture*, sized 6¼ by 9⅜ inches, boasted twenty-seven pages, and featured three photographs—by Lange, Adams, and the Viennese-born Lisette Model. Minor and Nancy did all the writing: two extended essays. A few additional photographs illustrated Minor's "The Exploratory Camera: A Rationale for the Miniature Camera." Nancy's piece was titled "The Caption: The Mutual Relation of Words/Photographs," and it remains one of the definitive essays on the subject.

Perhaps the most compelling aspect of the new publication was the statement of *Aperture*'s raison d'être in its first editorial. There, the Founders laid out their intentions for a "mature" journal that would communicate with "serious photographers and creative people everywhere, whether professional, amateur, or student":

> Every photographer who is a master of his medium has evolved a philosophy from such experiences; and whether we agree or not, his thoughts act like a catalyst on our own—he has contributed to dynamic ideas of our time. Only rarely do such concepts get written down clearly and in a form where photographers scattered all over the earth may see them and look at the photographs that are their ultimate expression.

Aperture, they concluded, was an open invitation to "a common ground for the advancement of photography."

Minor was a logical choice for editor; he already edited the periodical *Image* (and besides, he was the only candidate). Like Stieglitz, he had a rather unworldly attitude toward money; during the next fifteen years of his editorship, he never received a penny for his often prodigious efforts on behalf of *Aperture*. Nor did any of the contributors of photographs, essays, or reprints. Nor did Ernest Louie, the designer for the first few issues, nor Melton Ferris, who volunteered as production manager for several years. Minor did get something in return because he, in fact, *was Aperture*. Informally organized, it was copyrighted in his name. And the periodical was headquartered wherever Minor lived: first in San Francisco, where Ansel had found him a teaching post; subsequently in Rochester, New York.

Editors can be either despots or puppets; Minor was definitely, if on most occasions civilly, the former. It was up to him to interpret and realize the Founders' intentions. As with most complex individuals, time has yielded commentators who reduce the extraordinary to the banal in their labeling. In Minor's case, the sticking commonplaces are "mystic"—usually as a pejorative—and homosexual, in either the pejorative or the celebratory sense. His editing reveals a man of originality, practicality (as far as photography was concerned), and near-limitless curiosity.

During the next few years, the quarterly reflected the taste, sweep, and quirks of Minor's view of photography. There were, of course, those artists now revered as masters of the medium, though little exposed to public view at the time. Among them: Weston's last photographs of the endlessly evocative cove so associated with his name, Point Lobos; a portfolio from Mexico by Manuel Alvarez Bravo—a selection later recognized as among his masterpieces; and indelible images including Wynn Bullock's pastoral nudes, Pirkle Jones's poetic land- and seascapes, and Paul Caponigro's supernal rocks and stones. An issue in 1953 concentrated on Chinatown in San Francisco with a photo-essay by Charles Wong, "The Year of the Dragon," a mysterious contemplation of a kind of metaphorical kidnapping; and "Chinese New Year," a selection of works by members of the California School of Fine Arts, where Minor taught.

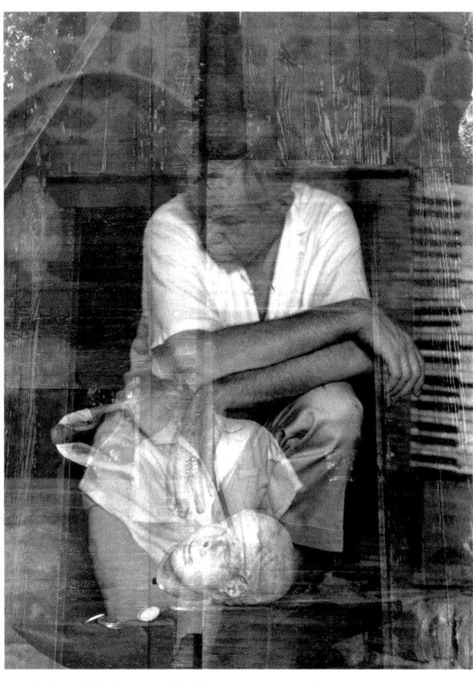

Minor White, 1957. Photograph by Walter Chappell.

In reproducing *Aperture*'s imagery, White looked over the shoulders of engravers, compositors, and printers at presses at the San Francisco (and later Rochester) printing houses where the quarterly was published. He meticulously went over every page, making endless, expensive, subtle and not-so-subtle corrections and alterations. Even so, he cautioned his readers that the best reproductions were inevitably poor imitations of the original prints.

Unpaid, the photographers appearing then (and now) in *Aperture* had hopes of awakening interest, possibly exhibition and purchase of their work. Some images were offered for sale. In the early 1950s, an astute subscriber could have bought Weston's fiftieth-anniversary portfolio of twelve prints for one hundred dollars, and a reproduction of Adams's classic *Moonrise, Hernandes, New*

Mexico, for six dollars plus tax. No such rewards accrued to the (unpaid) writers Minor needed. For the professionals, Dr. Johnson's admonition that only blockheads ever write except for money probably spoke to their very genetic makeup. Minor was constantly trying to prize out articles, critical essays, reports from conferences, and "advice." That he managed to do so was a credit to his persistence and patience. The Founders helped with essays but, with the exception of Nancy and Beaumont, seldom more than once.

Lange and her son Daniel Dixon coauthored an essay, "Photographing the Familiar," which, typically for Lange, emerged as a manifesto. Decrying the "fear, worship, convenience or custom" that led photography to seem more concerned with illusion than reality, she exhorted, "It is the nature of the camera to deal with what *is*—we urge those who use the camera to retire from what *might be*." Morgan contributed an analytical description of her working technique in the essay "Kinetic Design in Photography," which concluded, "Essentially, kinetic design is a channeling [of] one's discoveries of the central energy of any subject and as such it is a way of being in unison with life." Ansel offered an extended, thoughtful, ten-point plan for the education and training of photographers, reflecting his lifelong commitment to the medium's future practitioners. In it, he included a gamut of requirements—from a thorough training in photographic processes to a solid general education with emphasis on the humanities. He called for experience in community efforts, including relationships to museums and related organizations, which would prove an insight into the nature of *Aperture*'s future way of working. Adams's essay also provided a curious academicism that photography required "severe standards of professional training and professional certification to establish itself as an Art."

White, of course, weighed in with much of the writing—so much so that he began to use pseudonyms to give readers a sense of variety. One of his noms de plume was "Myron White"; another was in the guise of an ambiguously ancient and wise Chinese poet named "Sam Tung Wu," whose verse accompanied photographs of White's own choosing.

Reviews of publications always formed part of *Aperture*'s perceived mission, and in the second issue, Minor revealed himself as a willing controversialist. The object of his polemic was the book *Advanced Photography* by Andreas Feininger. Minor praised Feininger's descriptions and advice on the technical aspects, but deplored what he viewed as Feininger's subjection of the aesthetics and art of photography to the manipulation of such techniques. He criticized the book for misleading truly creative artists.

Minor asked for a reply to his critique of *Advanced Photography,* and Feininger obliged. He engaged issues of the "eternal" versus the "transitory" in photography, and of the "accidental" as opposed to the "controlled" and delved into the meaning of "cre-

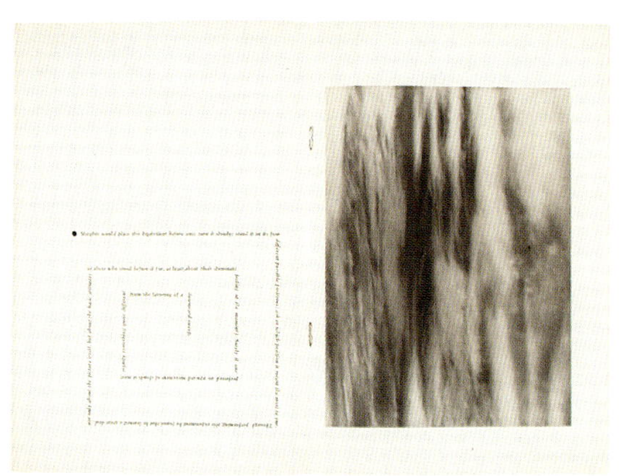

"Every photographer who is a master of his medium has evolved a philosophy . . . and whether we agree or not, his thoughts act like a catalyst on our own—he has contributed to dynamic ideas of our time. Only rarely do such concepts get written down clearly and in a form where photographers scattered all over the earth may see them and look at the photographs that are their ultimate expression."

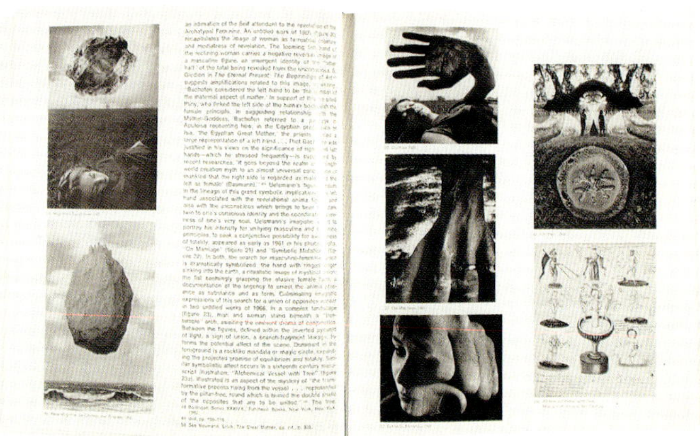

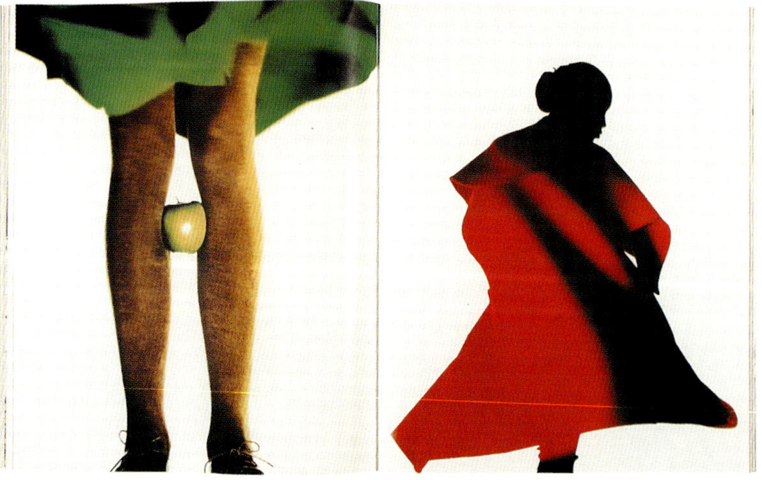

TOP: *Aperture* vol. 3, no. 4, 1955, pages 20–21: photograph by Alfred Stieglitz. MIDDLE: *Aperture* vol. 13, no. 3, 1967, pages 22–23: photographs by Jerry Uelsmann, except (bottom left) painting by René Magritte, and (bottom right) alchemical vessel with tree, manuscript, France, sixteenth century. BOTTOM: *Aperture* 122, 1991, pages 63–64: photographs by Nick Knight.

ative." And he thoroughly objected to being characterized as "naïve" and "pedestrian" on matters of aesthetics. Minor postscripted by accusing Feininger of imposing dogmatic formulae upon creative photography. A few years later, Minor bashed Feininger's *Creative Photography* on much the same grounds, ending with the observation—which must have been a relief to both men—that the author henceforth intended to publish only picture books.

Variety in *Aperture*'s texts was achieved by soliciting reprints, provided for free in that more generous age by the *New York Times*, the *New Yorker*, and other distinguished sources. Thus, Minor was able to publish articles by architect Frank Lloyd Wright on press photography and how he felt about being photographed; by Elizabeth Bowen on the writer's unpremeditated search for a subject; and Kenneth Clark's views on the relations of photography and painting.

Perhaps the most memorable title in *Aperture*'s entire history was from James Thurber's *New Yorker* piece "Has Photography Gone Too Far?" The answer from a nun in a Minnesota priory was unequivocal. It had. She named the photograph that had taken the medium over the edge . . . and its maker could not have been more pleased. Frederick Sommer delighted in mischief.

Born in Angri, Italy, in 1905, Sommer had a remarkable education, was fluent in several languages, and possessed considerable talent in drawing and painting. He had received encouragement from no less a personage than Stieglitz himself, and later from Weston (who according to some accounts gave Sommer his first camera). Almost entirely self-taught, he devoted himself to painting and photography at a young age, became a U.S. citizen, and settled in Prescott, Arizona, where he made his home for the rest of his life.

If there was ever a photographer who, as Aperture's founding mandate invoked, had created "dynamic ideas" and "photographs that are their ultimate expression," it was Sommer. To begin with, he had a long list of "anti-'s." He was anti-organized religion, anti-organized belief, anti-creeds of art and aesthetics, anti-philosophy, and, rather stunningly, anti-metaphysics! He was devoted to the act of attention, to its quality rather than span. And he was a champion of combinatory art—of bringing things together that seemed unrelated, of discovering possibilities within possibilities.

Into his studio Sommer brought "found objects," some that might remain untouched for years until he discovered their coalescing with others, and from these linkages he created photographs of mystery and lingering beauty. It was one of these combinations, containing a severed foot loaned by a medical friend, which so aroused the ire of Sister M. Noemi, O.S.B., of St. Scholastica Priory in Duluth, Minnesota. The ardent eloquence of her letter, written in 1956, would be revisited by *Aperture* editors for decades.

She had recommended *Aperture* for the college library—in itself a rare act as the journal had only a few hundred subscribers—but withdrew the issue from the periodical room because the Sommer print "so trespasses on holy property, so profanes that which is sacred." She had nearly lost her own foot a year earlier to infection, had come to realize how precious it is to its owner and, if lost, how it deserved respectable disposition. Sister M. also noted that as a photographer in the college hospital she had taken "pictures of infections, skin diseases, and surgical cases" that made the Sommer print look mild, but with the intent of a realism that would help doctors in their practice. "That," she added, "is the photographic use of a part of the body in the spirit of Holy Service. But this particular foot [Sommer's] was exploited by a mind that was PERVERTED . . . the motive distortion and EVIL" [capitalization hers].

Sister M. was not Sommer's only detractor. He disliked both Newhalls—Beaumont for his pedantry and Nancy for her sentimentalism—and they thoroughly disliked his work. They wrote an indignant letter to Minor for publishing Sommer's photographs in *Aperture*, and he responded with the only answer he ever offered to Founders or others: "If you don't like it, you can do it yourself." No one ever took up the challenge.

The only time Sommer ever provided a description of his approach to photography was at the first Aspen Conference in 1951, when he suggested the term "imaginative realism." But that might have been to shut up, or at least annoy Lange, for whom photography such as his was as anathematical—although for different reasons—as it was to Sister M. Like Stieglitz, Sommer never met an "ism" that he liked.

As for Minor, he and Sommer were good friends; Sommer had the gift of friendship—even with people he thoroughly disagreed with—and he maintained his delight in mischief up to his death at age ninety-three in 1999.

The cumulative effect of those first few years of publication was for *Aperture* slowly to acquire an identity—and something more. Any periodical originating in ideals and values and purpose begins to take on an organic quality, to have a life of its own. In the pages of *Aperture*, images and writings began to convey a sense of photography as a palpable, living entity. And from the beginning there was a sense of struggle. The cover of the very first issue had been emblazoned with Ansel Adams's own passionate conviction in launching the endeavor: "We have nothing to lose but our photography!" To today's ears, that may have the ring of mock heroics. Fifty years ago, it had a precise, stirring meaning to the few members of the Aperture community who truly understood. If there was such a thing as a living, vital force called Photography, they were engaging a battle for its soul.

Probably the most mature idea ever presented to picture-making photography was the concept of Equivalence which Alfred Stieglitz named early in the 1920s and practiced the rest of his life. The idea has been continued by a few others, notably at the Institute of Design in Chicago under Aaron Siskind and Harry Callahan, and at the former California School of Fine Arts in San Francisco under the efforts of the present author. As a consequence, the theory is in practice now by an ever increasing number of devoted and serious photographers, both amateurs and professionals. The concept and discipline of Equivalence *in practice* is simply the backbone and core of photography as a medium of expression-creation.

At one level, the graphic level, the word "Equivalence" pertains to the photograph itself, the visible foundations of any potential visual experience with the photograph itself. Oddly enough, this does not mean that a photograph which functions as an Equivalent has a certain appearance, or style, or trend, or fashion. Equivalence is a function, an experience, not a thing. Any photograph, regardless of source, might function as an Equivalent to someone, sometime, someplace. If the individual viewer realizes that for him what he sees in a picture corresponds to something within himself—that is, the photograph mirrors something in himself—then his experience is some degree of Equivalence. (At least such is a small part of our present definition.)

. . . At the next level the word "Equivalence" relates to what goes on in the viewer's mind as he looks at a photograph that arouses in him a special sense of correspondence to something that he knows about himself. At a third level the word "Equivalence" refers to the inner experience a person has while he is remembering his mental image after the photograph in question is not in sight. The remembered image also pertains to Equivalence only when a certain feeling of correspondence is present. We remember images that we want to remember. The reason why we want to remember an image varies: because we simply "love it," or dislike it so intensely that it becomes compulsive, or because it has made us realize something about ourselves, or has brought about some slight change in us. Perhaps the reader can recall some image, after the seeing of which he has never been quite the same.

—Minor White, from "Equivalence: The Perennial Trend" (1963), *Aperture* 95, 1984

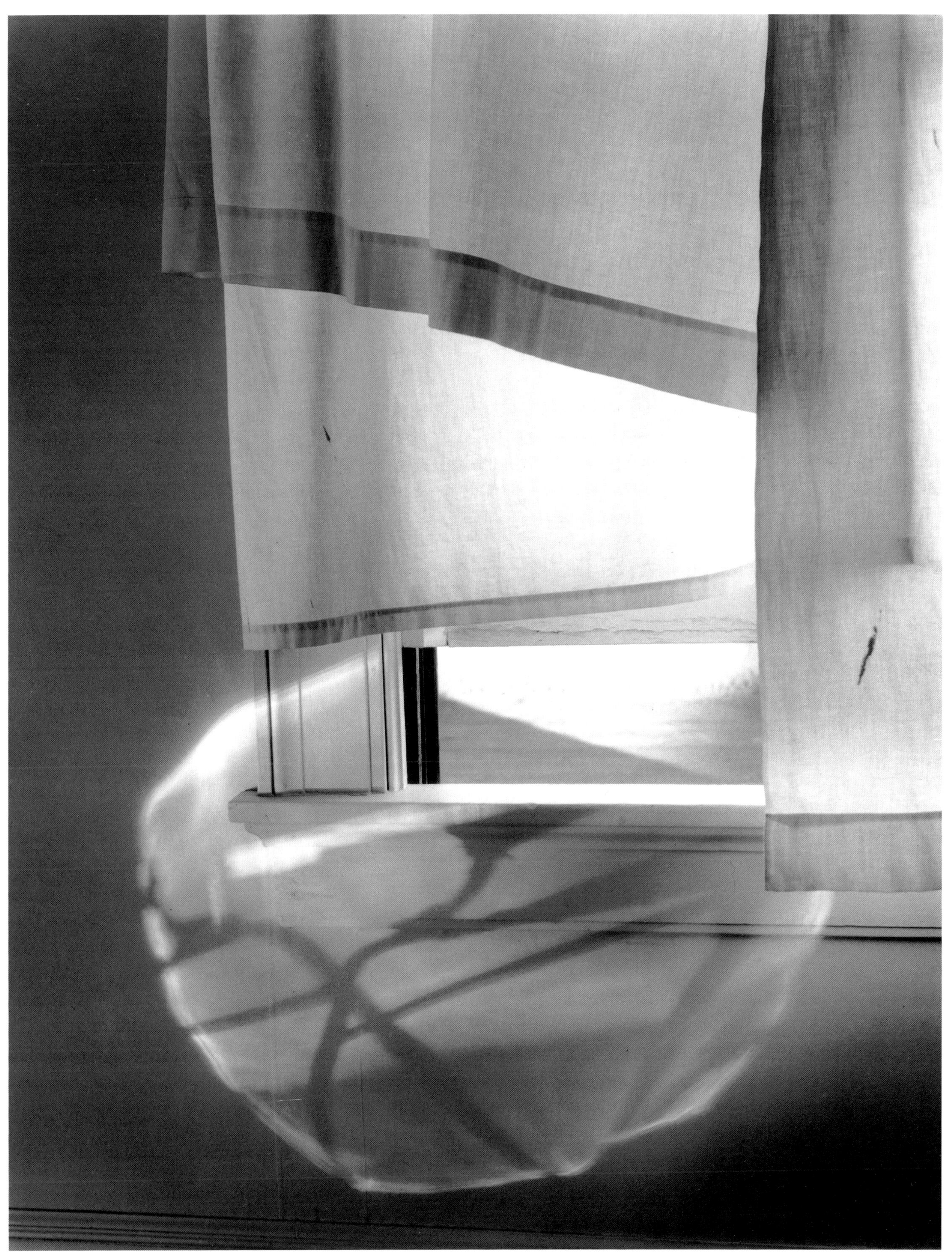

Minor White, *Windowsill Daydreaming*, Rochester, New York, July 1958; from *Aperture* 80, 1978.

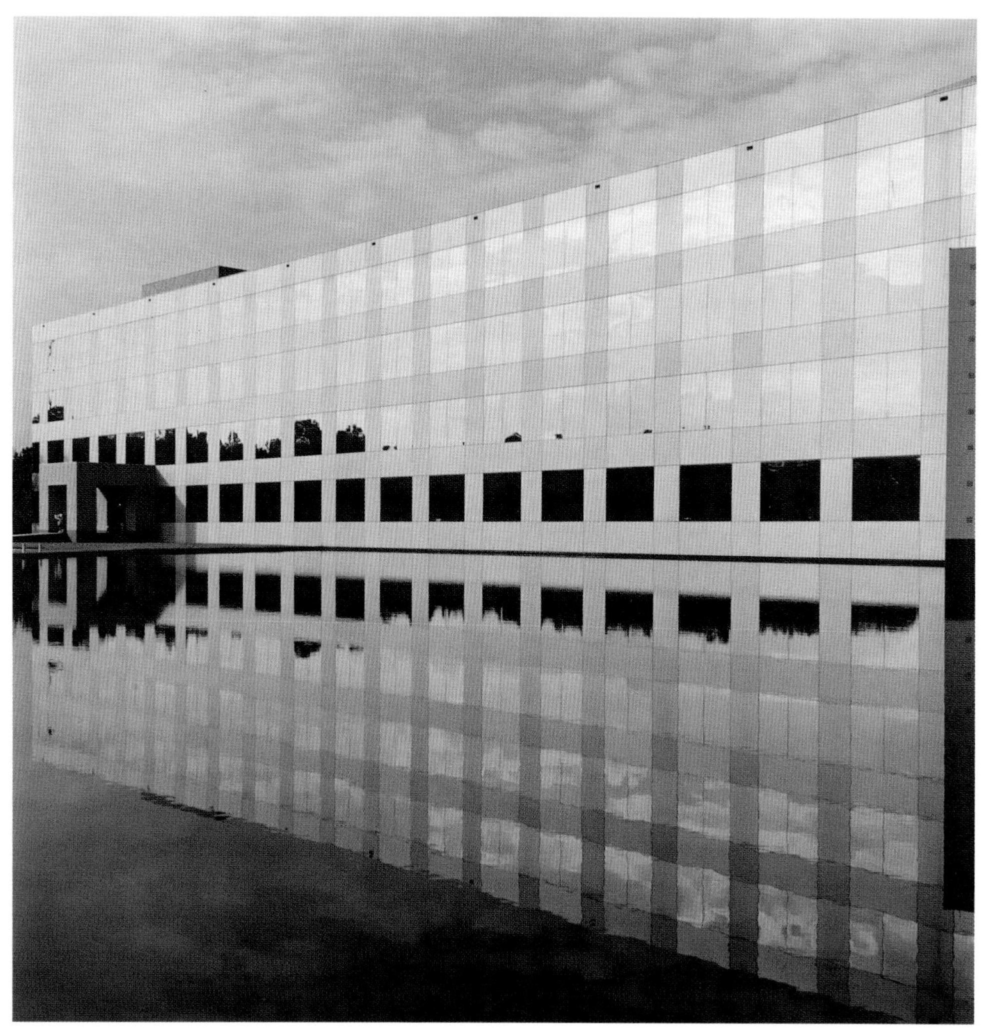

THIS PAGE: photographs by Lynn Davis.
TOP: *Team Disney*, Orlando, Florida, 1998.
LEFT: *Jonas Salk Institute*, La Jolla, California, 1999.

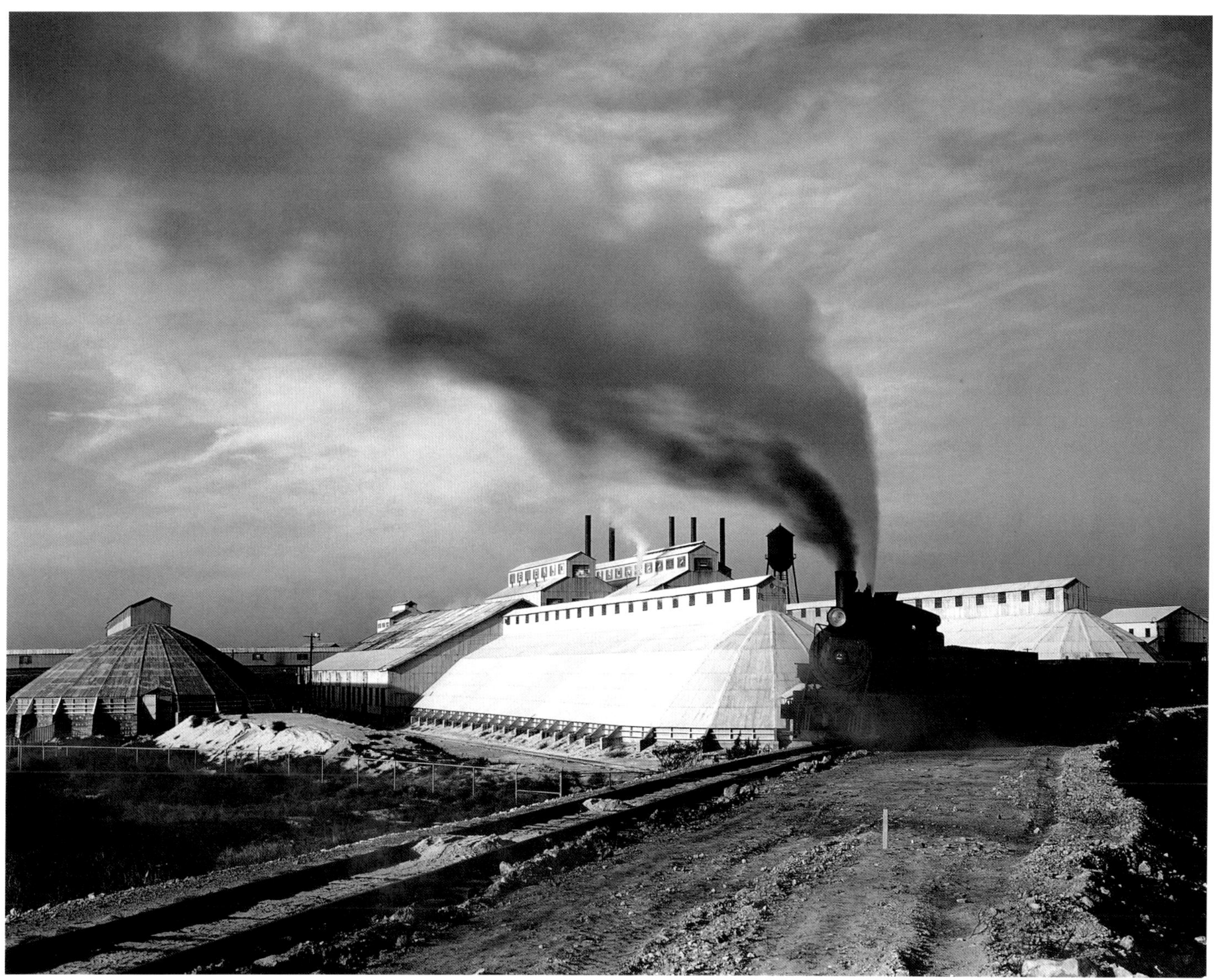

Ansel Adams, *Plant of the U.S. Potash Company*, Carlsbad, New Mexico, 1941; from *Aperture* vol. 1, no. 3, 1952.

Movement of contemporary life cannot be thought of without the machine. Our viewpoint is through a windshield, through reflected images on plate glass, blurred snatches through an elevator door. We watch quilted land patterns slowly shift far below our propeller blur, and the vibrating wing tip. Time is cogged, margins are tightened, spirit is pressured. Pavement is a child's backyard and the moon is less familiar than a street lamp. If it takes a thief to catch a thief, the camera is the machine to catch the machine age. . . .

—Barbara Morgan, from "Kinetic Design in Photography," *Aperture* vol. 1, no. 4, 1953

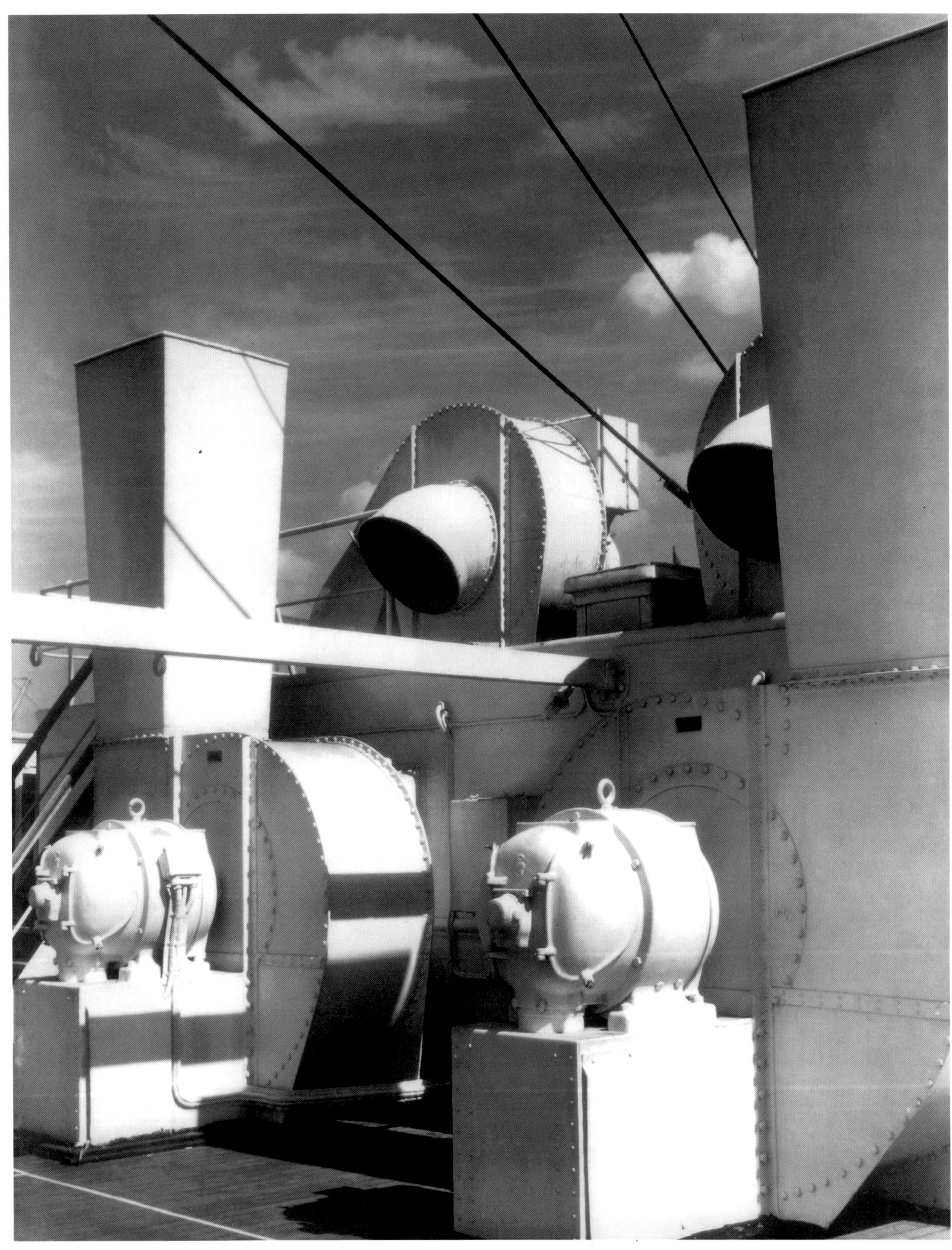

Charles Sheeler, *Upper Deck*, 1928; from *Aperture* 106, 1987.

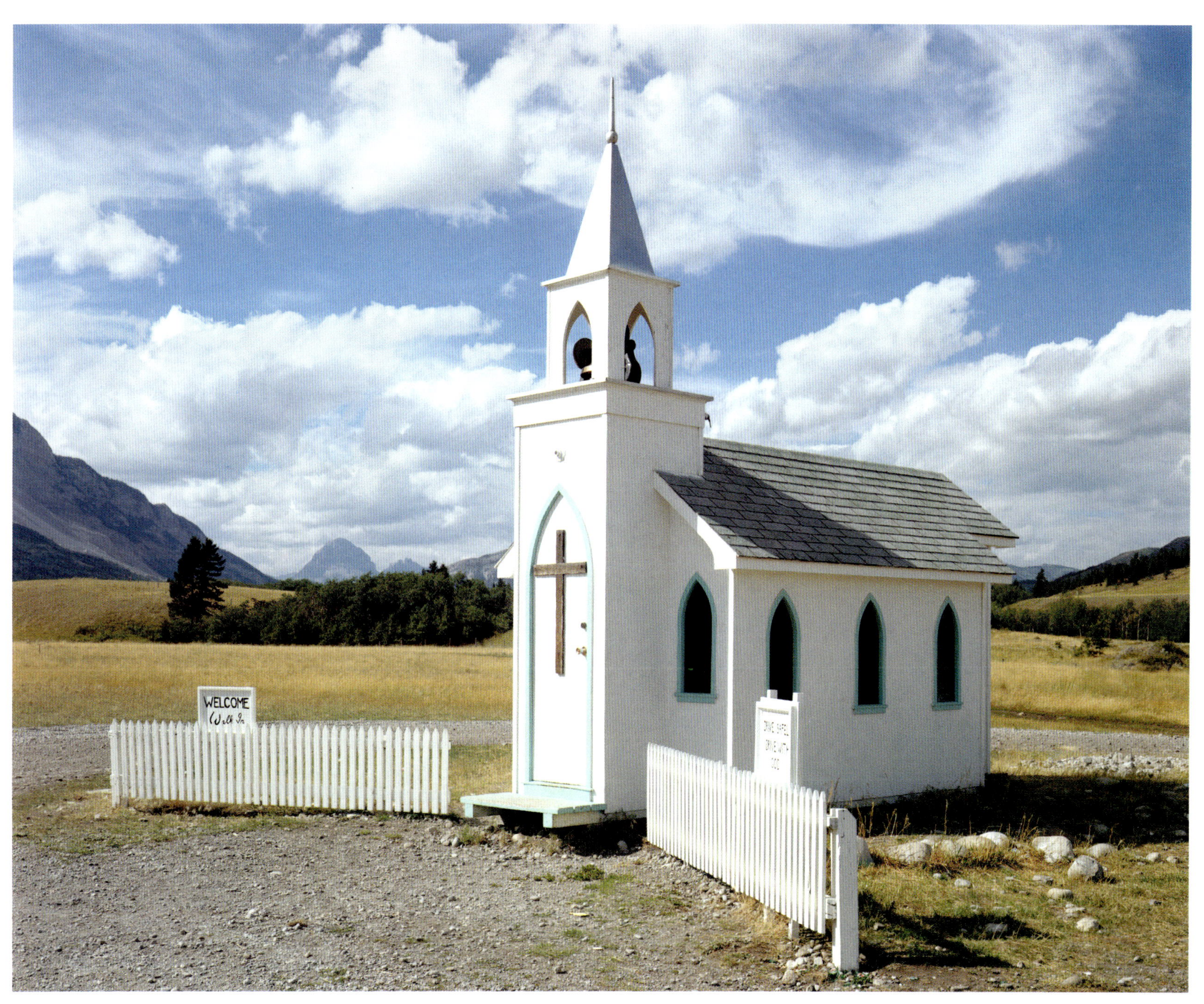

Stephen Shore, ***Bellevue, Alberta***, August 21, 1974; from ***Aperture*** 77, 1976.

The small towns of North America are a far cry from what they used to be. While cities like New York, Los Angeles, and Miami have been, effectively, third-world capitals for some time, now the thousands of smaller towns also reflect this new national character. The combined impact of our nationally subsidized highway program, the once-mighty auto industry, and the new multicultural mix have changed "our towns" into something strange and wonderful. . . .

We are at a critical moment. Our national resources are becoming depleted, our old self-image doesn't exactly jive with what we see in the mirror, our economy is shaky, and our status among nations is questionable. And yet we hold the seeds of cultural rebirth and rejuvenation . . . if we are flexible and cool enough to accept a new definition of what we are. We can go down with the ship, proudly saluting the flag and quoting the pledge of allegiance, or we can get on the tramp streamer bound for who knows where. . . .

In a way, these photos are of a nation on the brink. A fond, or angry, goodbye to a dream that never manifested in reality. A myriad of ghettoized cultures about to confront one another. Pictures of a chemical reaction about to take place. All the right elements are here, but there's no precedent for the new polymer they'll create. It's a new primordial soup. A funky ooze. Good luck to us all, amigos.

—David Byrne, from "Funky Town," ***Aperture*** **127, 1992**

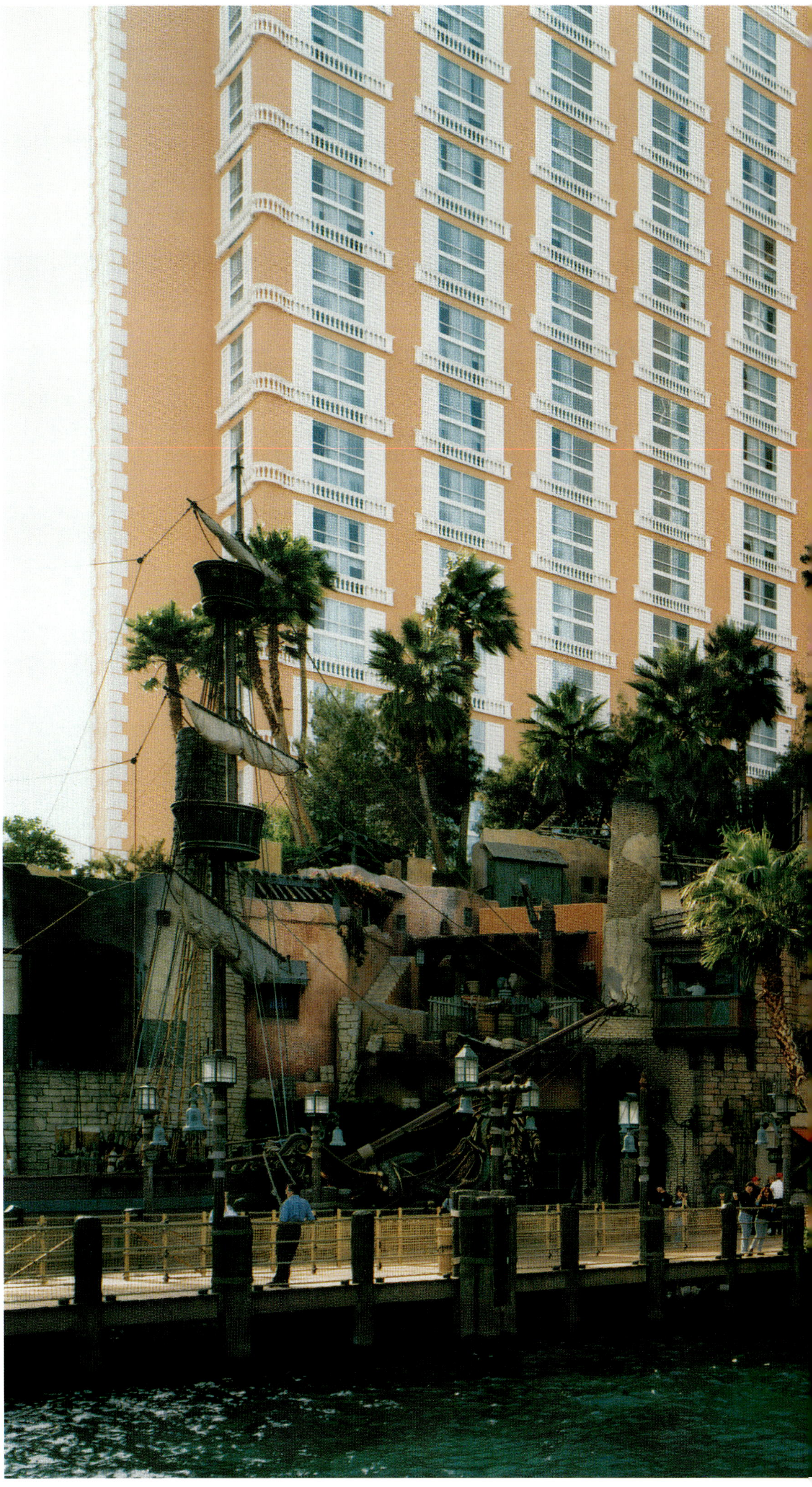

Thomas Struth, *Las Vegas, Nevada*, 1999.

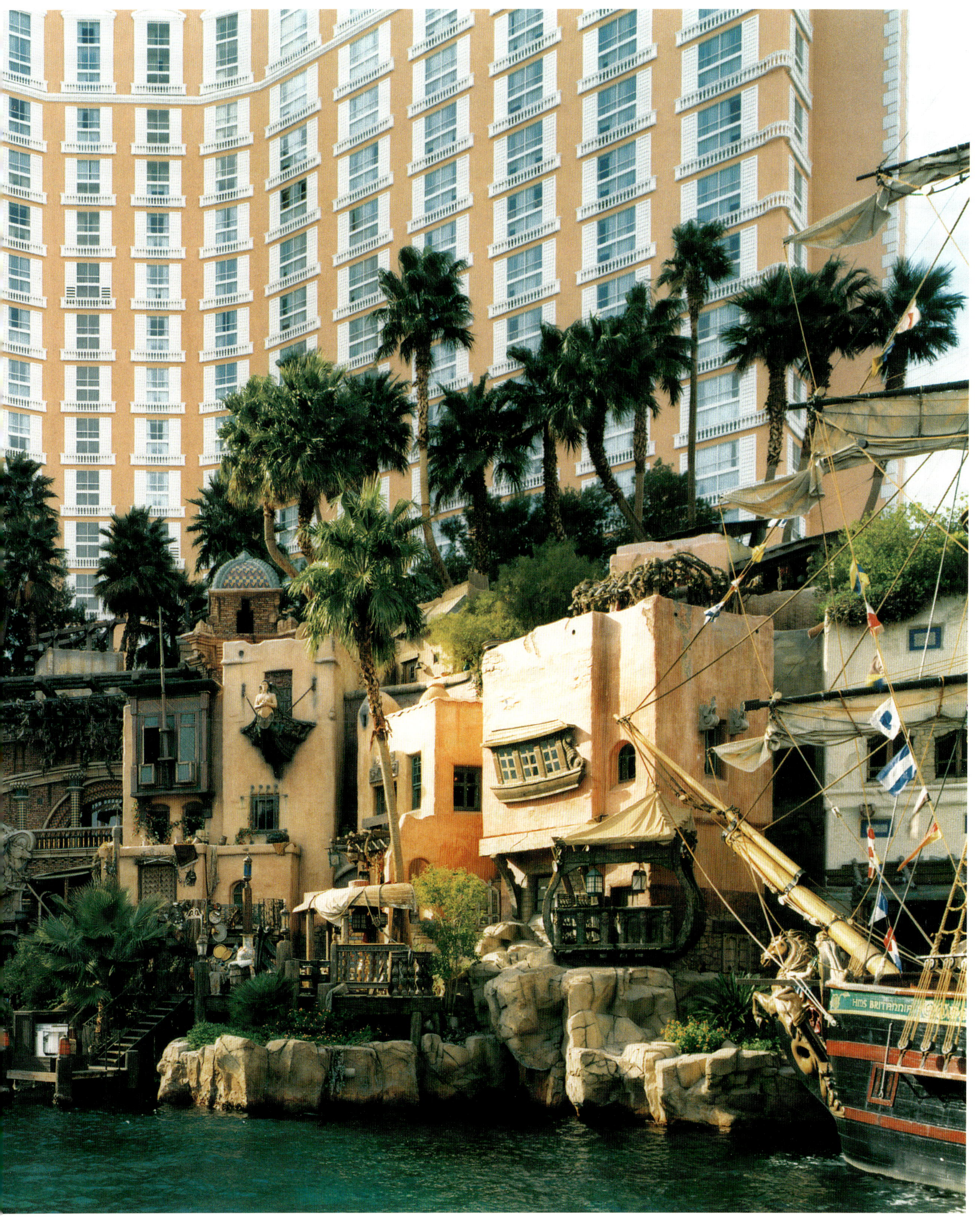
HMS BRITANNIA

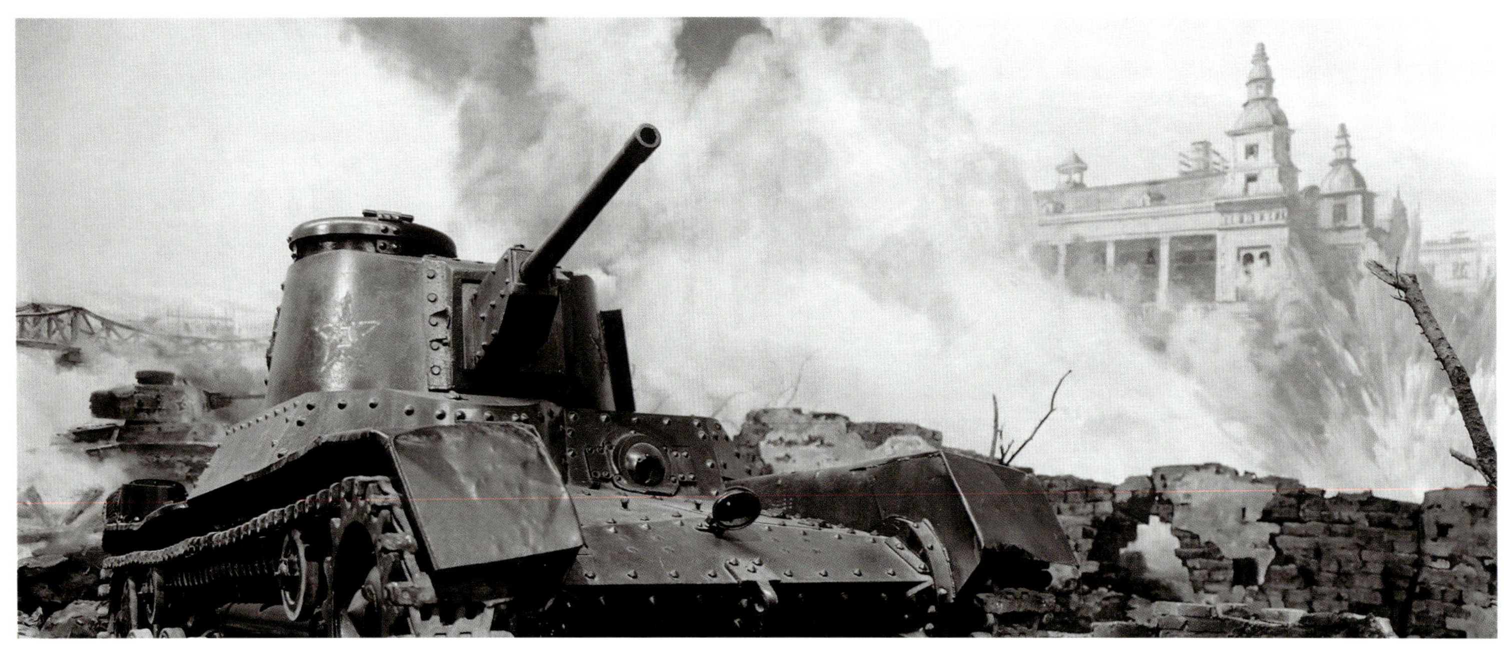

THESE PAGES: photographs by Lois Connor. **ABOVE:** *Military Museum*, Beijing, China, 2000. **BELOW:** *Sydney Opera House*, Australia, 2000.

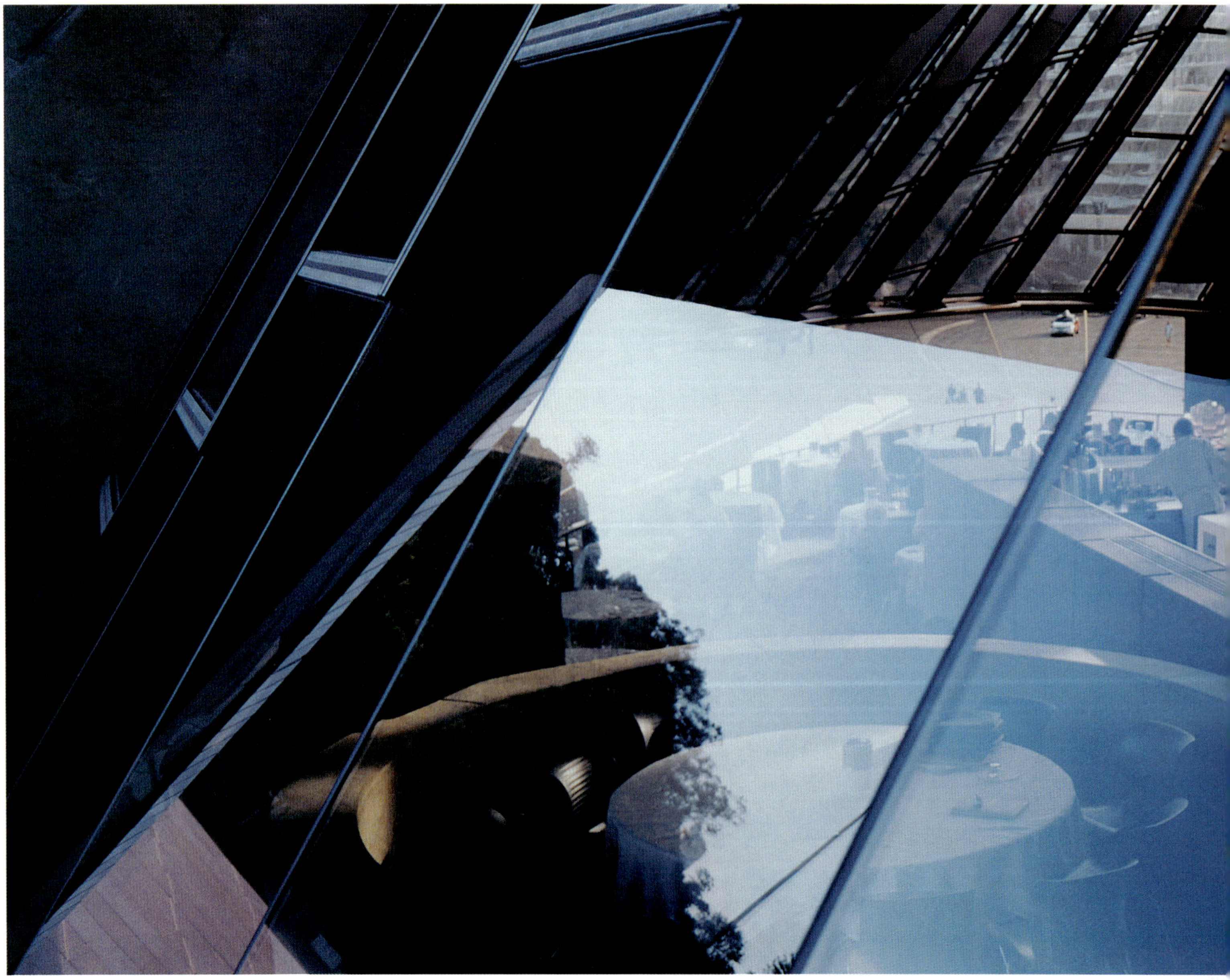

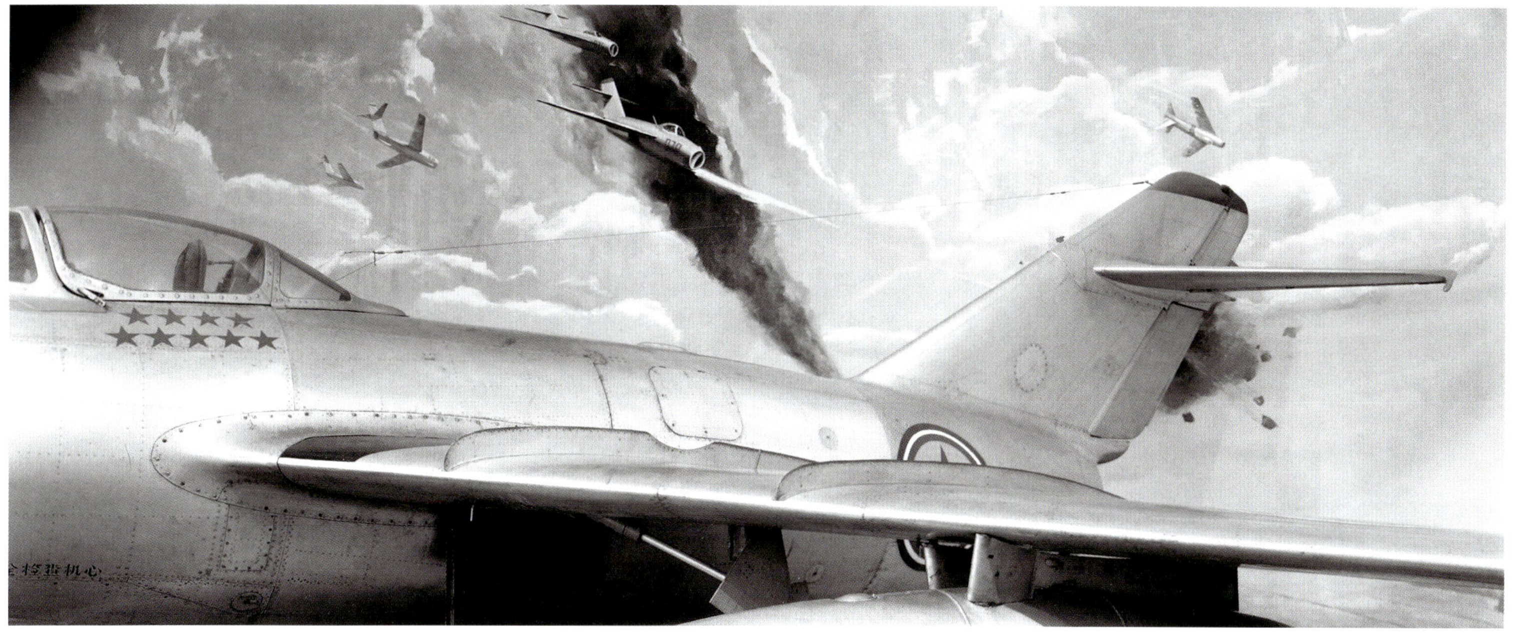

ABOVE: *Military Museum*, Beijing, China, 2000.

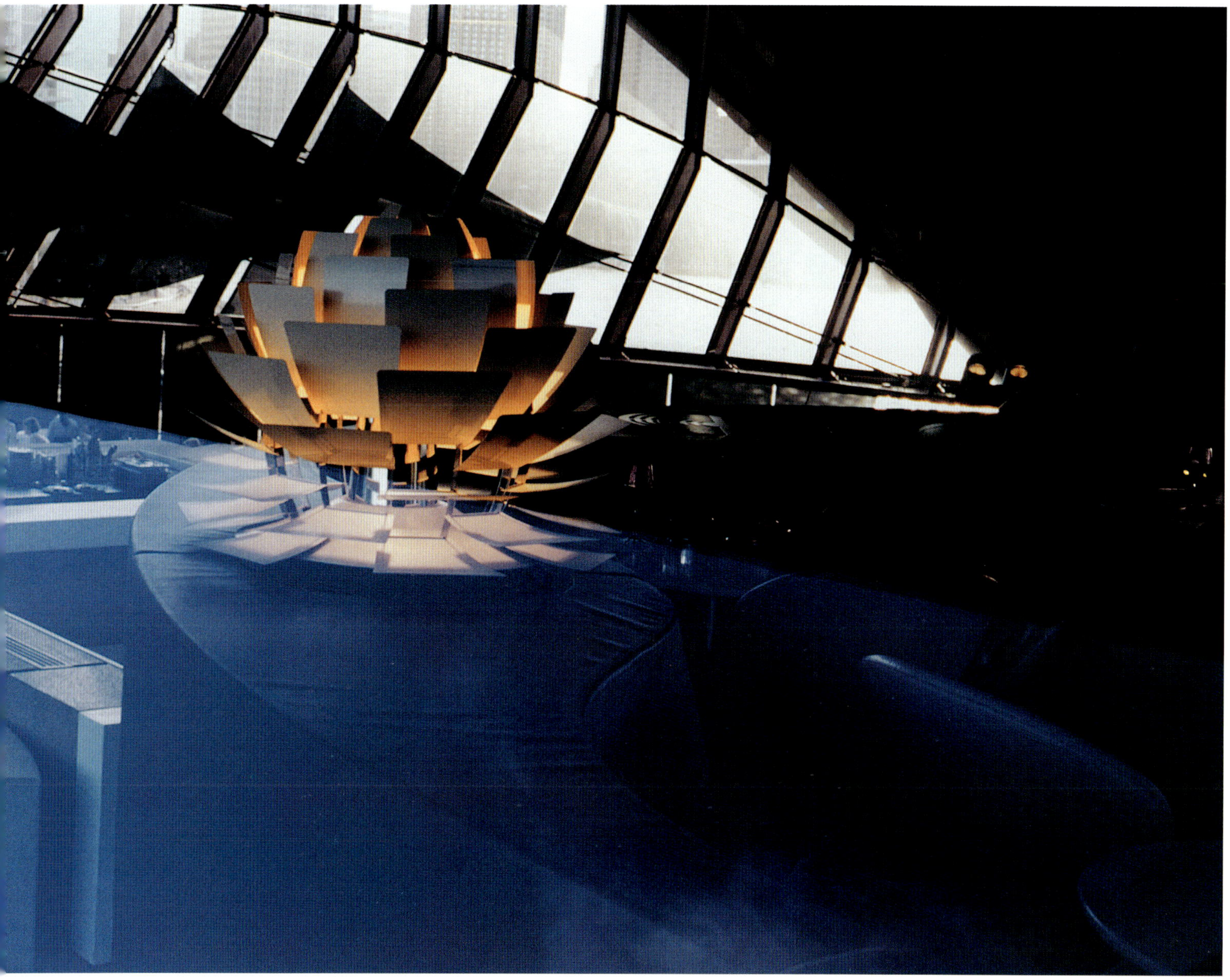

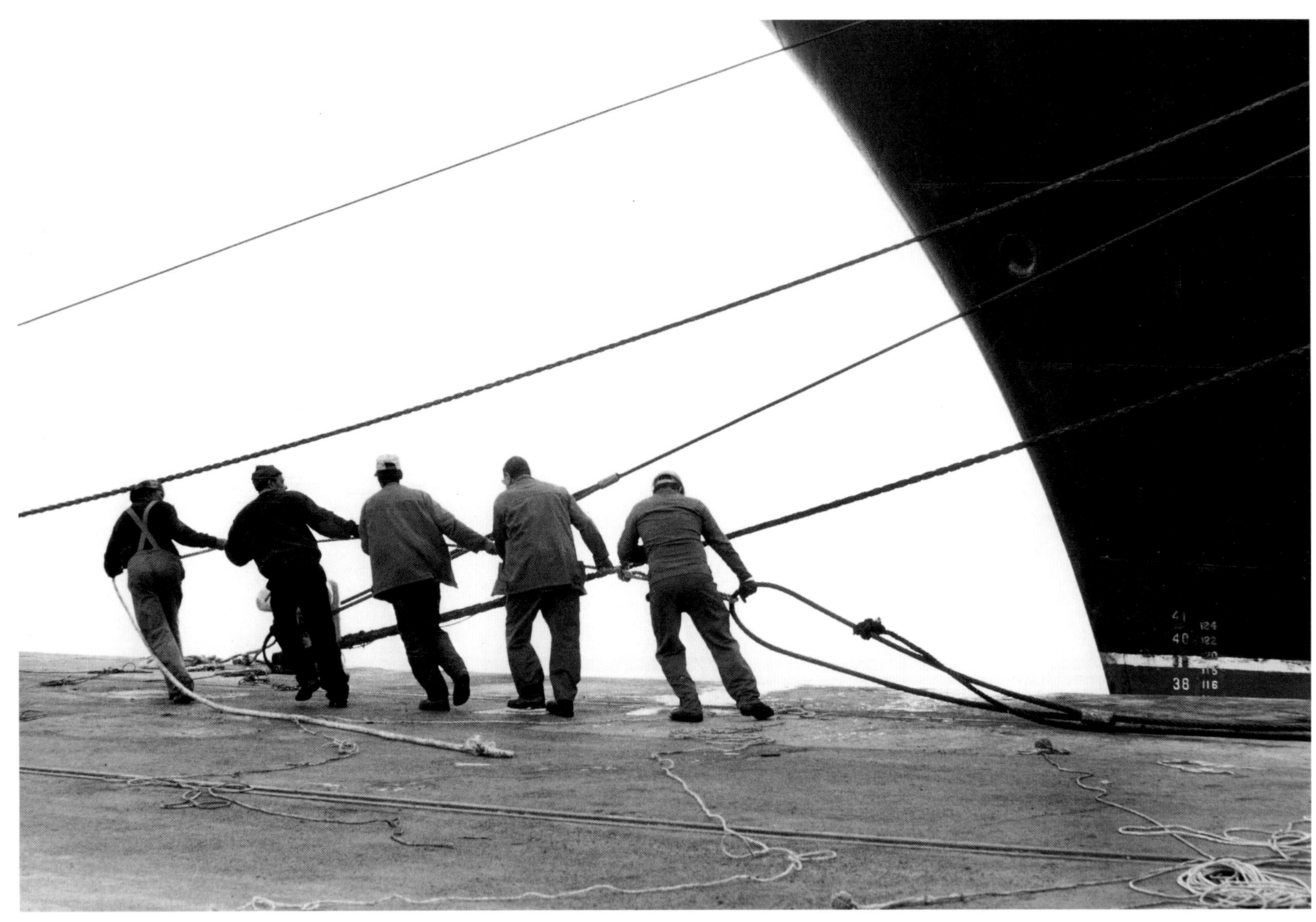

THESE PAGES: photographs by Bruce Davidson.
ABOVE: Securing mooring lines for the *Queen Elizabeth II*, Capetown, South Africa, 1998.
OPPOSITE: The *Queen Elizabeth II* during sand blast operation while in dry dock, Southampton, England, 1996.

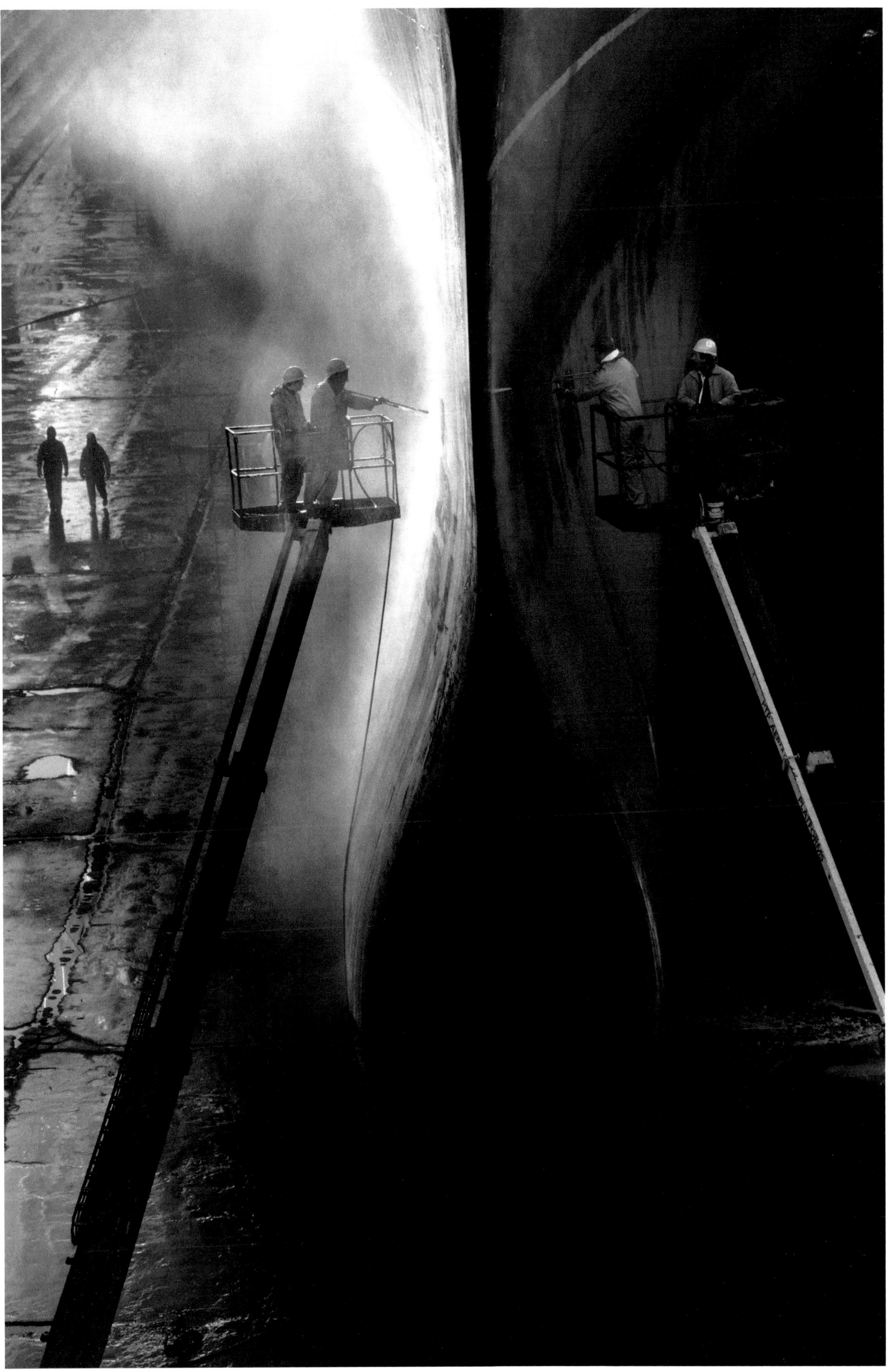

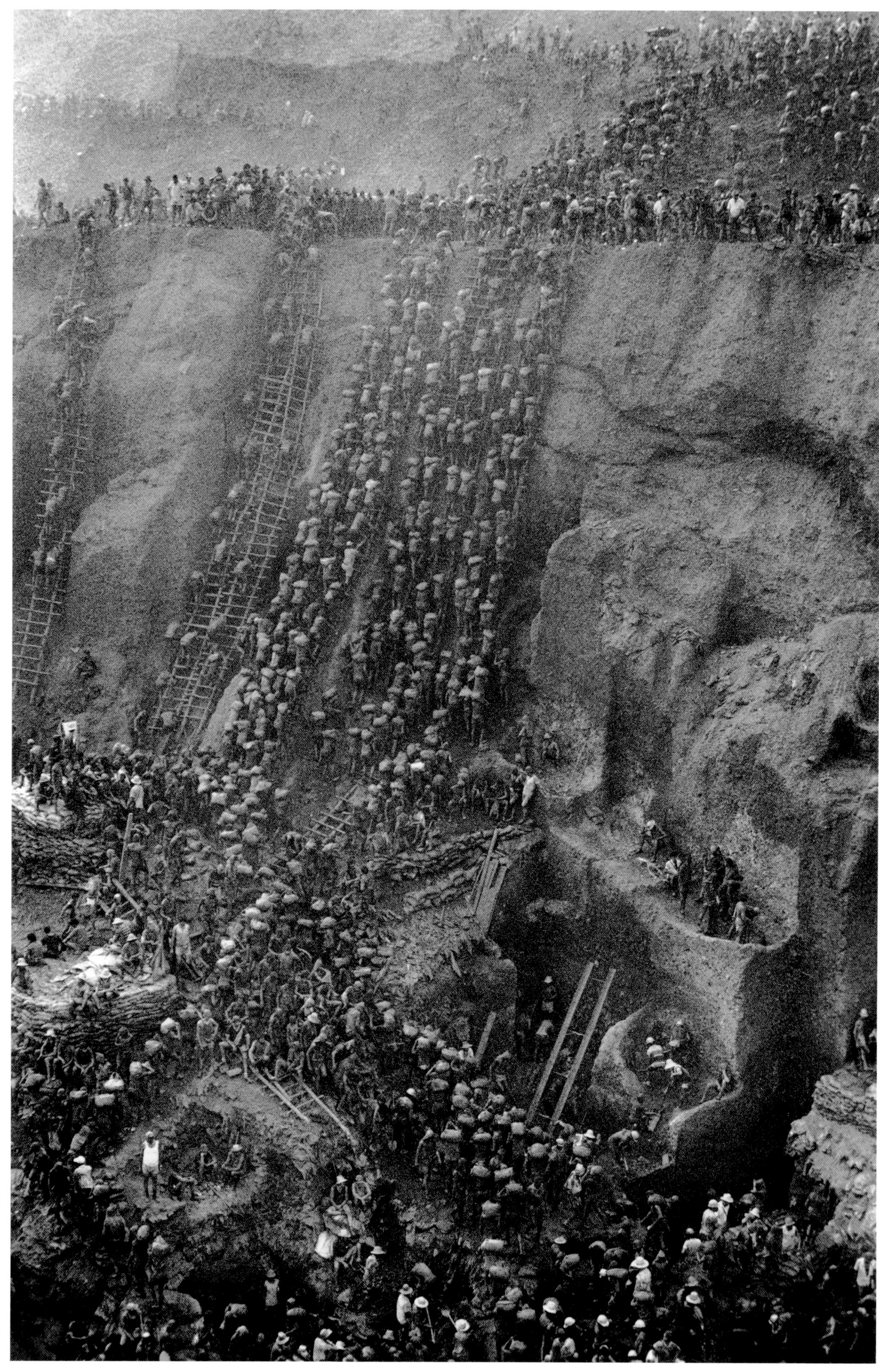

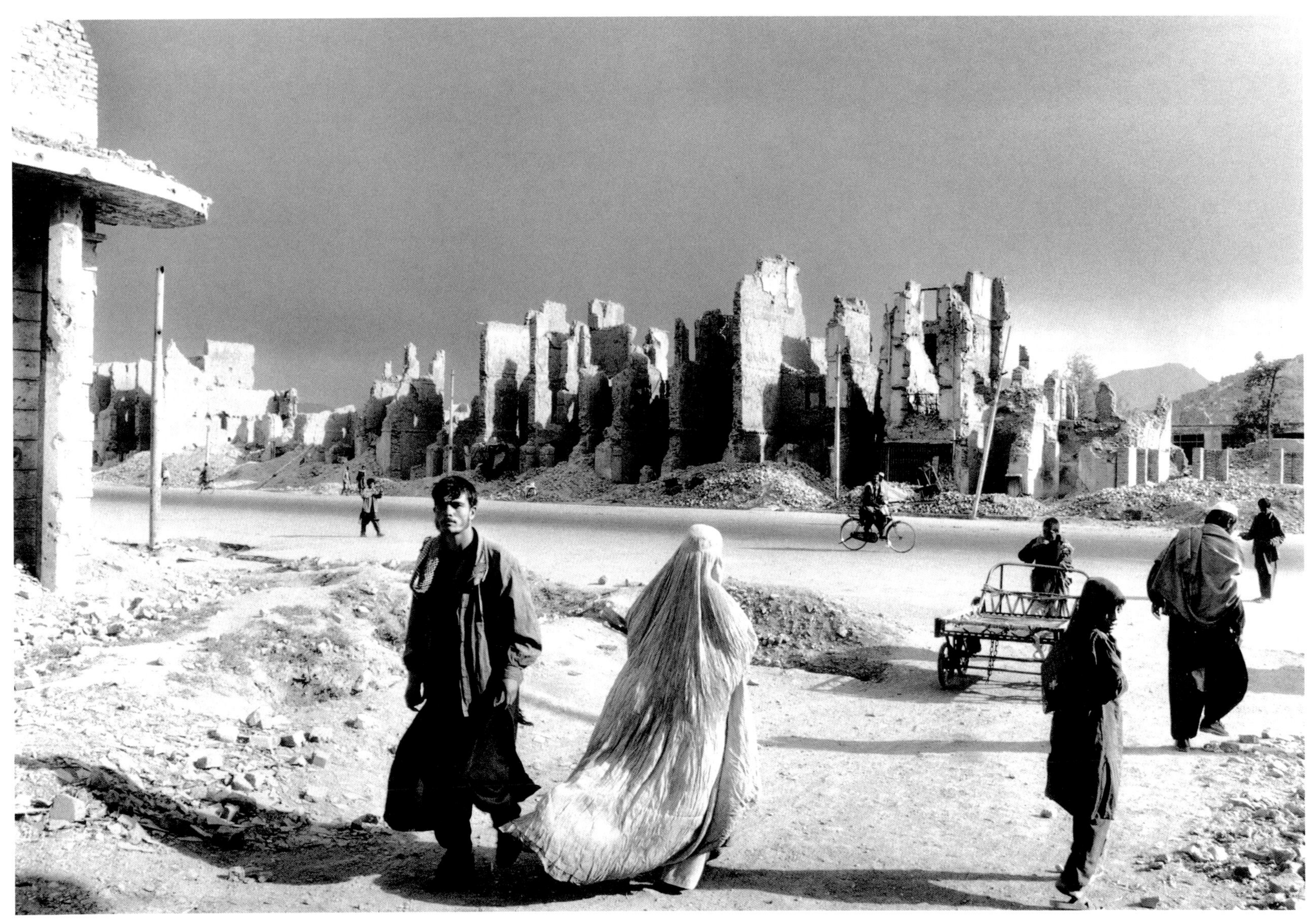

THESE PAGES: photographs by Sebastião Salgado.
OPPOSITE: *The gold mine.* Serra Pelada, State of Pará, Brazil, 1986; from *Workers: An Archaeology of the Industrial Age* (Aperture, 1993).
ABOVE: *Kabul, Afghanistan*, 1996; from *Migrations: Humanity in Transition* (Aperture, 2000).

And never have I found the limits of photographic potential. Every horizon, upon being reached, reveals another beckoning in the distance. Always, I am on the threshold. . . .

—W. Eugene Smith, *Aperture* vol. 14, nos. 3–4, 1969

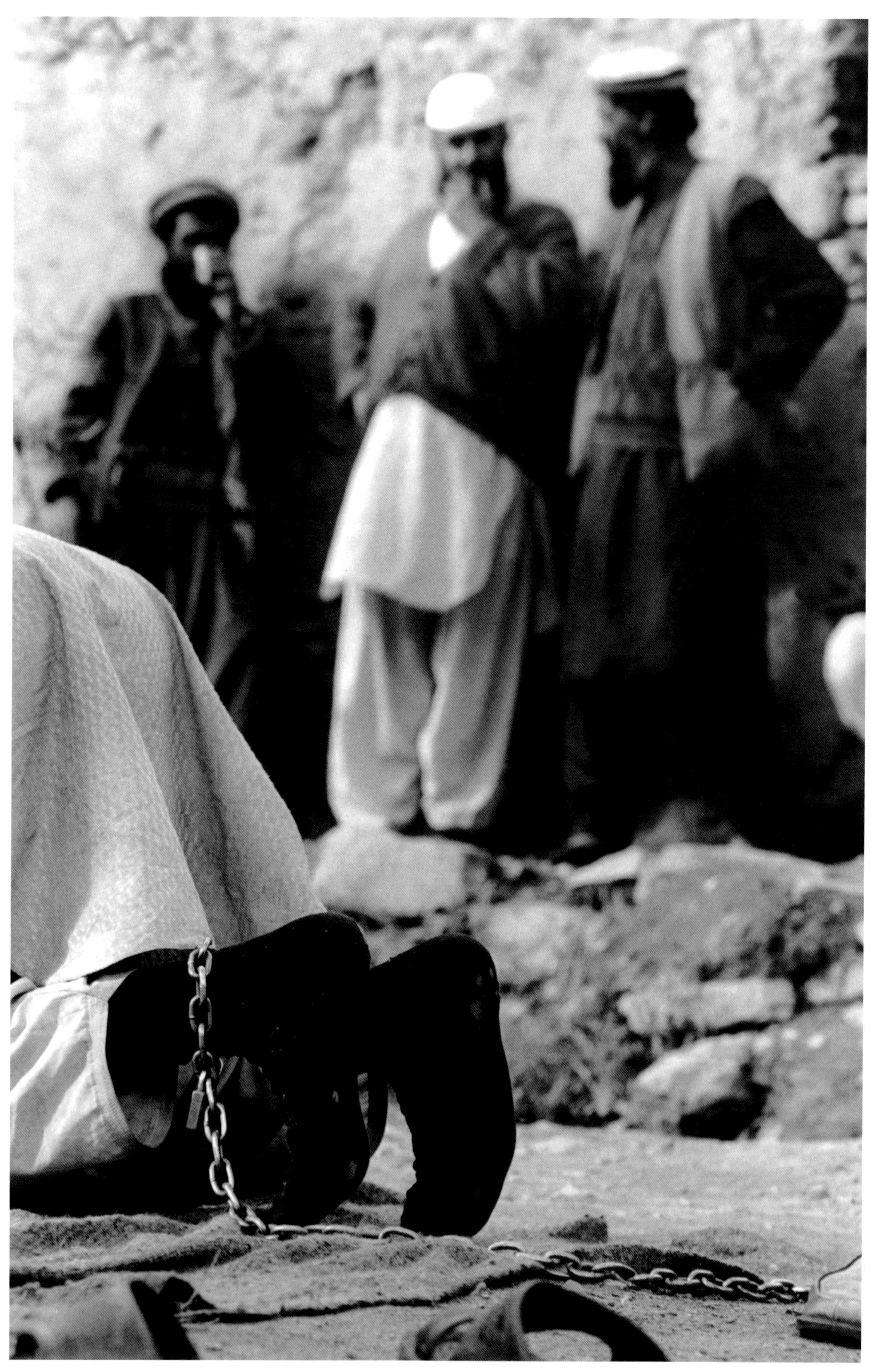

Chris Steele-Perkins, Captured Taliban prisoners held by Massoud's forces, Afghanistan, 2001.

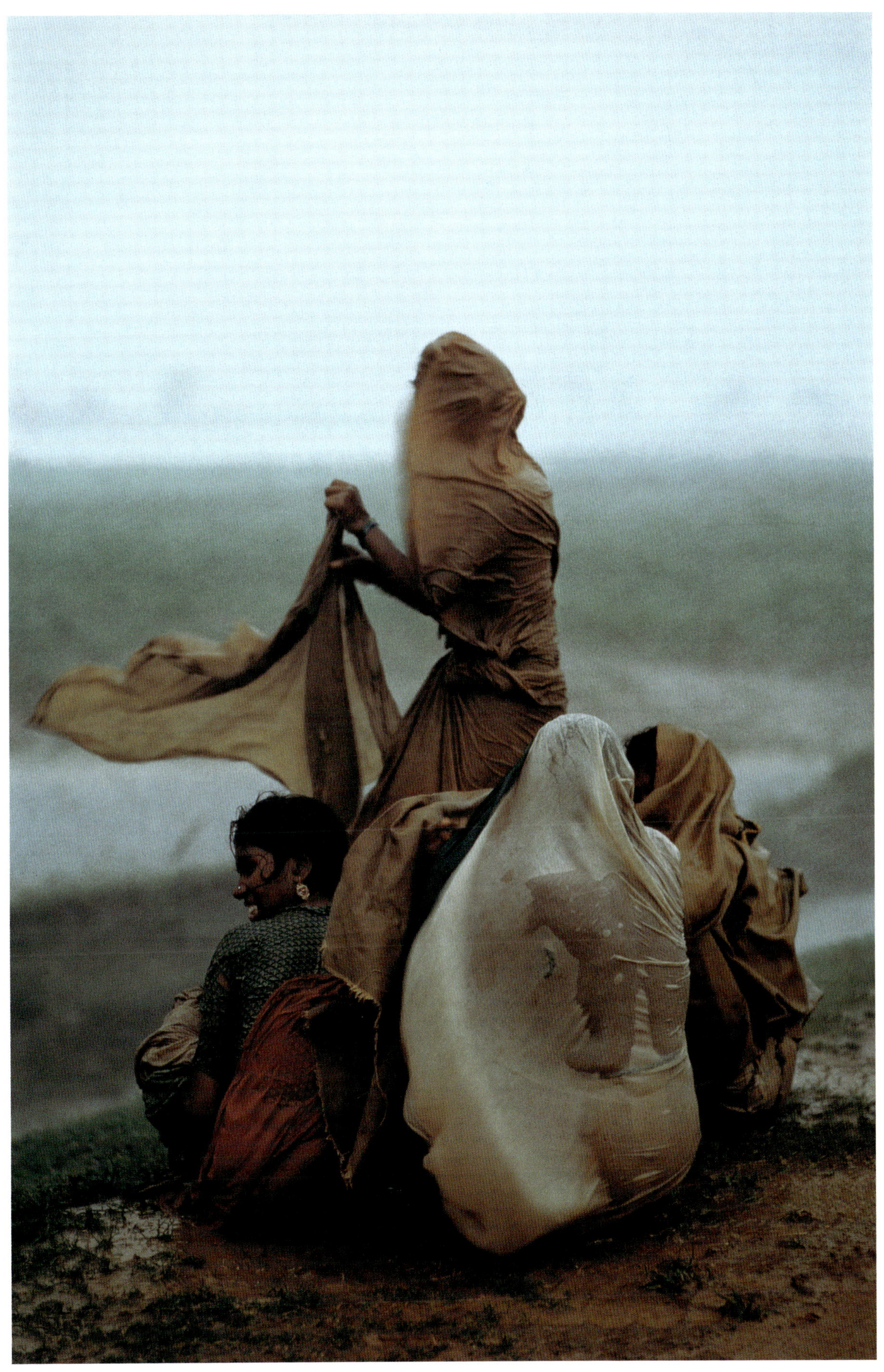

Raghubir Singh, Women caught in monsoon rains, Bahir, 1967; from *Aperture* 105, 1986.

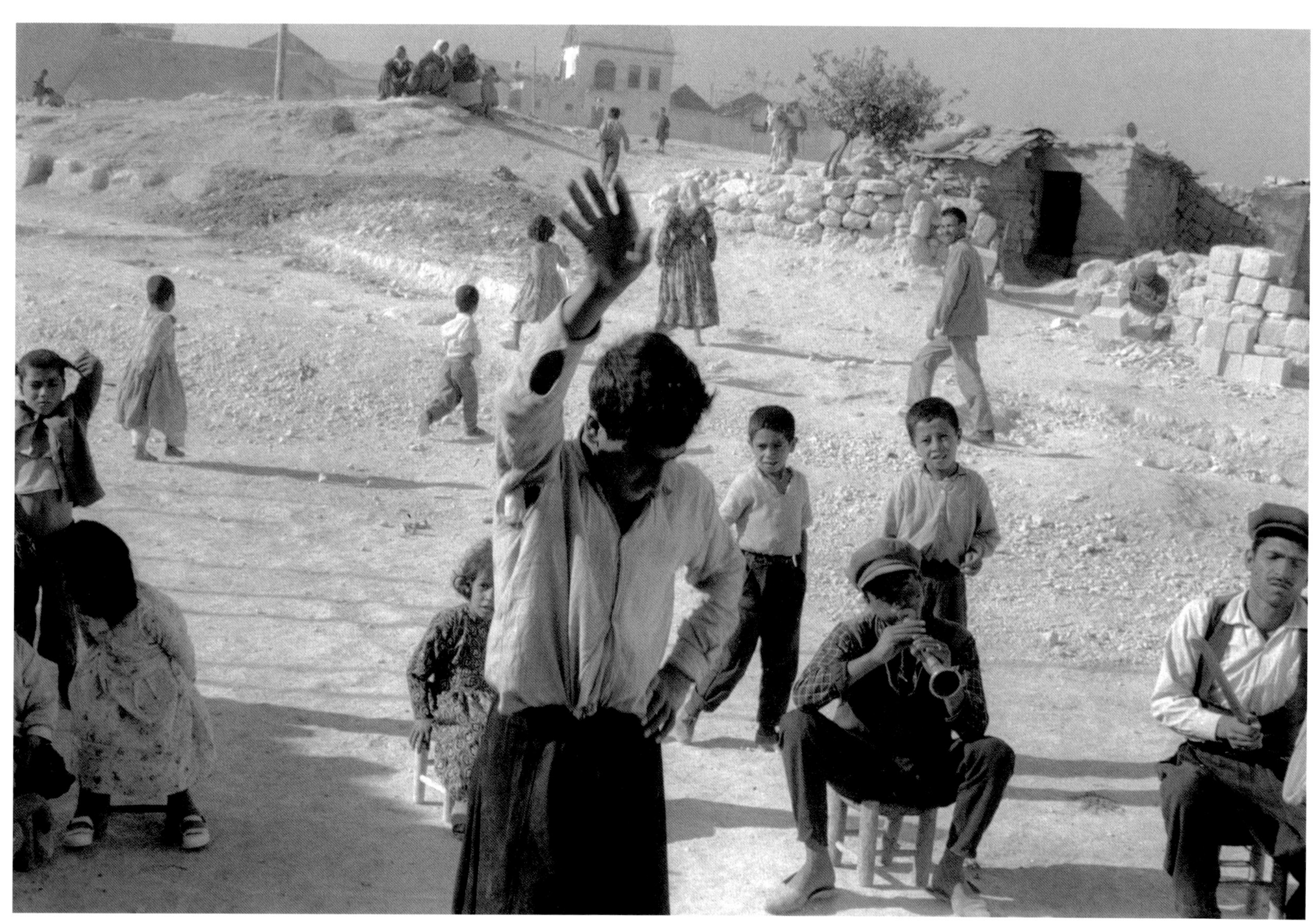

Henri Cartier-Bresson, *Turkey*, 1964; from *Aperture* vol. 13, no. 4, 1968.

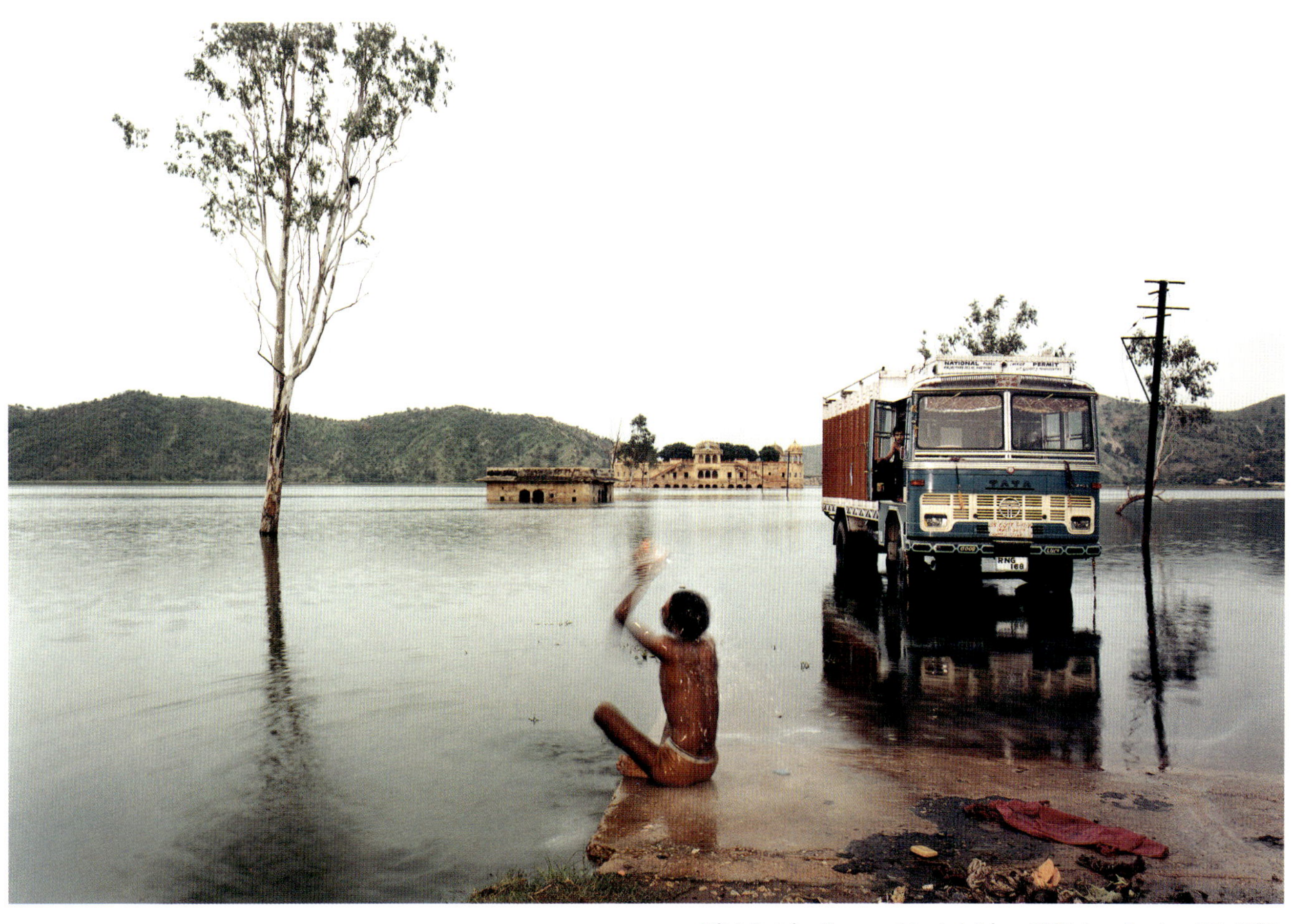

Mitch Epstein, *Monsoon*, Jalmahal, Jaipur, 1985; from *Aperture* 105, 1986.

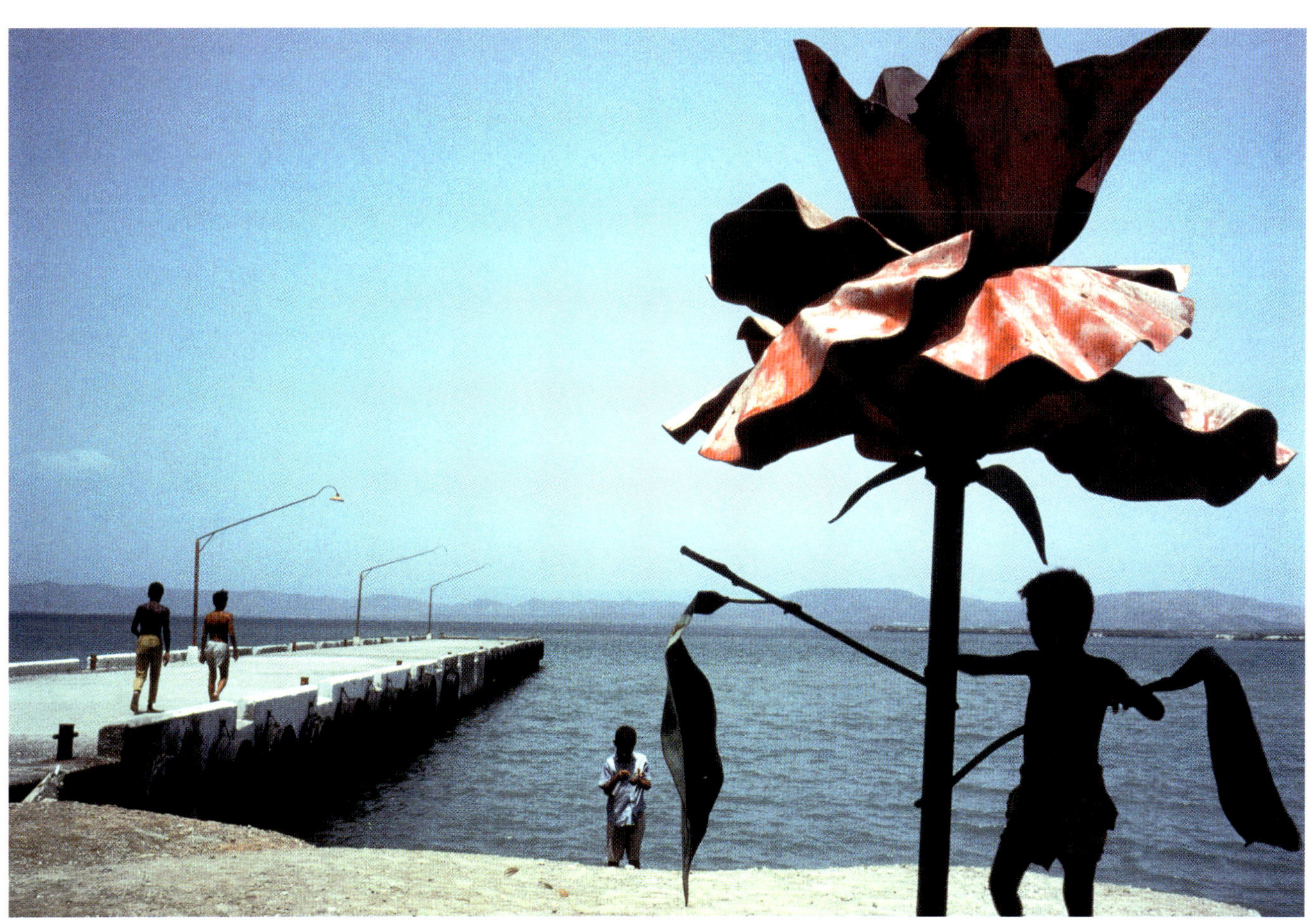

Alex Webb, *Guantanamo Bay, Cuba*, 1993; from *Aperture* 141, 1995.

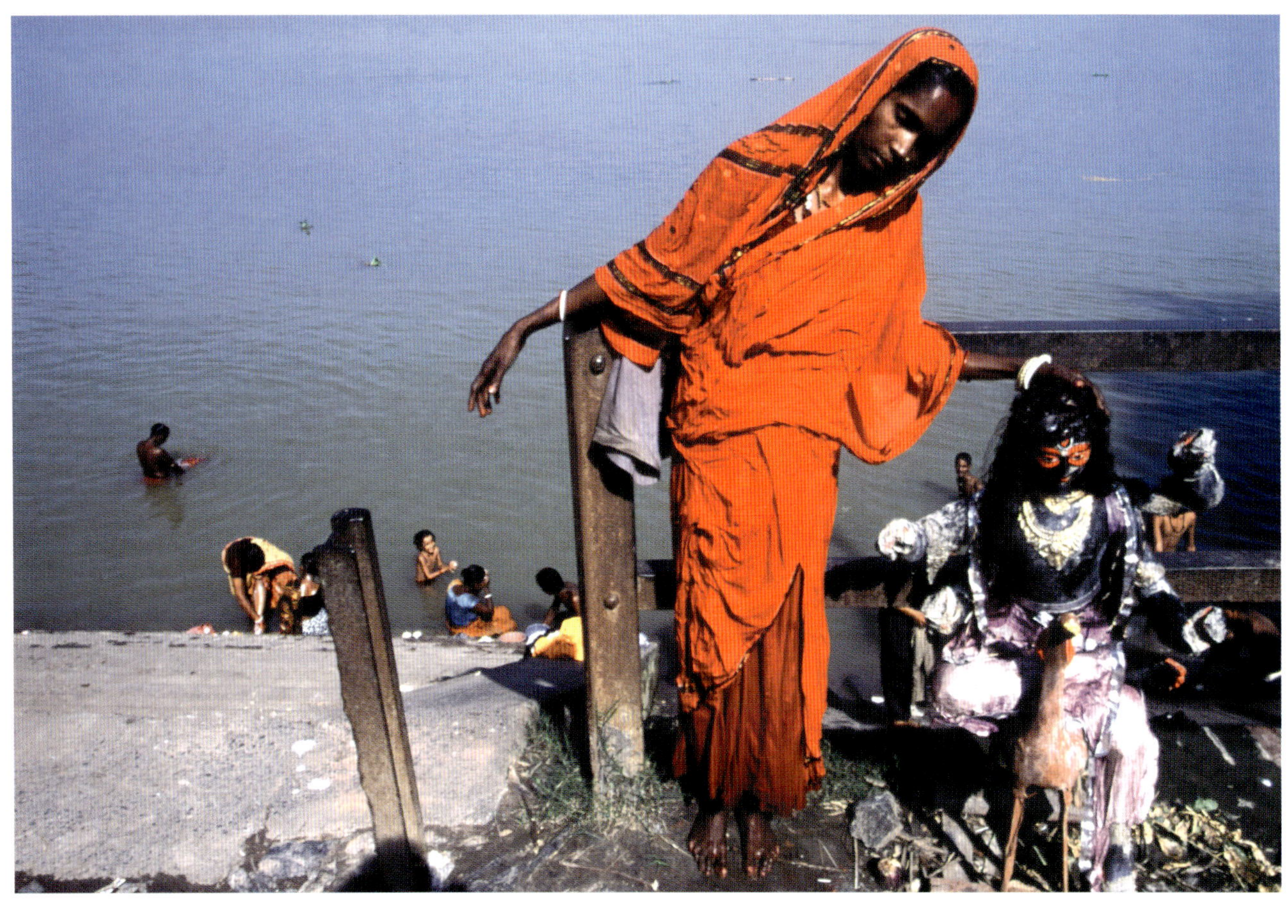

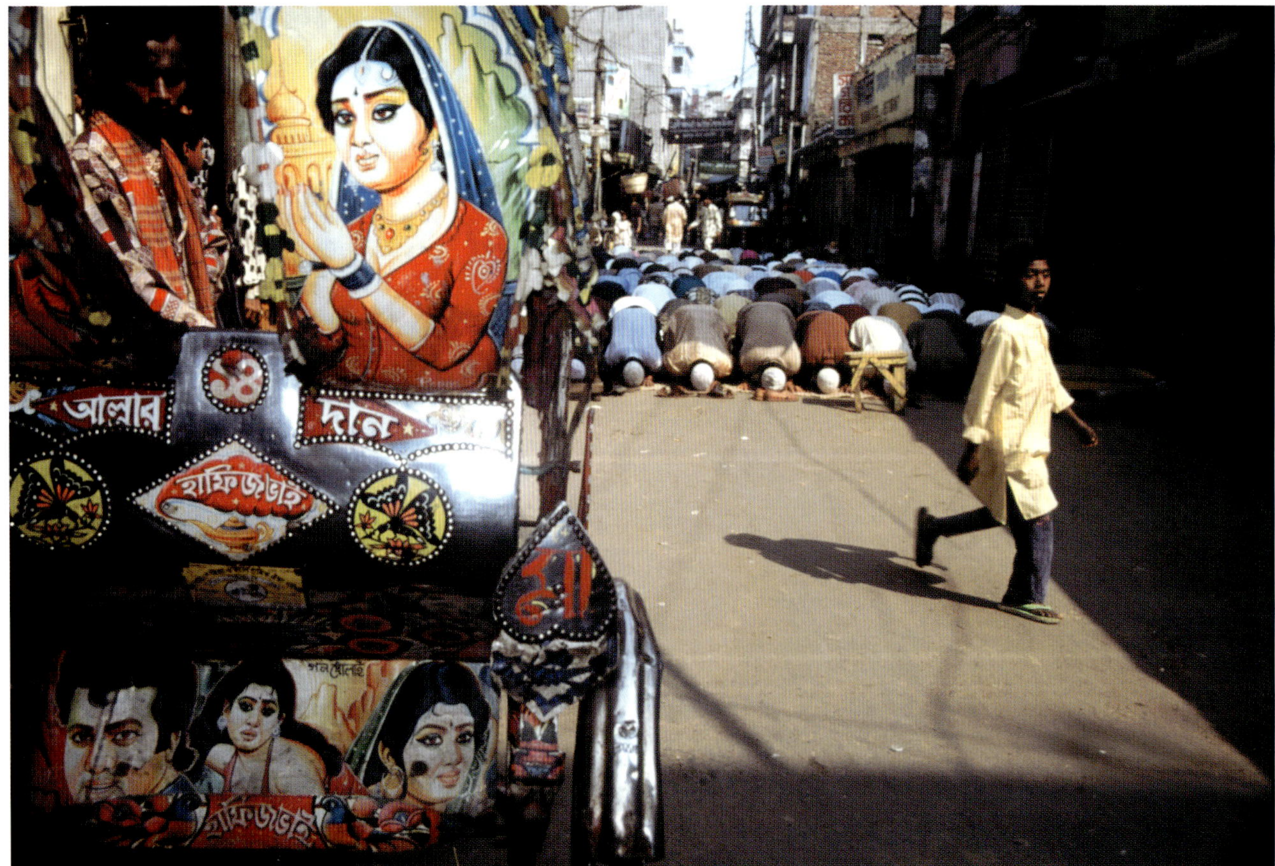

THIS PAGE: photographs by Raghu Rai. TOP: ***With Goddess Kalima*****, Calcutta, 2000. BOTTOM:** ***Prayer time,*** **Dhaka, 2000.**

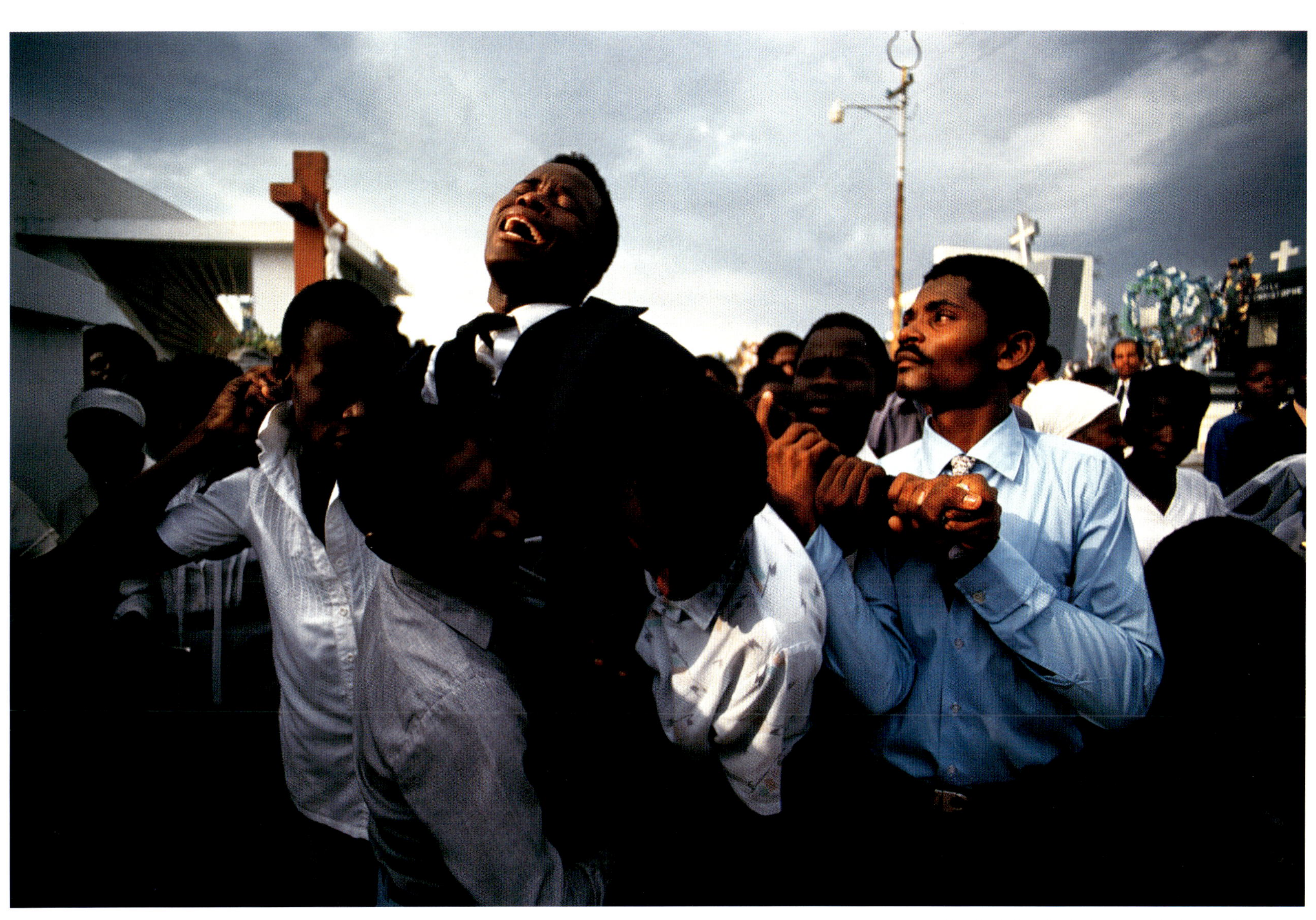

Maggie Steber, *Mother's Funeral*, 1987; from *Dancing on Fire: Photographs from Haiti* (Aperture, 1996).

Castro reappeared. He had just spoken to a women's conference, and now spoke spontaneously for more than an hour and a half about photography, and about health care and baseball and video cassettes and other subjects, quickly moving back and forth from one to the other. During his talk, almost no one moved; a large group of photographers remained standing in the front of the hall.

At the end of his talk, Fidel Castro greeted Manuel Alvarez Bravo, considered Latin America's greatest photographer, who had not lectured but sat through the conference like any other delegate. For many delegates it was a major historical moment—Latin America's greatest photographer being presented to the man whom many consider its greatest politician.

The following text is an excerpt from Castro's speech. —Fred Ritchin

. . . But I have seen many books of Cuban photography containing nothing but pictures. There is a recently printed book called *Twenty-five Years Under Revolution*, designed with only photographs. It is wonderful, it has immense value for us. Even if it is difficult to picture an idea, a crowd that sustains its fight for an idea eventually achieves it.

We are very sorry that we didn't have a photographer with us during the revolutionary war or during the first years of struggle, while we were underground, or during the advance to Moncada. We should have taken some photographs but we didn't think about it. There are a few pictures of those days, but there should have been more. We would now be able to write the history of our revolution with those pictures alone.

Unbelievable as it may sound, we have no pictures from when we were on board the *Gramma*, not one. We would have loved it if only an amateur had photographed us. Even Che, who was an amateur photographer and liked to try almost everything, didn't have a camera with him at the time. If only we had a camera with us that day on the *Gramma*, maybe we would now have photographs of the *compañeros*, of the thrilling moments, of the disembarkment, and of all the revolutionary war. Now, after almost thirty years, you feel sadness and regret for not carrying a camera with which you could have taken the pictures that would now speak for themselves. On those occasions, as on so many others, it is only after time passes that people realize that they have been through historical moments that will never be repeated, and that the memory fades. We are not so pretentious as to think that people will talk about us sixty years from now, but at least our relatives and descendants will have some interest in knowing what really happened during those years. We must preserve these moments through photography.

Time passes so quickly and the world changes so much within a short time that we ought to be conscious of the things we do, to make them as good as possible, so future generations will not think badly of us. At least we have the duty to leave a testimony about how we spent our time. Sometimes one regrets that photography was such a recent invention. When was photography invented? 1839? What a delay for man to discover such an interesting activity!

. . . The point is that the role of photography is very important for the development of progressive ideas and for the struggle of the poor nations of the world.

—From the Colloquium on Latin American Photography, Havana (1984), *Aperture* 100, 1985

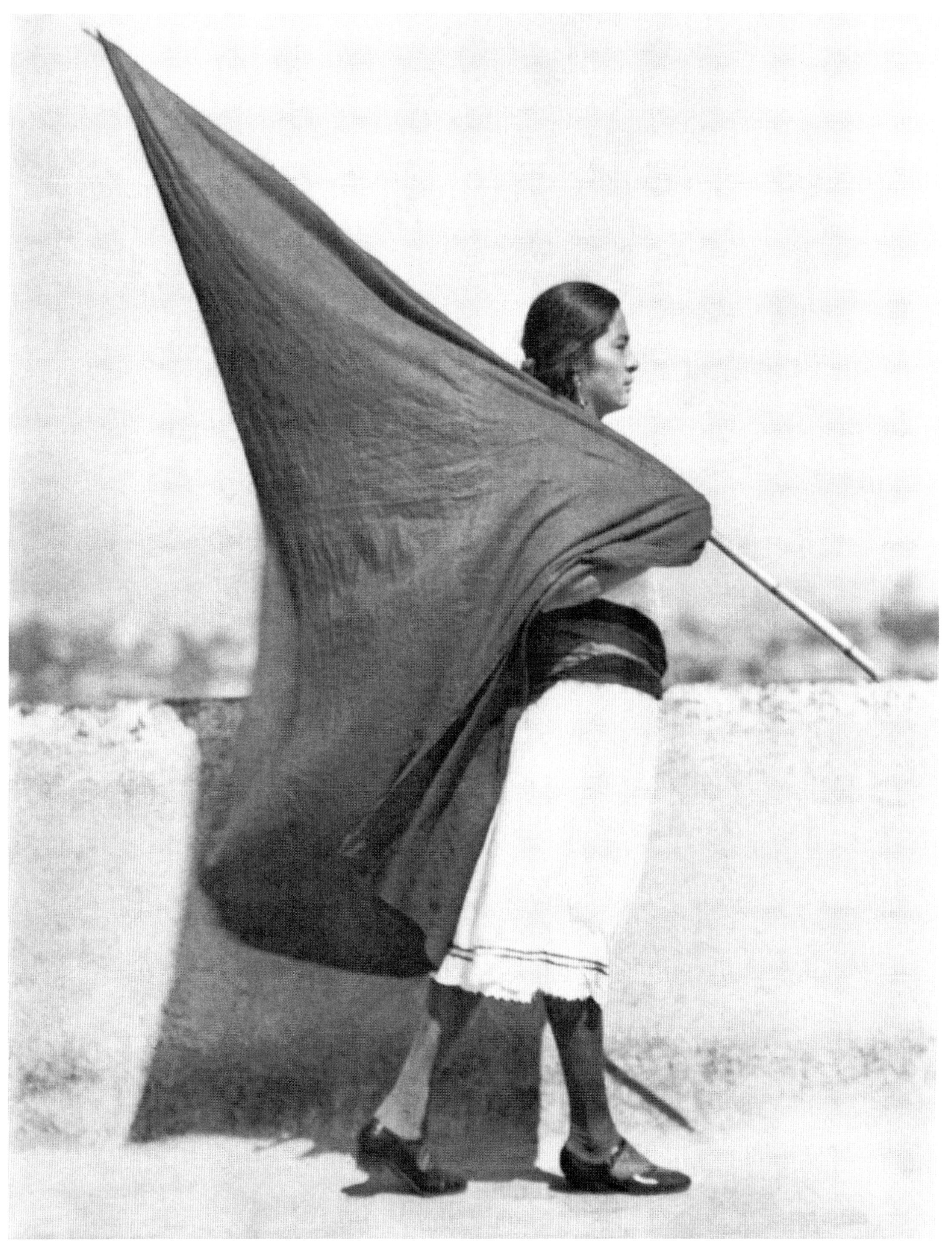

Tina Modotti, *Woman with Flag*, 1928.

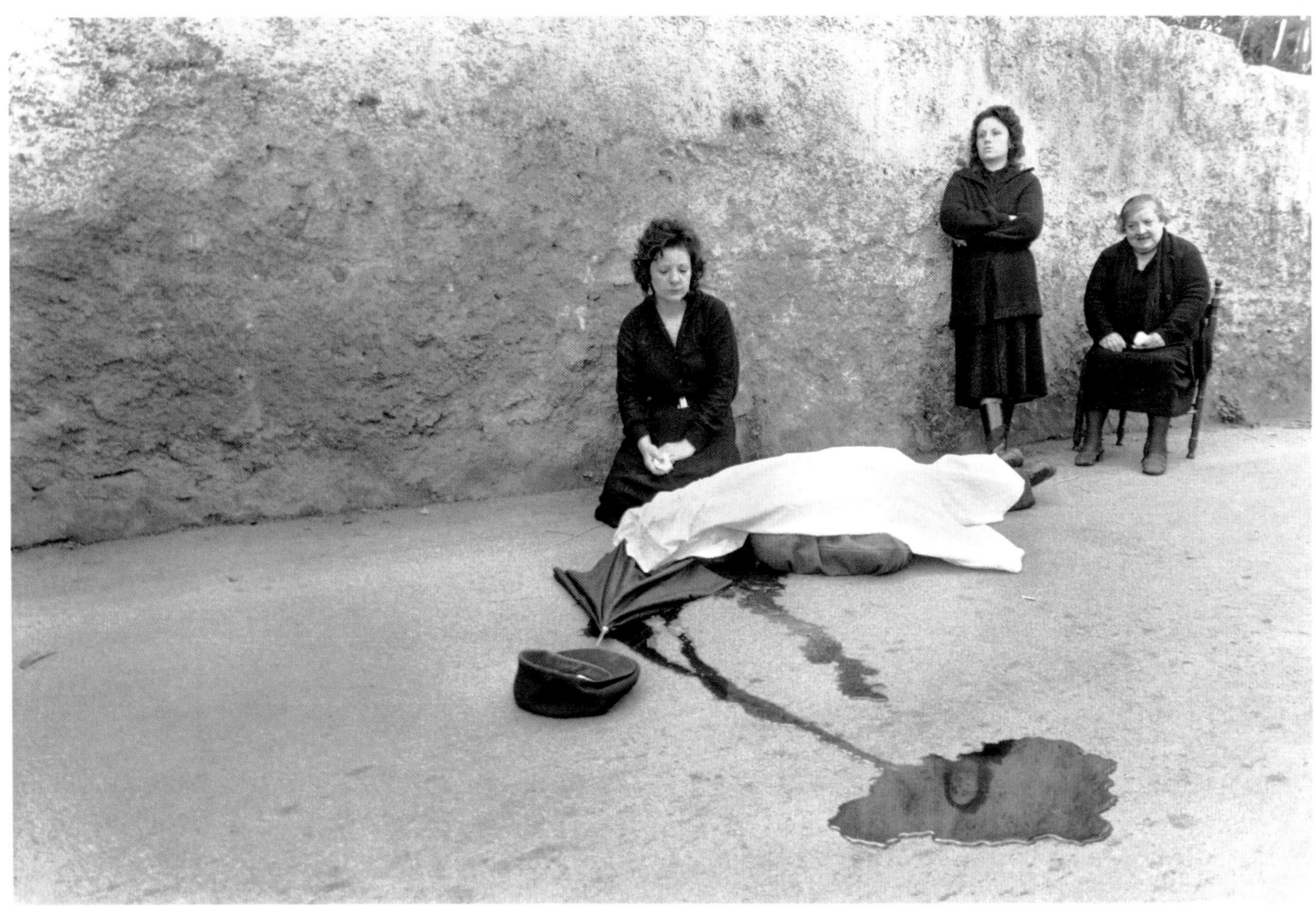

Franco Zecchin, The wife and daughters of Benedetto Grado at the site of his murder, Palermo, November 11, 1983; from *Aperture* 132, 1993.

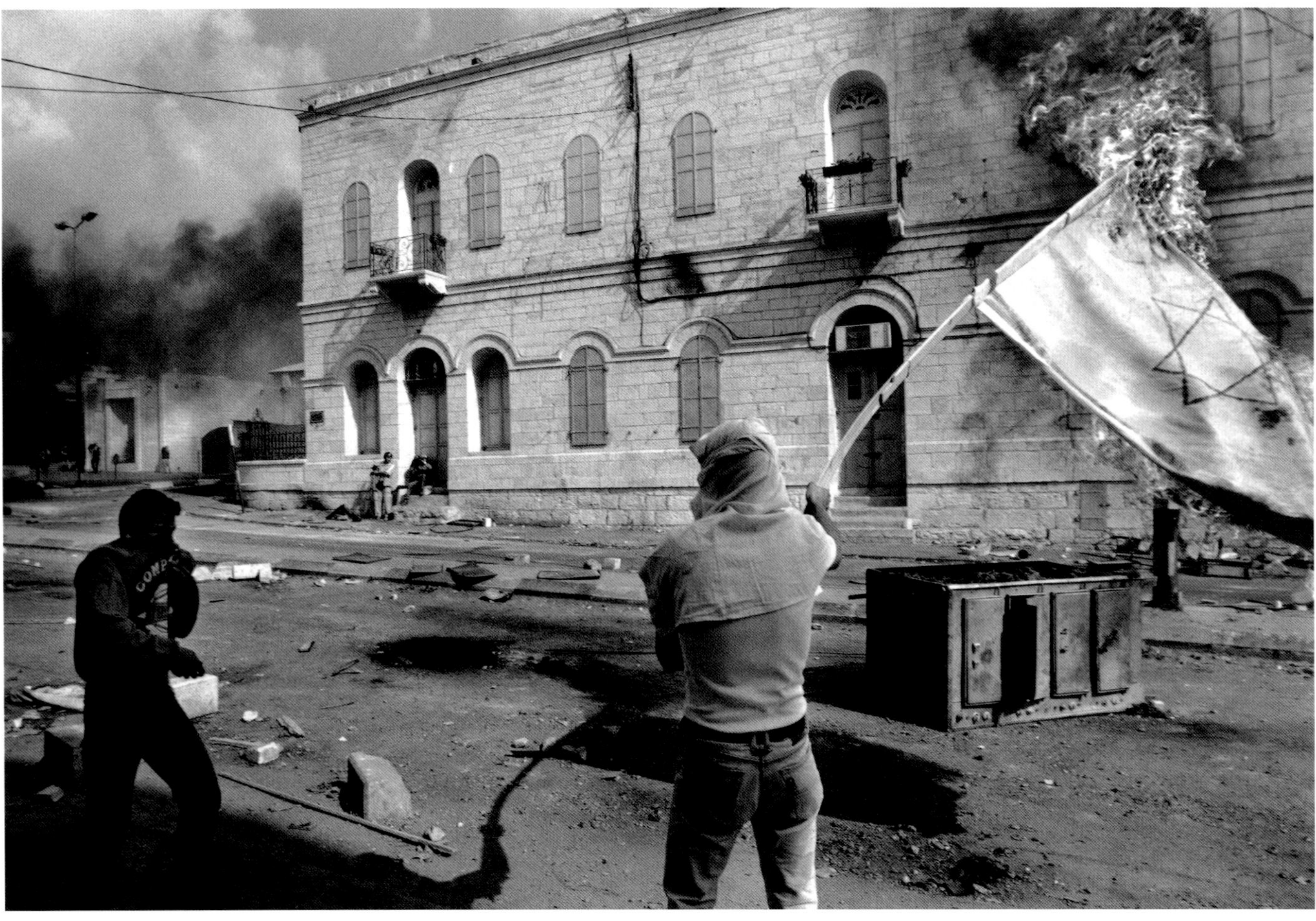

Larry Towell, Demonstrators burn a homemade Israeli flag in protest, Bethlehem, West Bank, 2000.

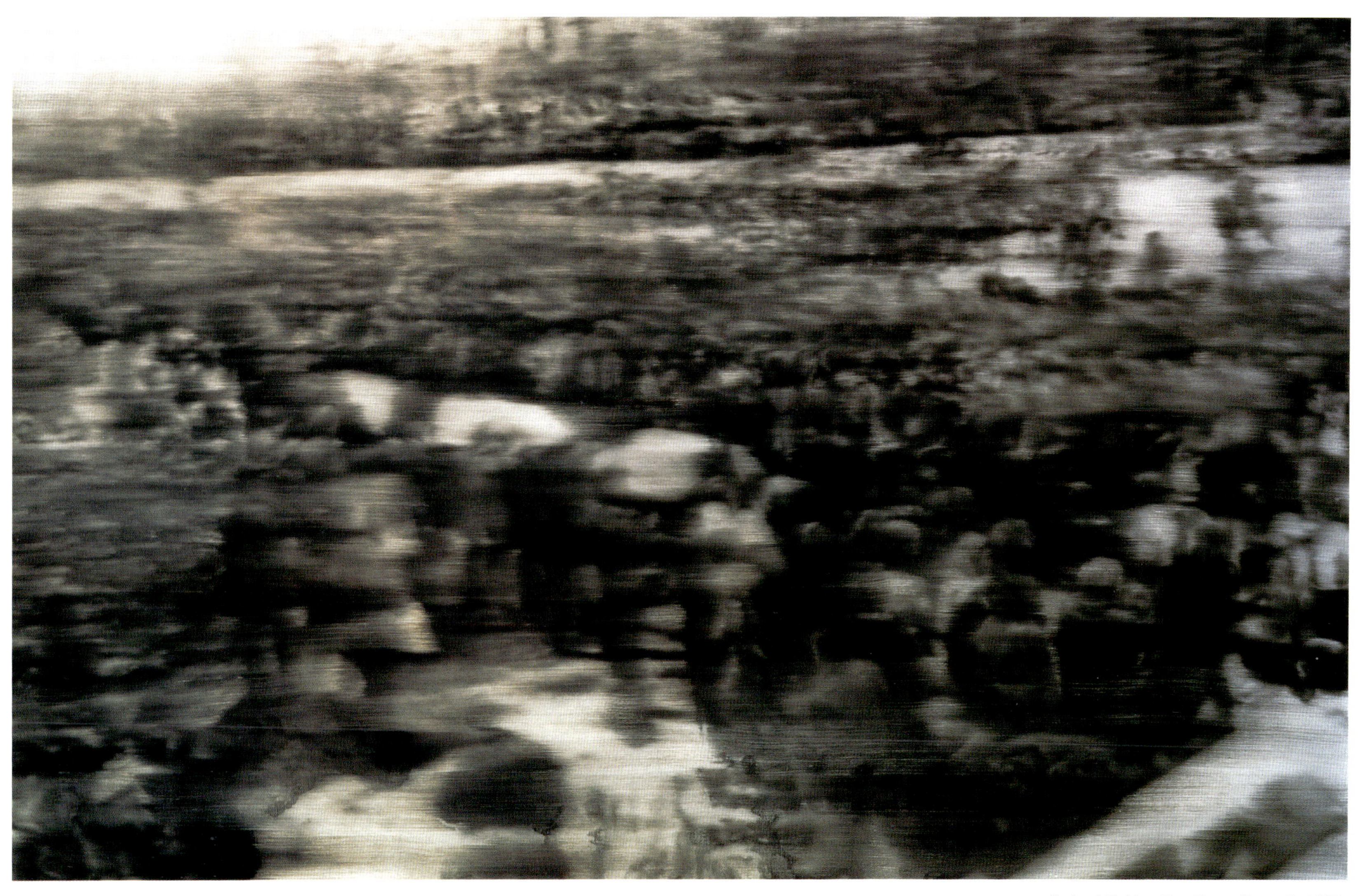

Gerhard Richter, *Beerdigung* (Funeral), 1988;
from *Aperture* 145, 1996.

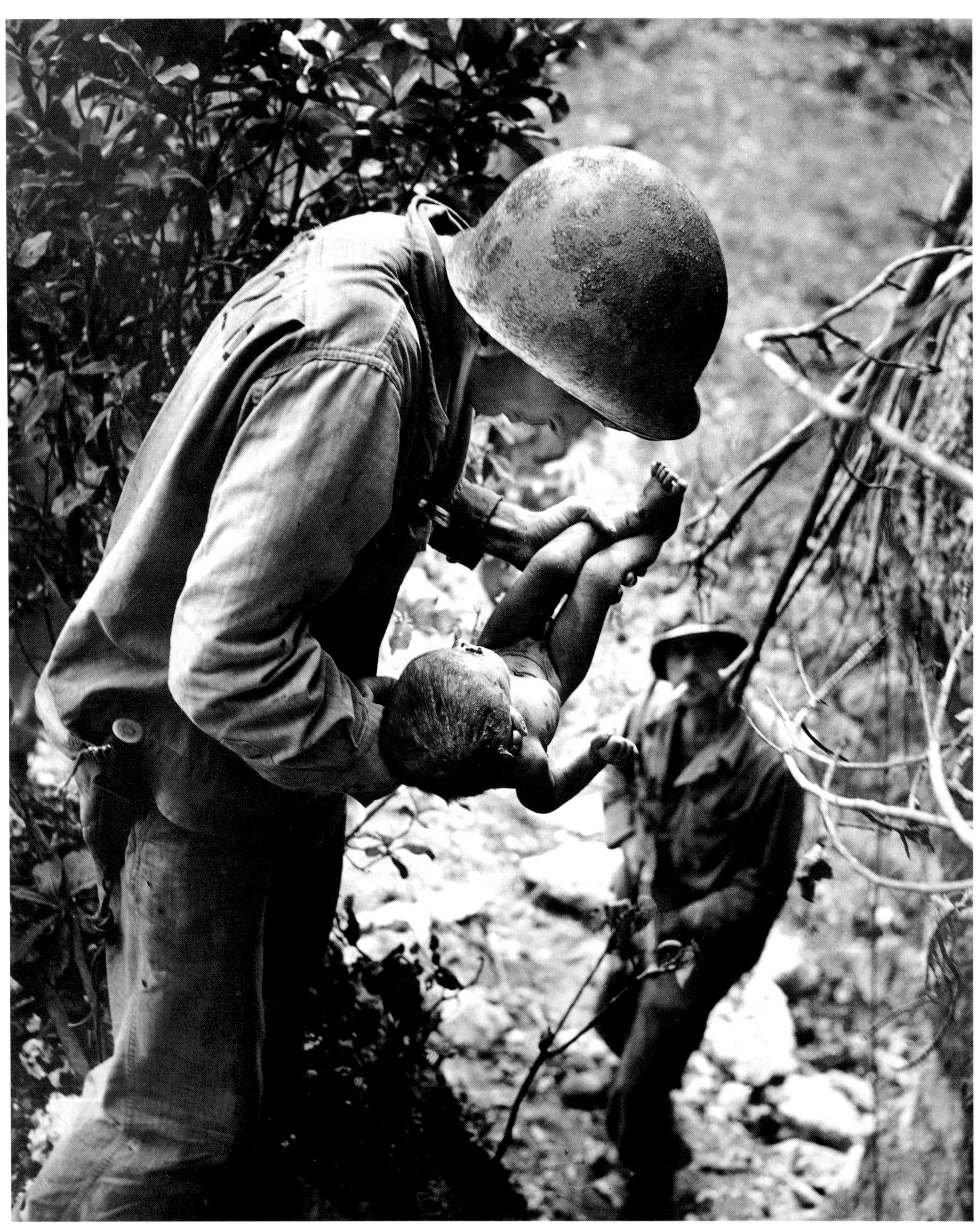

W. Eugene Smith, Wounded, dying infant found by American soldier in Saipan Mountains, June 1944; from *Aperture* vol. 14, nos. 3–4, 1969.

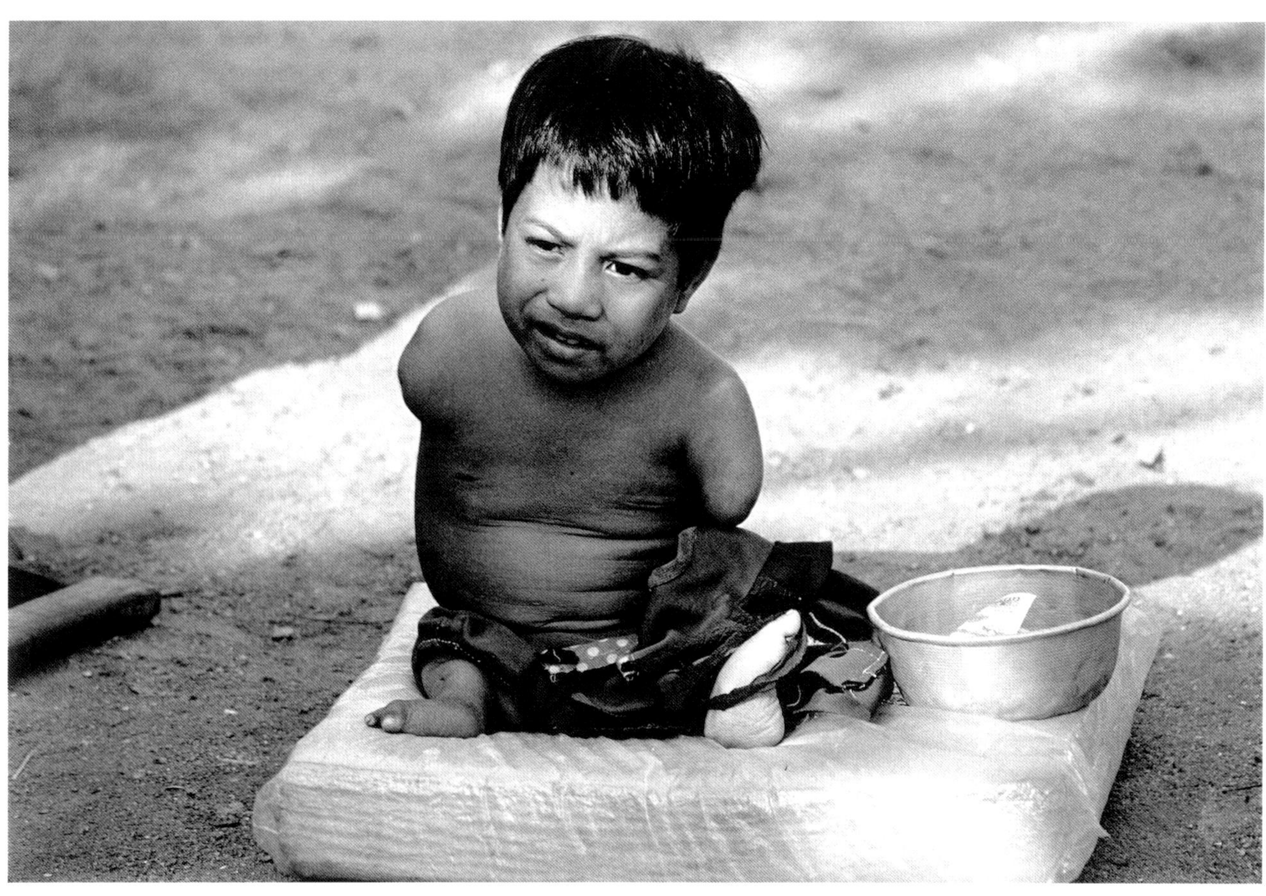

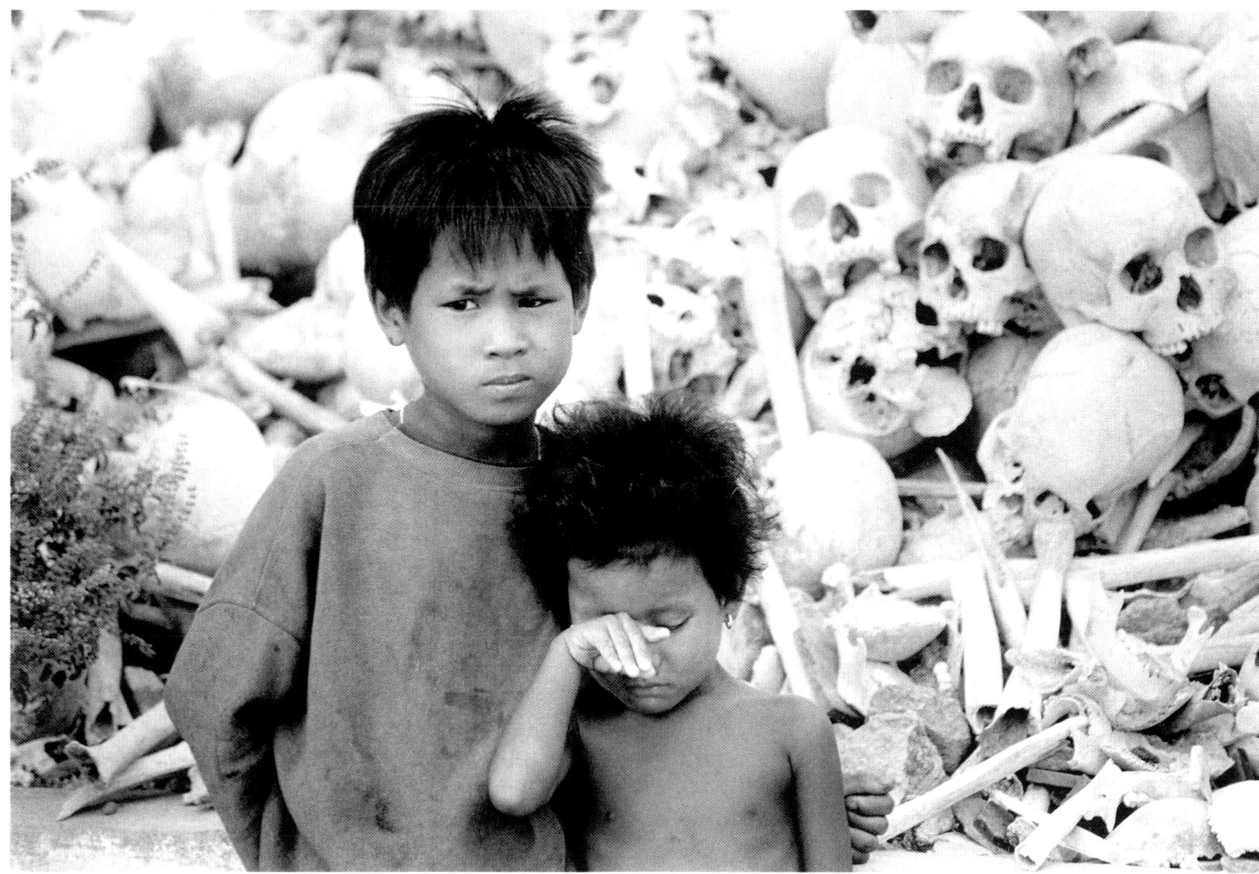

THIS PAGE: photographs by Philip Jones Griffiths.
TOP: A twelve-year-old boy from Svay Rieng, a Cambodian province adjoining Vietnam that was widely sprayed with Agent Orange by American airplanes. Many of those who were exposed to this poison during the Vietnam War remain seemingly healthy, yet their offspring will bear the effects of American chemical warfare for generations to come. This boy was brought to Phnom Penh to beg—as are many others—because the money he collects in this center of Western tourism will help support his family trapped in the poverty of the countryside, 1995.
BOTTOM: Village children before one of the many mounds of skulls that are scattered around Cambodia, 1996.

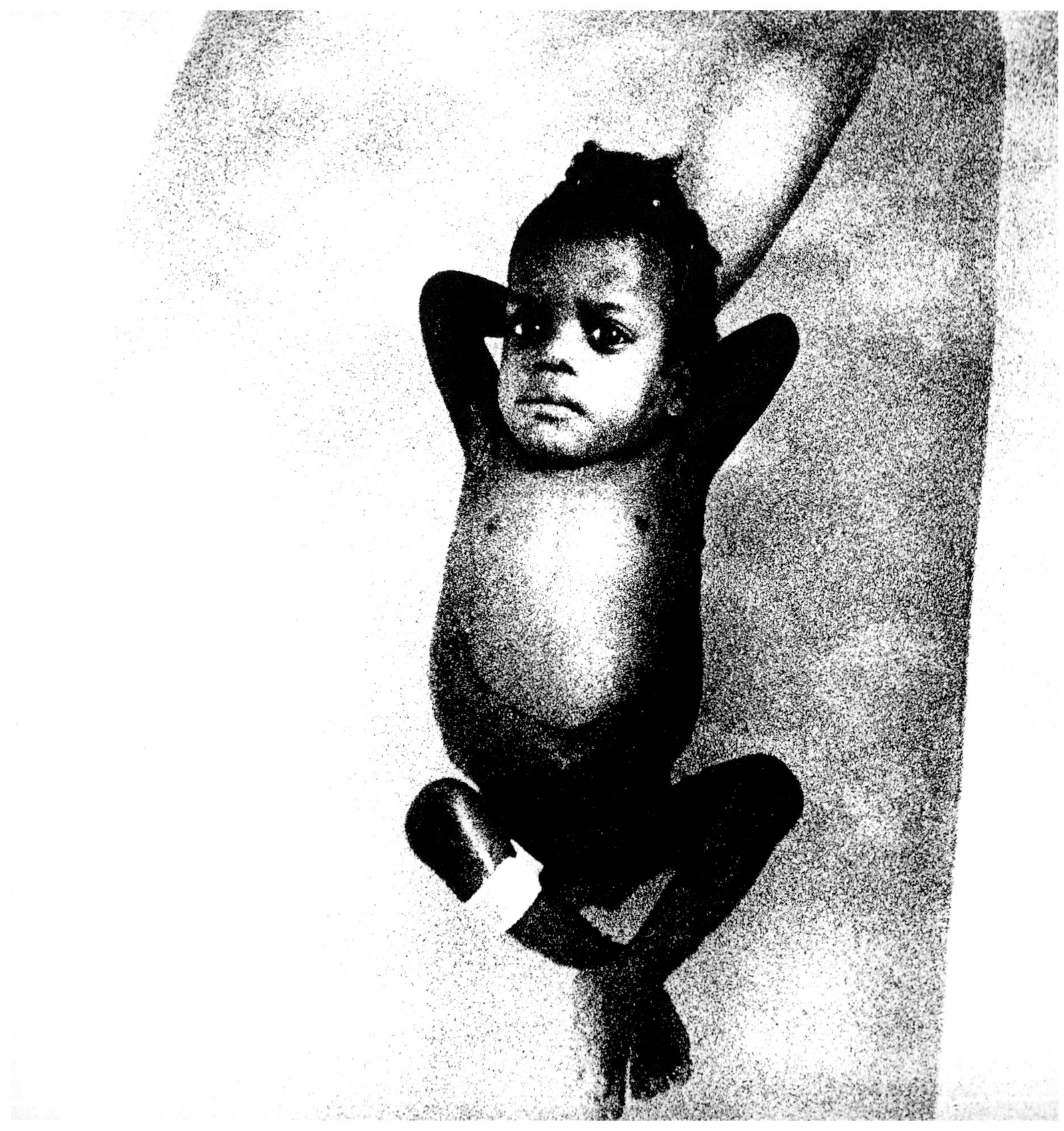

Brian Weil, *Prince, Two-year-old with AIDS*, New York City, 1986; from *Every 17 Seconds: A Global Perspective on the AIDS Crisis* (Aperture, 1992).

History is made by and for particular classes of people. A camera in some hands can preserve an alternate history.

—David Wojnarowicz, from "Close to the Knives," *Aperture* 137, 1994

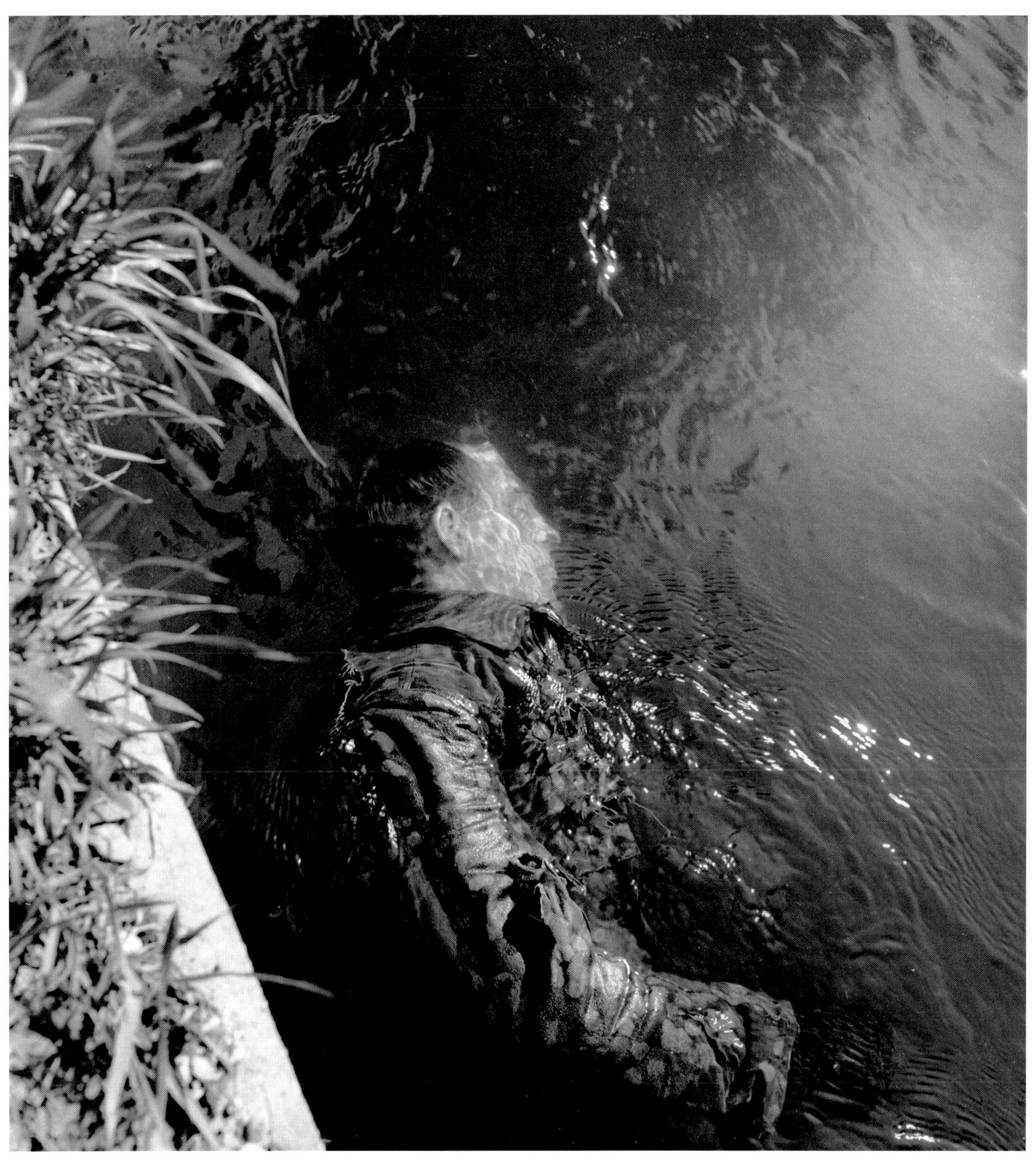

Lee Miller, *Dead German S.S. Prison Guard*, Dachau, April 30, 1945; from *Aperture* 103, 1986.

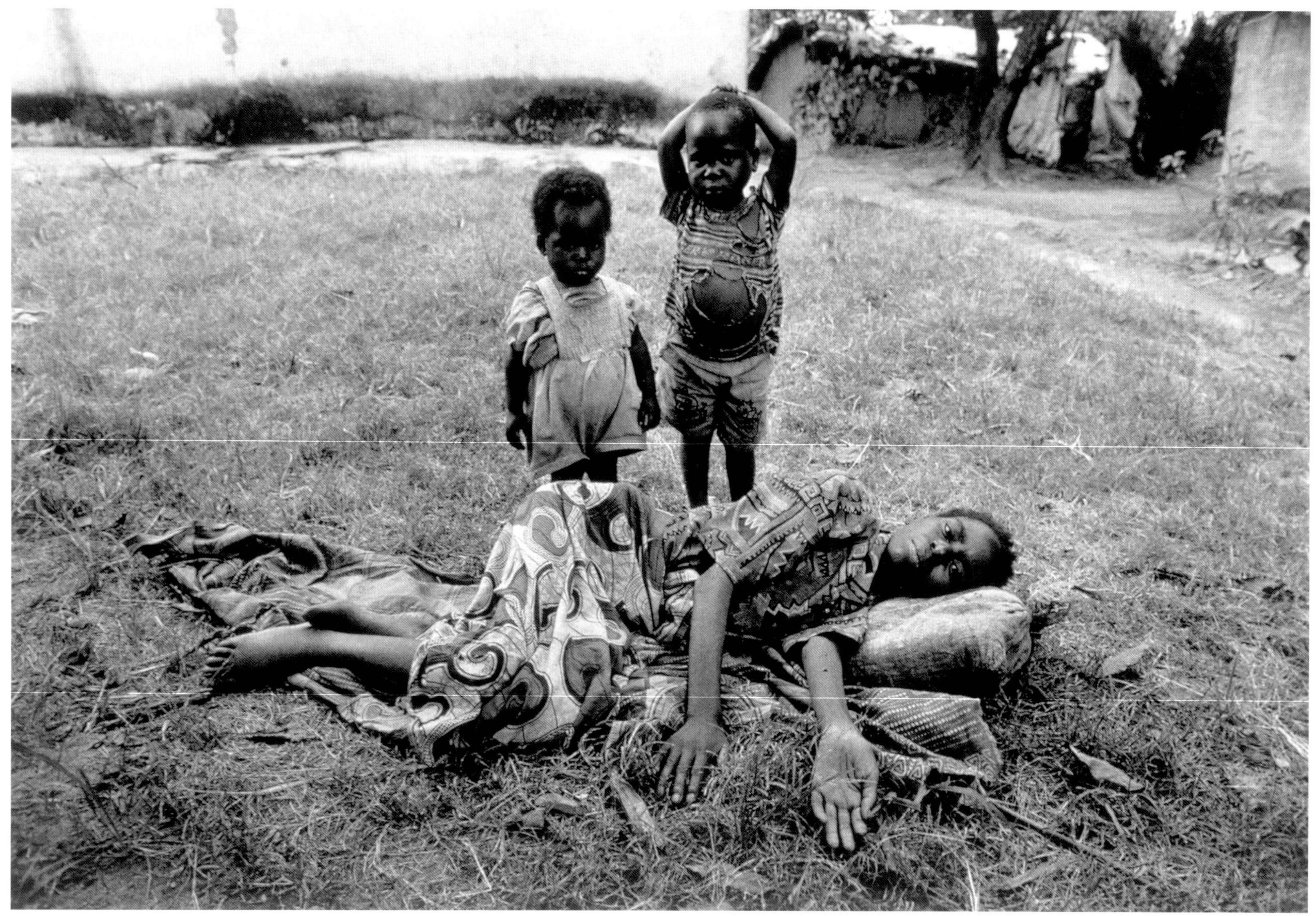

THESE PAGES: **photographs by Don McCullin, from a series on AIDS. Nkwazi compound in Ndola, Zambia, Justina Mkandawila with son Gift, five, and daughter Naomi, eighteen months old, February 2001.**

There are two courses open to the photographer. He can make the uncommon common. Or he can make uncommon the common.

The classic example of the photographer who aims to make the uncommon common is the news photographer. His goal is not to record the ordinary and the everyday, but the extraordinary and the unusual. Wherever there is disaster, the newsman is there. If he cannot find disaster, he searches for the odd and the peculiar, the exotic and the unfamiliar. His photographs, seen by millions, make momentary events and strange occurrences all over the world our common property. What more striking evidence could be offered of this power of photography than the atom bomb? The mushroom cloud, the very symbol of nuclear fission, has become known through photographs.

—Beaumont Newhall, from "Photographing the Reality of the Abstract," ***Aperture*** **vol. 4, no. 1, 1956**

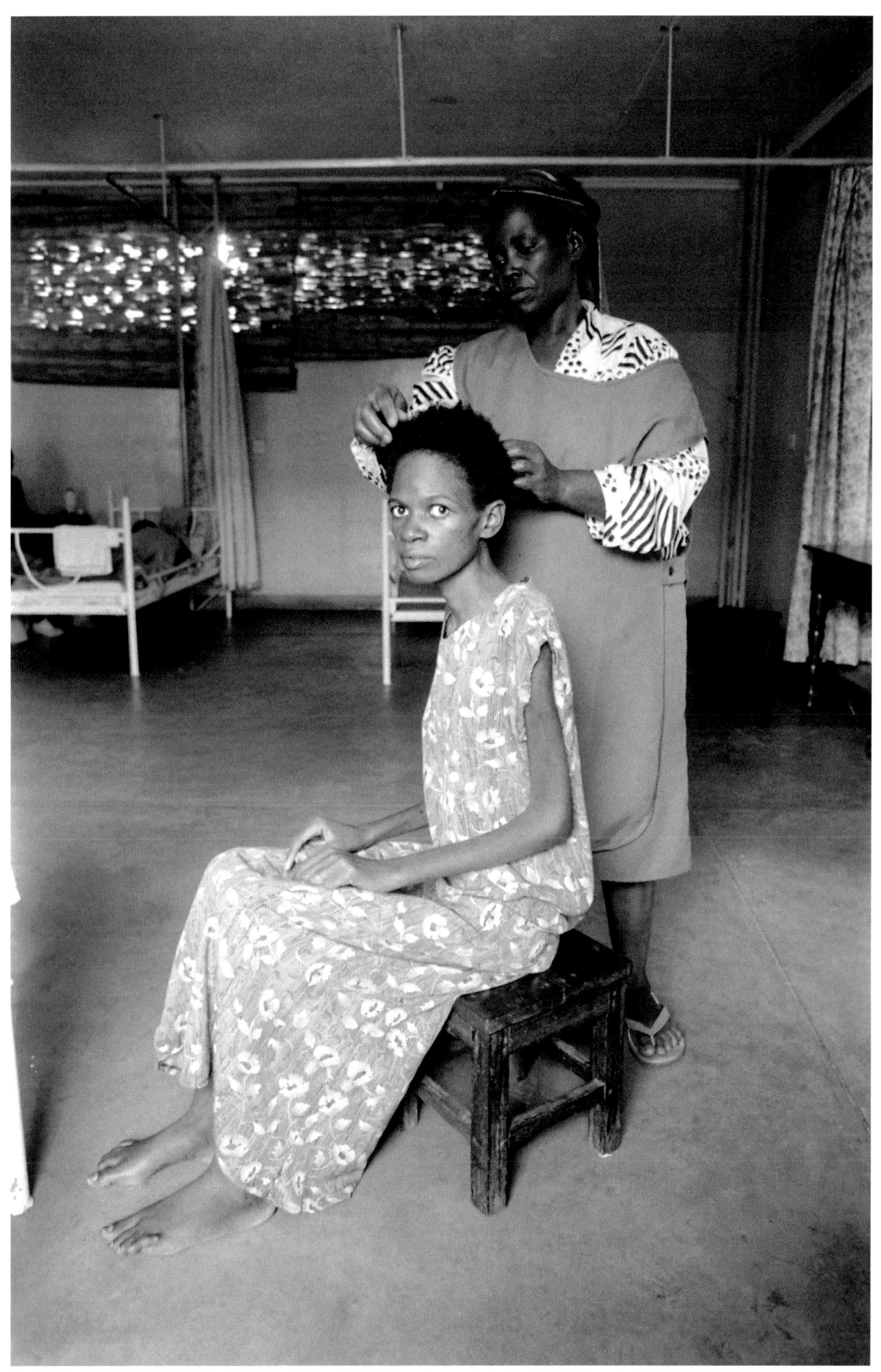

Cicetekeio Hospice, Ndola, Zambia, Hospital patient Mildred Moyo, twenty, has her hair styled by a volunteer worker, February 2001.

PART II

Contexts, Conflicts, and Congeries

Eternity is in love with the productions of time.
—William Blake, *Proverbs from Hell*

Comprehending the history of anything is largely a matter of context, and what is left out can be as revealing as what lies within. A viewer/reader of *Aperture* in its early years wouldn't find a hint that the United States was in the thrall of an anti-Communist witch-hunt. Or that it was involved in a slaughterhouse war in Korea. Or that people throughout the world had begun the decades of living with the nightmare of nuclear holocaust.

Nor was there much concern in the journal with art in general. No glimpse of the furor caused by Allen Ginsberg's riotous poem "Howl." Nor with the indignant reactions to the thrusts and drips of color on Jackson Pollock's "Action Paintings." Nor with the dismaying arrival from France and Italy of a new wave of erotic, existentialist filmmaking. It was a time when popular art comforted with Norman Rockwell illustrations in magazines, *I Love Lucy* on television, and paint-by-numbers kits that had hobbyists by the millions daubing coded colors onto numbered diagrams from which emerged manufactured scenes of dire sentimentality. It was a period of art when the elite was outraging the proletariat which, in turn and fairly enough, was appalling the elitists. It was not a new story.

Exactly thirty years before *Aperture* was founded, Stieglitz put forth his ideal in art of "equivalents." And it was also in 1922 that Sinclair Lewis published his novel *Babbitt*, whose hero was to become the immortal spokesman of the American cultural philistine. As George F. Babbitt memorably points out in his speech to his business community's hail-fellow Booster Club:

> In other countries, art and literature are left to a lot of shabby bums living in attics and feeding on booze and spaghetti; but in America the successful writer or picture painter is indistinguishable from any other decent businessman . . . [and] has a chance to drag down his fifty thousand a year, to mingle with the biggest executives on terms of perfect equality, and to show as big a house and as swell a car as any Captain of Industry.

It was within a context of Babbittry that Stieglitz had devoted his efforts to the "shabby bums," the visionaries both foreign and domestic of twentieth-century art. A generation later, *Aperture* was giving its pages to a visionary ideal of photography; it was an ideal charged with challenges and conflicts aplenty.

When Ansel proclaimed, "We have nothing to lose but our photography," he was not speaking about photographs and photographers. He was in broad strokes warning about the overpowering context of "their" photography. "They" were those who used the medium for purposes other than the artist's intent. "They" included art directors, designers, and photo-editors of magazines, advertising agencies, and other commercial or propagandistic enterprises. "They" engaged individuals of enormous talent, and the results were often brilliant: the riveting photo-essays of *Life* magazine, the lush color explorations in *National Geographic*, and the hypnotic fashion shoots of *Vogue* and *Harper's Bazaar*, to mention only a few. "They" also paid the bills—which "art photography," as it was then called (often disparagingly), did not. But these had always been the background conditions in the struggle to advance photography as an art form. The more serious threat, as some viewed it—Ansel among them—was emerging closer to the source in the person of one of the century's early champions of the art of photography, one of its foremost practitioners: Edward Steichen.

It is open to question whether Alfred Stieglitz was the most influential figure in American photography throughout much of the twentieth century. It is less arguable that his protégé Steichen was the most commanding.

Fifteen years younger than Stieglitz, Steichen was the son of immigrants from Luxembourg who settled in Milwaukee. His sister Lillian became a brilliant teacher and socialist activist, and the wife of poet Carl Sandburg. As for Edward, he was in every sense of the word self-made. After apprenticing as a lithographic designer and photographer for an advertising agency, Steichen at age twenty-one set out for Paris to study and establish himself as a painter and photographer. En route, he paid a call on Stieglitz, beginning an extraordinarily fruitful twenty-year collaboration to advance the art of photography and the Modernist movement in all of the plastic arts.

Theirs was a close kinship during most of those years, when Steichen divided his time between New York and his beloved Paris, and Stieglitz held forth in Manhattan. Stieglitz from the outset believed in Steichen as both painter and photographer. For his part, Steichen's independence was tamed to the older

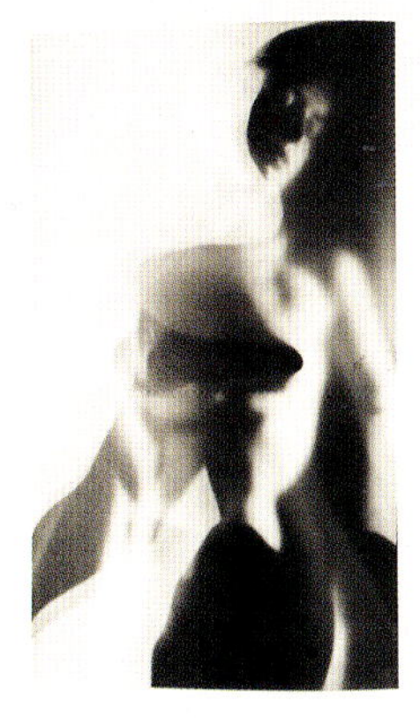
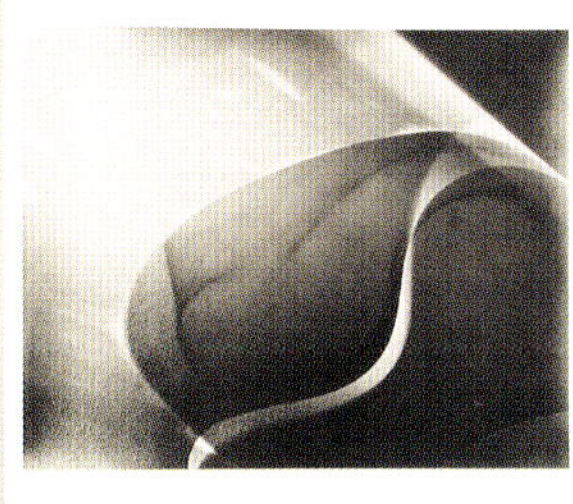

Stieglitz and Steichen had fought side by side for their vision of the medium, under the rubric of the Photo-Secession, which was generally what Stieglitz deemed it to be: a break from the past, a way of making photographs to be seen as pictures *and not as illustrations, documents, or derivatives of painting.*

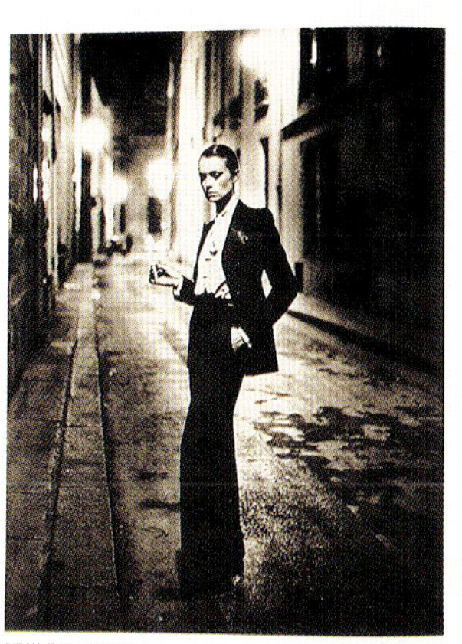
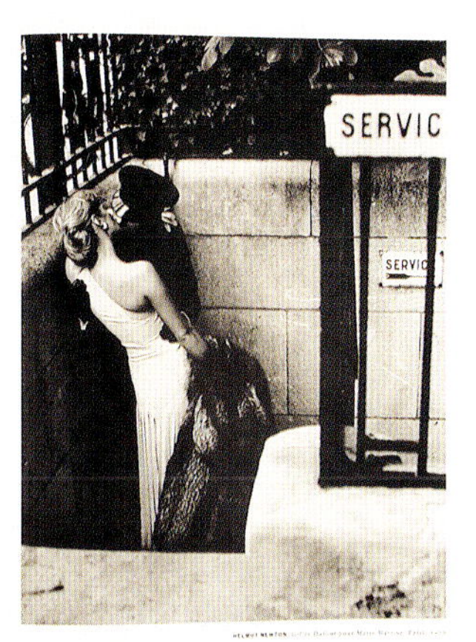

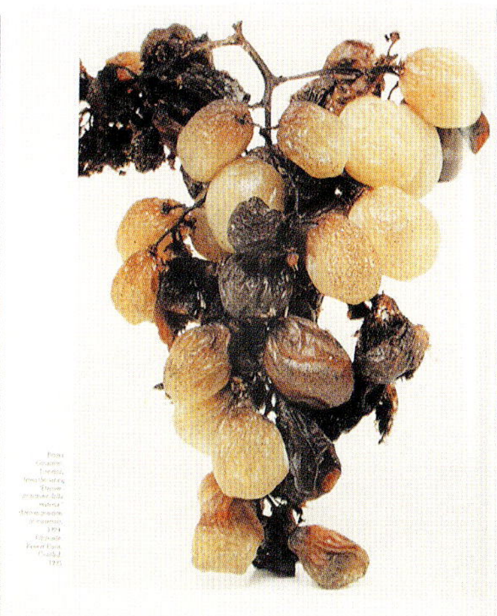
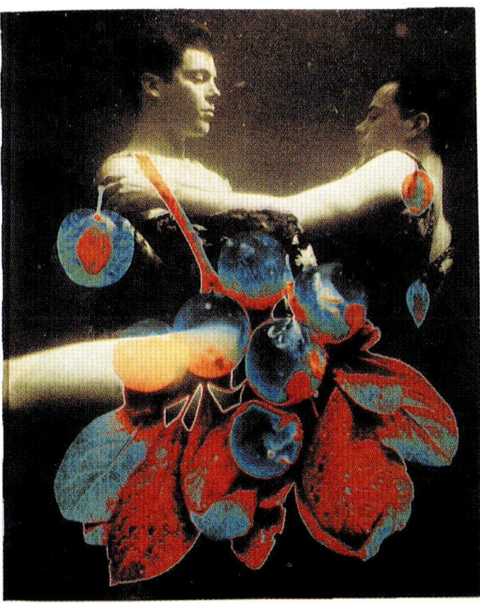

TOP: ***Aperture*** **vol. 14, no. 1, 1968, pages 28–29: (left) photograph by Ruth Bernhard; (right) photograph by Lotte Jacobi. MIDDLE:** ***Aperture*** **122, 1991, pages 94–95: photographs by Helmut Newton. BOTTOM:** ***Aperture*** **143, 1996, pages 24–25: (left) photograph by Bruna Ginammi; (right) photograph by Robert Flynt.**

man's taste, judgments, and adversarial stances. While Stieglitz is credited with introducing American audiences to the works of Rodin, Matisse, Picasso, and other European Modernists, it was Steichen who introduced them to Stieglitz—arranging for their works to be transported for exhibition at the 291 Gallery (which Steichen and his wife Clara had designed) and reproduced in *Camera Work*. This occurred in 1908, five years before the legendary New York Armory show that is purported to have launched Modern art in America.

By Steichen's twenty-second birthday, he had already achieved considerable renown in Europe, particularly for his flawlessly rendered "Impressionistic" pictures. His concentration upon a subject was obsessive. He spent a year photographing Rodin once or twice a week in his studio, then countless hours in the darkroom to create the picture of the master with his sculptures of *The Thinker* and Victor Hugo. By the end of World War I (and continuing into the following years), Steichen had created a body of photographic works that are among the medium's finest achievements.

The rupture between Stieglitz and Steichen began in the 1920s. It was inexorable, painful to both men, and had a profound effect on photography for decades. They had fought side by side for their vision of the medium, under the rubric of the Photo-Secession, which was generally what Stieglitz deemed it to be: a break from the past, a way of making photographs to be seen as *pictures* and not as illustrations, documents, or derivatives of painting. Stieglitz and Steichen also were generous, indefatigable promoters of other artists. They both had suffered, and supported one another through difficult first marriages. They were friends.

But there was an important difference between the two men. Stieglitz had been born to money, married money, and in his later years was supported by his successful second wife, Georgia O'Keeffe. Steichen had worked for every dime he ever made, and supported not only an ex-wife, a wife, and two daughters, but also his parents. Tired, as he said, of starving, he began after World War I to devote his energies to commercial photography. As the 1920s progressed, he became America's foremost, and most highly paid, portraitist and advertising photographer, and the senior photographer for Condé Nast's *Vogue* and *Vanity Fair*. But even more unforgivable than this, from Stieglitz's point of view, was Steichen's glorification of commercial photography as "art." The two men seldom, if ever, spoke to one another for the last twenty years of Stieglitz's life.

In his sixties during World War II, Steichen led the U.S. Navy's aerial combat photography units, and his cameramen captured the historic, breathtaking scenes of battle in the skies over the Pacific. It was in the war's immediate aftermath that he made the boldest move of an already adventurous career.

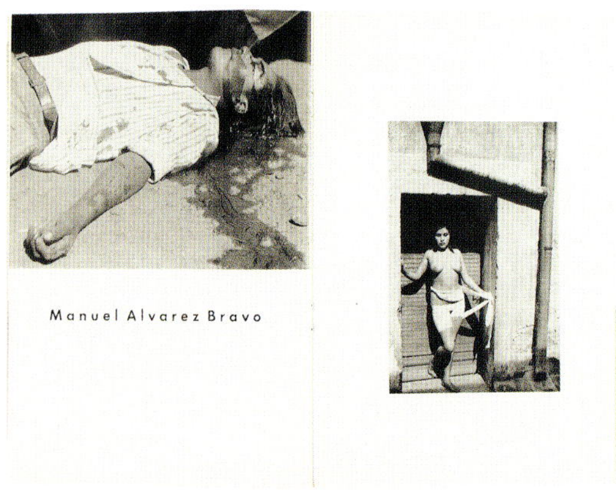
Manuel Alvarez Bravo

"To see through, not merely with, the eye, to perceive with the inner eye, and by an act of choice to capture the essence of that perception. This is the very core of the creative process."

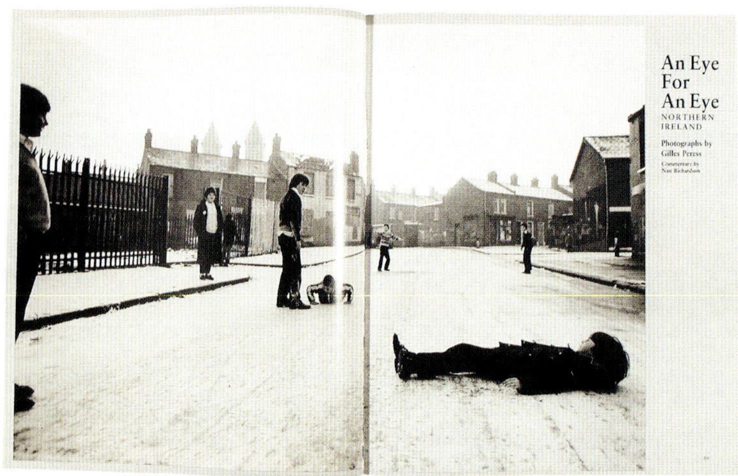
An Eye For An Eye
NORTHERN IRELAND
Photographs by Gilles Peress
Commentary by Nan Richardson

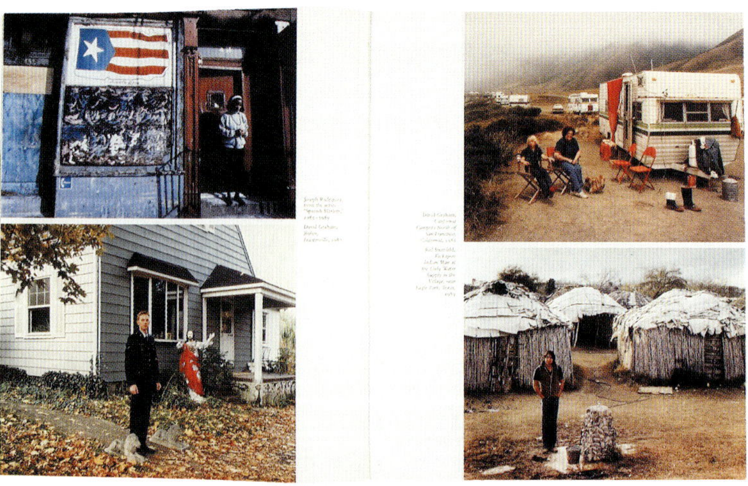

TOP: *Aperture* vol. 1, no. 4, 1953, pages 28–29: photographs by Manuel Alvarez Bravo. MIDDLE: *Aperture* 97, 1984, pages 28–29: photograph by Gilles Peress. BOTTOM: *Aperture* 127, 1992, pages 10–11: (top left) photograph by Joseph Rodriguez; (bottom left and top right) photographs by David Graham; (bottom right) photograph by Joel Sternfeld.

Throughout the war, Beaumont and Nancy Newhall exchanged a slew of lengthy letters discussing their plans for the photography department of the Museum of Modern Art, which Beaumont fully expected to head. They looked forward to expanding the collection, which they had created, and to furthering what Beaumont always referred to as "our" photography—devoted to dignified exhibitions of the medium's masters, past and present. Steichen's biographer Penelope Niven evenhandedly renders the ensuing events.

The first intimation that Steichen was interested in taking over the reins at the museum surfaced just after the war's end, when Stieglitz warned Nancy Newhall, "Look out for Steichen . . . he wants your department." The warning was soon a fait accompli, engineered by Steichen enthusiasts among the museum's administrators and trustees. Steichen's "coup" took place behind the backs not only of the Newhalls, but also of the museum's thirty-member Photography Advisory Committee, led by Ansel Adams. The Newhalls and the entire committee resigned, and Ansel wrote to the administration of his "profound shock and disappointment." He described the new regime as "inevitably favorable to the spectacular and 'popular'. . . a body blow to the progress of creative photography." Steichen claimed innocence of conspiring for the new post as director of photography.

Then, in his seventies and a survivor of many battles of peacetime arts and wartime combat, Steichen launched a three-year project to mount the greatest spectacle in the history of photography exhibitions—"The Family of Man." It was unabashedly a "message" show: the anodynes to the horrors of war were the innate goodness of the individual and the common bonds that unite all of humanity into a single family. From more than two million images, Steichen and a colleague, *Life* photographer Wayne Miller, culled a final selection of 503 photographs submitted by 273 professionals and amateurs from 68 countries. The show was designed as a walk-through installation, with partitioned sections of giant blow-ups that displayed humanity at its "universals"—loving, playing, working, eating, dancing—and ended in a darkened room with a giant color transparency of a nuclear explosion.

Opening January 24, 1955, "The Family of Man" then hived off into traveling exhibitions that roamed the world for the next half-century. It ultimately attracted more than nine million viewers. The catalog was indifferently designed: cluttered pages of pictures, with a giddy, pseudo-Whitmanesque prologue by Steichen's brother-in-law Sandburg. But the publication was inexpensively priced to be available to the average buyer. It sold more than five million copies, and is still in print.

With the exception of Minor White, whose work would probably have been unsuited, all of *Aperture*'s photographer-Founders appeared in "The Family of Man" (including Ansel!). Years later, a fair body of conventional wisdom would hold that Minor was the adversarial epitome of "The Family of Man" and similar uses of photography. Such was not the case. In the pages of *Aperture*, Minor announced Steichen's early preparations, advised photographers how to submit images, and reported on progress. He publicized the tour schedule and devoted a large segment of a 1955 issue of the journal to a judicious selection of viewpoints pro and con. Moreover, as Niven retells, Minor described some of the show as "really magnificent aesthetically," and personally mounted the exhibition when it moved to Rochester, New York, where Beaumont was then head of the George Eastman Museum of Photography. Years later, Minor was asked by an interviewer if "The Family of Man" may have "put back the art of photography many years." He replied, "It may have put back the aesthetic thing a little bit, but that didn't hurt. It was good to have that setback." In retrospect, part of that good was that it helped *Aperture* evolve toward a more sharply defined identity.

The controversy had in effect cleared the air, and the divergence of views about photography were best summed up in affirmations of intent by Steichen and Minor. From Steichen: "These are photographs that talk to people. There is no esoteric appeal here—just man explaining man to man." And from Minor, in an introduction to a photo-sequence in *Aperture* titled "Perceptions": "Their [photographers'] attempt is to see through, not merely with, the eye, to perceive with the inner eye, and by an act of choice to capture the essence of that perception. This is the very core of the creative process." And as the ever-sensible Dorothy Norman observed in her commentary on "The Family of Man," photography was a generous enough medium to accommodate both approaches.

While Steichen garnered an audience in the millions, Minor had at his disposal a journal that—even if it reached only a few hundreds—could be used to explore and teach. And this he did not with polemics, but with demonstrations of the richness of photographic experience, for both makers and viewers of an image. *Aperture* devoted lengthy pages to ways of experiencing a photograph, of "reading" an image, and he emphasized the need for a new dimension of "greatness," as opposed to competence, in photographic criticism. Essays had titles such as "Photographing the Reality of the Abstract" by Beaumont Newhall; "Can Photography as an Art be Taught?" by William Rohrbach; and a lively, analytical excursion coauthored by Minor and colleague Walter Chappell, "Some Methods for Experiencing Photographs."

White knew that the ultimate method for conveying the less understood potentials of the medium lay in the photographs themselves. By the end of the 1950s, he had expanded the journal's format to 8 by 9½ inches, to allow for improved vertical reproduction. With few venues for exhibition of serious photography beyond metropolitan art centers (and only a handful there), he offered readers a chance to contemplate known images in a new way, and also introduced to his select audience a stream of artists many had never encountered. An example of the familiar viewed fresh was a portfolio in 1957 of portraits by *Life* magazine's Alfred Eisenstaedt—without accompanying text. For many, it was the first view of Eisenstaedt as artist, not illustrator of stories. There were essays, sometimes entire issues, devoted to the recognized masters, including Norman's first edition of the classic *Alfred Stieglitz: An American Seer*; portfolios by Imogen Cunningham, Harry Callahan, and Paul Caponigro, and early glimpses of artists later to be included in the first rank of photography's practitioners, such as Aaron Siskind, Ray K. Metzker, Robert Frank, and Bruce Davidson.

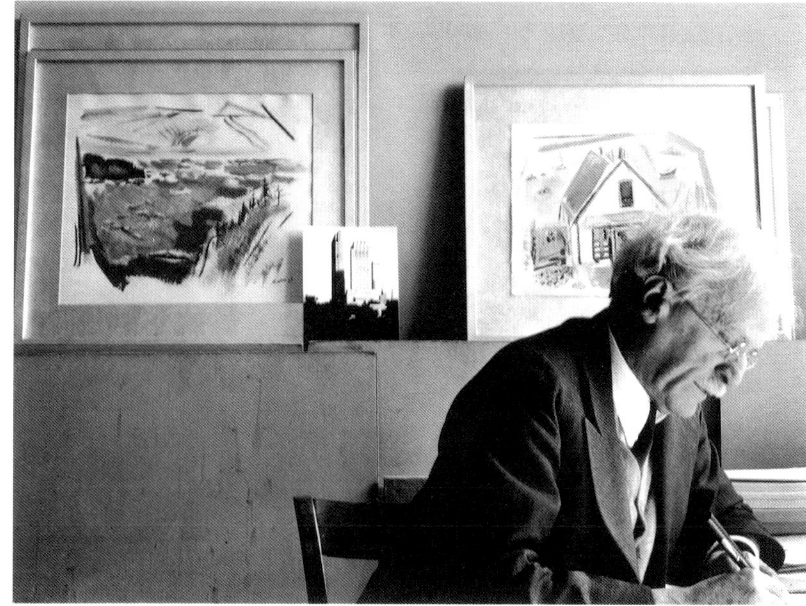

Alfred Stieglitz spotting portrait of Dorothy Norman (with John Marin paintings and Stieglitz photograph in the background), An American Place, 1930s. Photograph by Dorothy Norman.

In 1958, White published an issue destined to be one of *Aperture*'s most successful and influential efforts. At dawn of New Year's Day that year, the almost totally paralyzed Edward Weston had managed to pull himself into a rocking chair facing the Pacific at his home on Wildcat Hill in Carmel, and there his ten-year struggle with Parkinson's disease came to an end. White's testament appeared initially as *Edward Weston: Photographer*, with a selection of the artist's masterworks accompanied by excerpts, edited by Nancy Newhall, from Weston's *Daybooks*. As a monograph, later named *The Flame of Recognition*, it would become one of the best-selling photography books ever published. But even in the early years, the Weston issue would profoundly influence *Aperture*'s future, indeed its very survival—not least of all because it fell into the hands of a fifteen-year-old boy.

Michael Hoffman was, in every sense, an "interesting" child. Born July 5, 1942, in New York City, he was the only son of Myron and Dorothy Hoffman. His father was a transplanted Iowan who had built a successful career in an importing firm. His mother, whose family roots Michael later described as "Jewish-Calvinist from Kentucky," had widespread connections in the artistic and intellectual life of New York. Michael and his younger sister, Jill, were raised in a spacious Upper East Side apartment and summer vacations were spent in Westchester county and Connecticut.

Among his earliest recollections, Michael at age five wandered off into the woods near a vacation house and came across a fruit tree—he could not recall whether it was apple or cherry—in full bloom, a tree filled with a "radiant light" that held him transfixed. The next year brought another formative experience: a riding and jumping class taught by a former White Russian colonel named Gary. Hoffman had a gift with horses, and this was honed to a sense of discipline and personal growth by the colonel, whom Michael would ever after count among the decisive influences of his life.

Still, Michael often felt miserable and misfit. Sent annually to a summer camp of two hundred boys fanatically urged to competition, including boxing (which he hated), he ran away three out of four years. The following summer, his exasperated mother took him by train to a camp in northwestern Montana, which—he assumed this was unknown to her—was devoted to the reform of juvenile delinquents. It was a brutalizing environment ("I'd go to a special tree and cry"), until he met a grizzled cowboy named Sam Wicker. "Sam was on his eighth or ninth wife; rolled cigarettes with one hand, and lived by a bare-bones philosophy: 'It's a hard life if you don't weaken, harder if you do.'" Sam offered the boy a job as cook and flunky, and Michael simply drifted away from his camp and took a job among horse packers.

During his first summer working with horses Michael, thirteen years old, had another moment of visual and spiritual epiphany. "My horse had gotten away from me, and I'd hiked for hours trying to get back to camp. I wandered onto an Indian burial ground . . . and later came to an emergency landing field. It was late afternoon and suddenly everything seemed different: the sky was luminous, the trees and flowers filled with light. It was totally out of the ordinary. I just sat on a log and looked." Eventually, Sam, who had raised hell with the other wranglers for losing the boy, came and found him.

Michael's parents sent him to a progressive boarding school in upstate New York, the Millbrook School, founded by its headmaster, Edward Pulling. Pulling had created an environment rigorous in academics while tolerating his students' idiosyncrasies and urging them to explore their own interests. Hoffman's summers were spent in the West, leading horses packed with supplies into otherwise inaccessible camps for tourists and forest rangers. He also began breaking horses and doing stints as a rodeo rider.

Michael had received his first camera at age eight; in his teens he set up a photography service at Millbrook with Pulling's encouragement. For his fifteenth birthday, a friend named Florence Benedict gave him a subscription to *Aperture*—beginning with the Edward Weston issue. Hoffman was first drawn not to the pictures, but to Nancy Newhall's excerpts from the photographer's *Daybooks*. A bookish, predawn riser himself, Michael immediately identified with the opening photograph Weston had taken of his tall, book-crammed desk, with the hand-scrawled caption, dated February 2, 1931: "Peace again!—the exquisite hour before dawn, here at my old desk—seldom have I realized so keenly, appreciated so fully, these still, dark hours."

Otherwise, the pictures had little effect on the boy. "Then, one day I sat down to look at it . . . and three hours later I came back changed. I had never had such an experience of total immersion." In the next few years, he carefully studied *Aperture* and developed a deepening curiosity about its editor.

After high-school graduation, and despite his parents' misgivings, Michael broached the subject of his summer plans to Saul Siegal, the president of his father's importing firm. He wanted to sell glass beads—which the firm, Elliot Greene & Company, imported from Czechoslovakia—to Native Americans in the Western states. With a fifty-dollar loan, Michael bought a heavy-cruising 1939 Buick that he named "Antigone." His father relented enough to teach him to drive, and Michael set out for Montana. Over the course of his first summer on the job, he logged 25,000 miles in sales trips to tribal elders and artisans and trading posts in Oklahoma, the Dakotas, and New Mexico. "I wore shined cowboy boots, a shirt with mother-of-pearl buttons, and I was deeply tanned. I looked like an Indian, and my friends on the reservations gave me contacts and routes most people never knew about. It turned out that I was very successful at selling. The Indians loved the old Buick—they thought it was hilarious."

Michael attended a small college, St. Lawrence University in Canton, New York, near the Canadian border. Majoring in literature and religion, he came under the influence of a remarkable, demanding faculty. They inspired him to search for interrelationships in literature, religion, music, and science; it was a succession of mind-opening studies that fed into Michael's early encounters with Minor White.

The first of these occurred in the summer of 1962, when Michael diverted from his itinerary in Indian country to attend Minor's workshop in Denver, Colorado. The workshops were limited to ten participants. Minor asked for no photographs from applicants—only a general statement of background and interests. At their first meeting, Michael didn't recognize Minor: "When I arrived at the

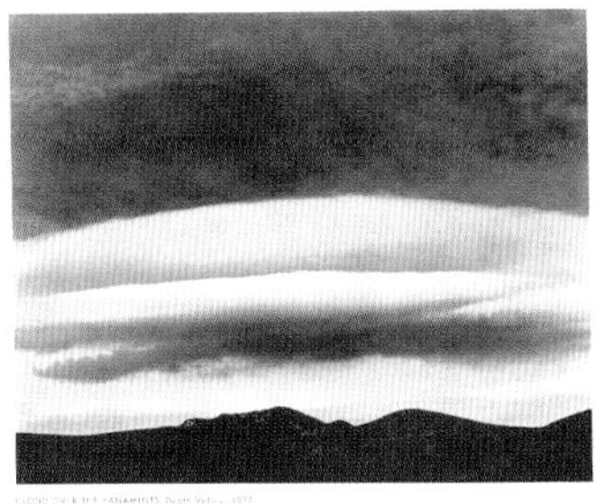

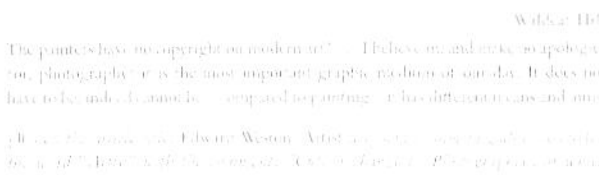

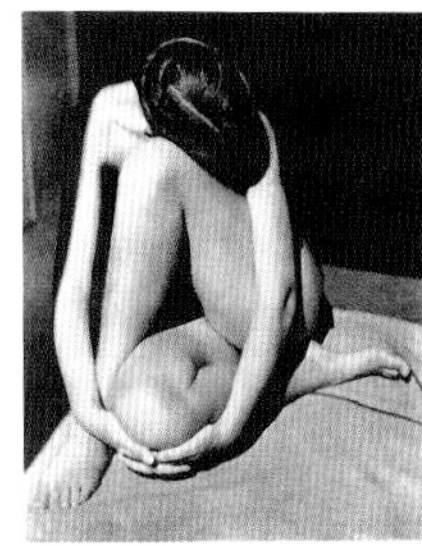

"Minor and the people around him really believed that if you sat down for an hour and looked at a great photograph such as Weston's Pepper No. 30 *. . . you'd be changed, and you'd be changed for the better, reaching into the heritage of intellectual and emotional tradition that was the mainstream of human endeavor."*

Aperture **vol. 6, no. 1, 1958, pages 40–41: photographs by Edward Weston.**

workshop, I found it to be quite a bohemian setting. In the room there was a tall man with a beard, rather handsome, rather formidable—and I was sure he had to be Minor White. To the right of the door there was another man with an open white shirt, loose-fitting trousers, and sandals. I remember thinking he was in the way and wished he would leave so we could get on with something important. Of course, the man in the white shirt was Minor." His manner, it turned out, was unassuming, gracious, and accepting.

Minor's workshops were devoted to the "art of seeing," with or without a camera. His ideas, processes, and techniques over the years usually divided his students into two groups: those who immediately or gradually came to understand what he was up to, and those who in dismay or annoyance headed for the door. His fundamental premise was that the ability to see well was inhibited by laziness, bad training, and constant exposure to badly organized images. All of these inhibitions might be overcome through work, discipline, and a nurtured openness.

Introductory exercises involved rapid sketching of a simple subject such as a strand of wire or a table leg, beginning an awareness of the relationships between what the eye sees and the kinetic motion of eye, fingers, hand, and body. The association of motion and imagery would remain a constant in Minor's teaching, involving preparation of the body through absolute stillness segueing into postures, then movement derived from theater and dance exercises. With photographs of his own making or those of other masters he would guide students into looking at an image with constant attention to the movement of the eye as it traveled within the subject and around the boundaries of the image. With this Minor introduced the concept of "dominant image," containing a documentary element but more importantly conveying both a summation and an essence of the subject.

Other exercises were devoted to seeing and sensing without camera or image. Particularly excruciating to Michael and others was a requirement to simply stand, alone and still, for a long period at a busy Denver intersection. Another involved a non-camera, a rectangular, open-ended box through which a student alternated looking as though selecting a subject, then looking without the box afresh at an entire scene. This was an introductory exploration of "camera eye."

Minor's students photographed in the morning, often with a break for a lecture, then spent afternoons in the darkroom processing film and printing. Evenings were devoted to presentations and discussions. Minor, throughout his years of workshops, constantly pressed students to articulate what they saw and felt in an image, "to use words freely because they are both expedient and expendable . . . useful in the learning process. The ultimate aim," he would add, "is visual experience visually grasped." He required, however, that certain words be prohibited, among them: *like*, *dislike*, *good*, *bad*, *right*, *wrong*, *interesting*, and *should*. He gently prodded his students toward words more precise, metaphors more meaningful—and through these metaphors to begin comprehending (although Stieglitz's name was seldom mentioned) the nature of "equivalents."

Michael almost abandoned Minor during the group's first photographic junket—to a garbage dump. "I thought, this is the limit, this is the end . . . and then things began to transform themselves before my eyes." At a later workshop excursion to a state park in New York, Michael's impressions take on more detail: "He talked

The association of motion and imagery would remain a constant in Minor's teaching, involving preparation of the body through absolute stillness segueing into postures. . . . he would guide students into looking at an image with constant attention to the movement of the eye as it traveled within the subject and around the boundaries of the image.

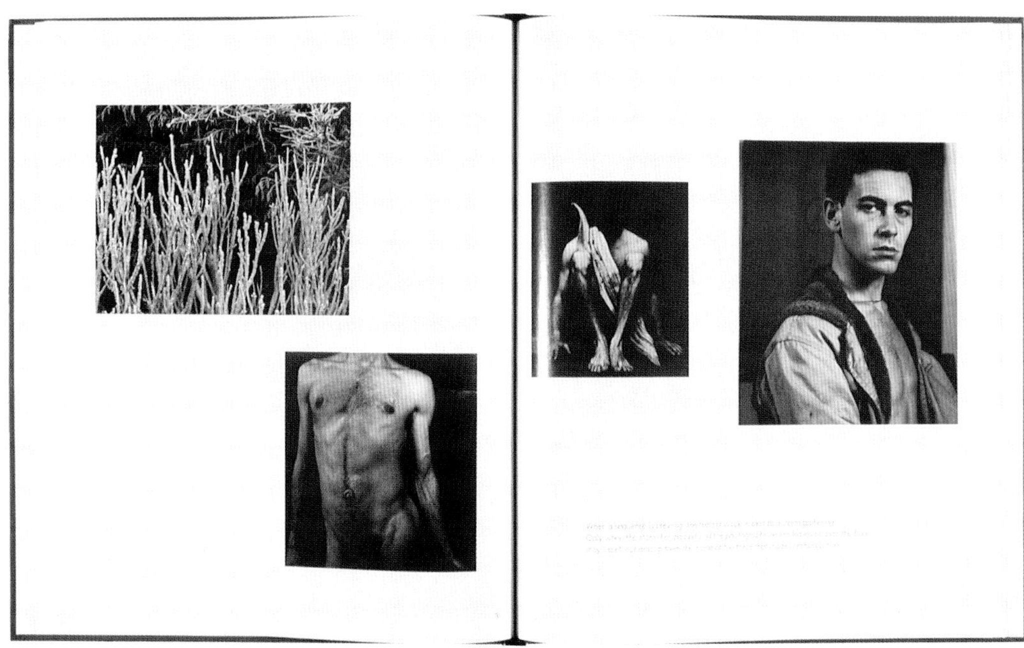

Aperture 80, 1978, pages 70–71: photographs by Minor White.

to us at length before we left, in such a way that you almost felt there were gremlins, pixies, and elves waiting, if only you were ready to see them. . . . A mood began to take hold. . . .The silence and spaciousness offered a new way of seeing. Different and significant forms emerged in the forest . . . forms skirted just off the edge of vision. They became subjects making themselves available to the camera."

Barely out of his teens, Michael discovered his personal quest, articulated in simple but adequate terms: "to live life beyond the ordinary." He decided Minor White was a needed guide and ally. The problem was how to turn Minor into something more than an instructor, into a true mentor. It wasn't easy because Minor, although the most generous of teachers and a creator of live-in workshops for his students, was also an intensely private man. Even his closest friends, colleagues, and lovers encountered boundaries. The sorcerer brooked no apprentices unless, as one of his earlier students discovered, one could make oneself indispensable—especially in the agonizing task of getting out issues of *Aperture*.

Peter Bunnell retired in 2002 from his post as McAlpin Professor of the History of Photography and Modern Art at Princeton University, after a long and distinguished career as teacher, writer, historian, and curator. As a freshman forty-seven years earlier, he had been one of Minor's first students at Rochester Institute of Technology, beginning a lifelong friendship and professional collaboration. Largely because of the Newhalls, Rochester then was the nexus of creative photography in the East—with an axis that extended to the publications and institutions in New York, and also to the Limelight Gallery, where Lisette Model, Berenice Abbott, Cornell Capa, W. Eugene Smith, Robert Frank, and Walker Evans, among others, were habitués. At Rochester, Bunnell's first close encounter with Minor came when he joined the Newhalls, photographer and mystic Walter Chappell, and a group of students for Minor's Thanksgiving party in 1955—where, Bunnell recalls, dinner "had a slightly Oriental touch, with broth in a porcelain bowl, and then out comes the roast with chopsticks. . . . You can imagine how bizarre we thought this was."

Minor accepted Bunnell as a working associate because he needed help.

> As far as *Aperture* was concerned, I started typing letters and organizing things, and then he says, "Look, why don't you take over circulation?" Which sounded like I was being given some executive position. It turned out that we typed every single mailing label by hand. We recorded every single check that came in. And then, of course, all the magazines would arrive from [the printers in] California, and we would stuff each one in an envelope, put the label on, buy stamps. Then—I still don't know why—we couldn't take them to the post office. We would have to drive all over Rochester dropping ten or fifteen issues in the mailboxes to get them out.

Bunnell and a couple of friends made the deliveries in Minor's old Chevy paneled truck, which they painted silver and white with the *Aperture* logo, the crossed lines and circle, on the door of the front cab. "Minor was horrified, but he stayed with it."

Minor worked like a horse, Bunnell recalls, but in those early Rochester days, "he was also as fun as hell. He drank like a fish, and had these quirky parties and dinners and loved to dance—particularly to Berlioz's *Symphonie Fantastique*." This he played at full blast on his only luxury, a well equipped hi-fi set. Otherwise in Minor's cold-water loft, there were no radio, newspapers, or television. Books purchased for research into *Aperture* essays were read, marked up, used, and then left in a cardboard box for any student who might want them. There was also, Bunnell adds, a sense of religious calling about *Aperture* . . . and an innocence. "Minor and the people around him really believed that if you sat down for an hour and looked at a great photograph such as Weston's *Pepper No. 30,* or a Siskind or Sommer print, you'd be changed, and you'd be changed for the better, reaching into the heritage of intellectual and emotional tradition that was the mainstream of human endeavor."

As he had done at the Millbrook School, Michael created a photography service at St. Lawrence. In 1963, he arranged for Minor to give a series of summer workshops at the university. Minor and the university—with its faculty devoted to ways of harmonizing intellectual, intuitive, and emotional potentials in their students—proved an ideal fit. St. Lawrence's president Andrew Bewkes agreed not only to pay for students to attend the workshops, but also later financed student travel and costs to attend Ansel's workshops in California.

Subsequently, Michael arranged for Minor's workshops at Millbrook and also at the prestigious Hotchkiss School in Lakeville, Connecticut. Michael handled all of the arrangements and Minor, he recalled, "sort of woke up to the fact that here was somebody who could accomplish something . . . that he didn't have to do everything himself. I could get things organized, get the mailings out, get the people there, collect the money, make sure Minor got paid and had assistants. I was a pretty good factotum." So good, in fact, that Minor invited Michael to join him for advanced study in photography and also to assist him upon Michael's graduation in 1964.

Viewed in retrospect, the next year of Michael's life takes on dazzling complexity. He studied with Minor; entered the U.S. Army; fell in love; and set in train the efforts that would save *Aperture* from extinction. An enduring characteristic of Michael's life, in youth and later, was a disinclination to indulge in even the briefest interludes of idleness.

Michael revealed in the workshops an uncanny way of apprehending images—as if he were seeing with Minor's eyes. Michael recalled that, working in Rochester on sequences, he had "almost out-of-body experiences." It was as though his time in the Western wilderness had awakened a sort of extrasensory awareness. Minor was amazed that Michael could interpret a sequence exactly the way Minor had experienced it.

> He would put these photographs up late at night and I would start speaking about how I related to them . . . allowing the rational mind to go to sleep and allowing the intuitive senses and emotions to gain greater prominence in exploring the metaphors represented in the images. I began to be able to read them and understand them more from the heart and the mind in a way that was equivalent to what Minor had been experiencing when he was making them. It was very spooky, and it unnerved Minor!

After an intense three-month association with Minor, Michael—who had belonged to the small group of ROTC candidates at St. Lawrence—began officer training. His motives were practical. With the draft inevitable, he knew life would be easier as an officer than as an enlisted man. In fact, he relished the discipline, the training, his newly discovered ability to meet the demands of military life. Receiving his commission during the incipient American buildup of the Vietnam War, he was posted as a transportation officer at the Brooklyn Army Depot. It was one of the cushiest assignments the military had to offer, and it allowed him enough free time to continue working with Minor—and to pursue a young woman named Katharine Perkins Carter.

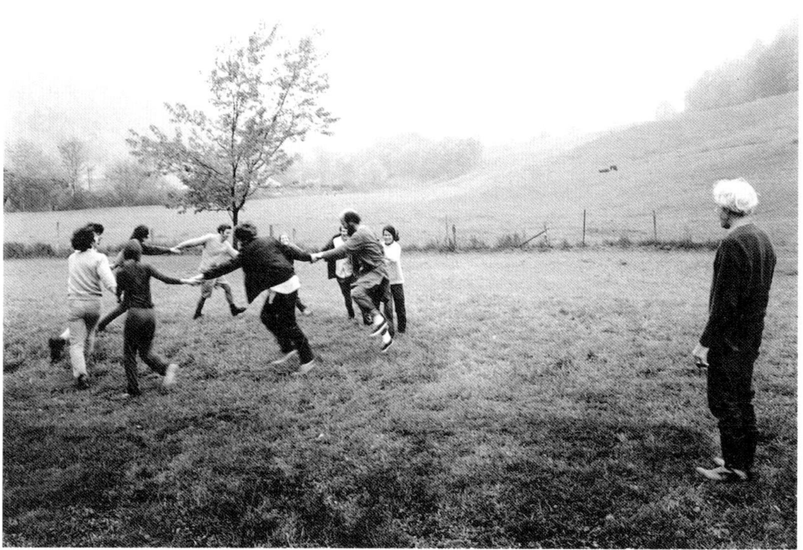

Minor White with students during a workshop in Rochester, New York, 1969–70. Photograph by Jonathan Saadah.

Michael met her in one of Minor's workshops at the Millbrook School. They discovered a range of mutual interests, and began dating—at first casually for her, intensely for Michael from the beginning. "I'd never met anyone like her," he recalled many years later. "She seemed absolutely unattainable . . . impossible that we could really be together." But another of Michael's intrinsic characteristics, persistence, ultimately paid off. A few months after he was posted to Brooklyn, he and Misty moved in together in a small walk-up apartment with a view of the harbor. Within two years, they were married.

Meanwhile in 1964, Minor was preparing the final issue of *Aperture*. The journal actually had folded ten years earlier at the behest of the Founders. With the exception of Ansel, none of them had any money to support the publication. In that ostensibly final issue of 1954, Minor had written to the subscribers a decidedly testy appeal:

> WHY APERTURE IS LATE: If you have wondered why this issue of *aperture* [*sic*] is ungodly late, the reason is that a thousand dollars had to be raised before it could be published . . . we feel that you would like to know the situation. . . . It is annoyingly simple . . . [the journal] costs $5,000 a year to produce. You subscribers number about 450 and account for about $2,600. . . . To continue the quarterly at its present standard . . . it is obvious that each present subscriber will have to find at least one more subscriber or take out a Retaining Subscription.

Otherwise, Minor warned, the subscribers would receive a refund for any monies due and the publication would end. The early "retaining subscriptions" were ten dollars—six dollars for four issues, the balance to help support "an ideal in photography for which the quarterly stands." Minor's relationship to his subscribers was always conceived as an act of service to a community of interest—but one that he felt imposed an obligation of support upon that community. Nevertheless, he laboriously sought out subscribers, gathering names, writing personal letters, and sending free issues to individuals he hoped would send back a six- or ten-dollar check. It was a process that over the next decade netted between fifty and one hundred new subscribers.

The decisive help, however, came from a photographer who was an "amateur" in the true sense: one who does the work strictly out of love. Shirley Burden was a Vanderbilt heir who was to become *Aperture*'s most enduring and important patron. In the 1950s, he picked up the deficit and published the journal jointly with Minor.

Still, each issue was a monumental task, in terms not only of financing but also of maintaining the extraordinary standards Minor set. There was at the time nothing comparable to *Aperture* in the world of photography, albeit Minor's vision of the ideal was not without detractors. As the 1950s progressed, the notion of a "quarterly" gave way to the reality that the journal was "published intermittently." There were occasions when few or no photographs appeared because there was no money to pay the engravers. And in 1963, not a single issue was published. At that point, Minor declared that it had always been his intention to shut down the journal upon its fiftieth issue—according to the tradition set, he said, by Stieglitz's *Camera Work*.

Michael later expressed the belief that Minor's decision reflected a profound shift in Minor's own interest and direction. "The spirit of *Aperture* was gone for him because he had been using it as a creative force in his own life." Minor progressively was turning his

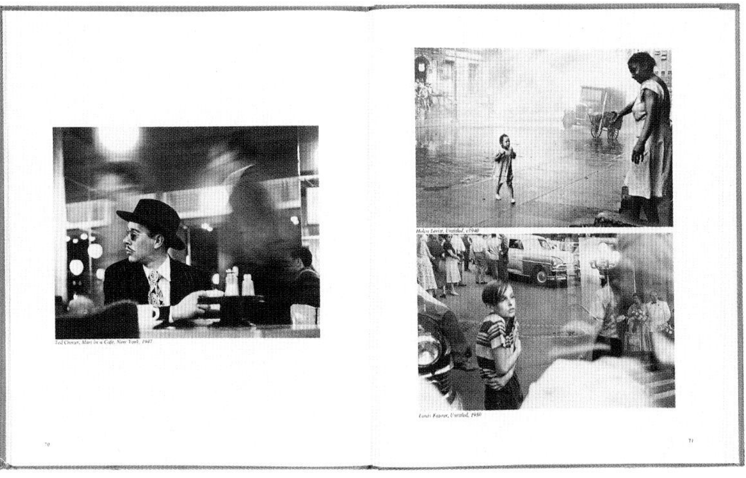

An image published in Aperture *was not intended to be a facsimile of the photographer's print. Minor said, "This is ink; it's not silver. You're going to have to intensify it . . . to make it deeper, richer than a silver print would be. You've got to make it more intense in order to give it the same resonance."*

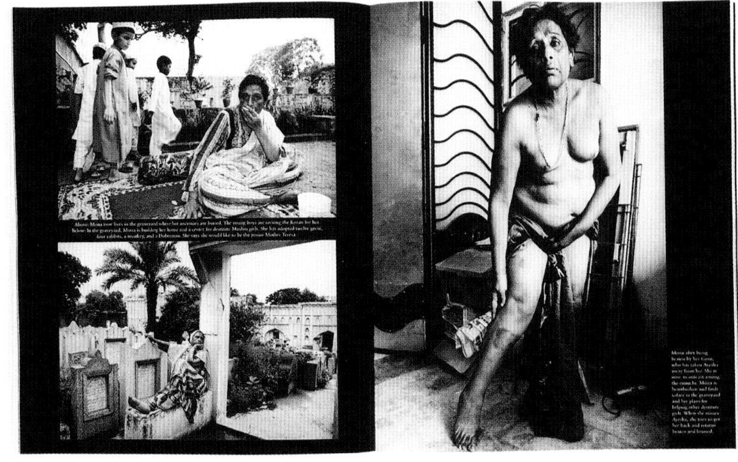

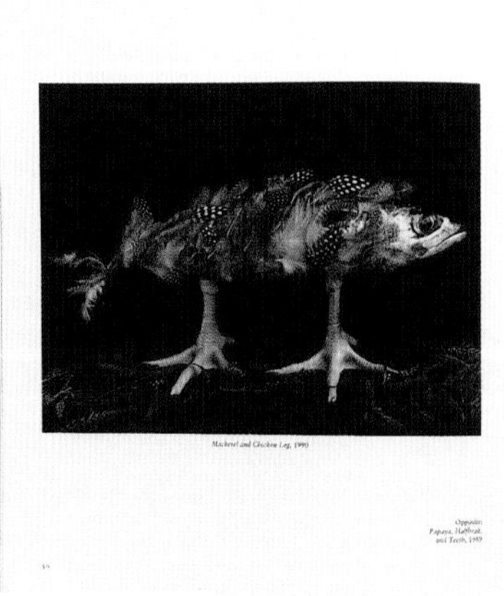

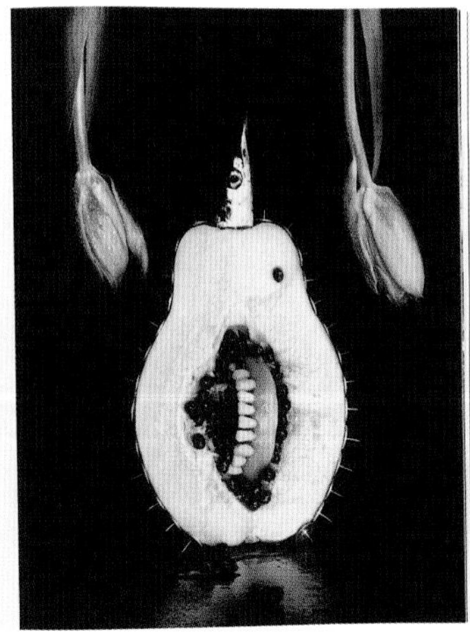

TOP: *Aperture* 81, 1978, pages 70–71: (left) photograph by Ted Croner; (top right) photograph by Helen Levitt; (bottom right) photograph by Louis Faurer. CENTER: *Aperture* 154, 1999, pages 18–19: photographs by Dayanita Singh. BOTTOM: *Aperture* 130, 1993, pages 56–57: photographs by Michiko Kon.

attention to his own photography; to his workshops, which might number as many as ten coast-to-coast sessions during the year; and to the further evolution of his theories and teaching.

He had published forty-four issues, and among them are some of the most original, provocative contributions ever offered to devotees of the medium. Most of these issues are now rare possessions of university, museum, or private collections. Or dimly viewable on microfilm. Only a few of the early issues, such as those devoted to Weston and Stieglitz, made the transition into monographs. Among the virtually lost classics are "The Substance and Spirit of Architectural Photography" (1958); "Death of a Valley (California's Water Problem)" by Dorothea Lange and Pirkle Jones (1960); and "Three Phantasts: Laughlin, Sommer, Bullock" (1961). After the publishing drought of 1963, Minor launched his intended final year with an issue devoted to Barbara Morgan and designed by her. The grand finale was to be another single-artist publication, "Imogen Cunningham," and he asked for Michael's help in producing it.

It was a daunting task, requiring lengthy commutes each weekend from his military duties in Brooklyn, and it was Michael's first involvement with the knotty details of the printing process. "Minor had a great sense of how things should look, and of course he was a magnificent printer." The first lesson was that an image published in *Aperture* was not intended to be a facsimile of the photographer's print. Minor said, "This is ink; it's not silver. You're going to have to intensify it . . . to make it deeper, richer than a silver print would be. You've got to make it more intense in order to give it the same resonance." It was an invaluable lesson, Michael recalled, because "all of the other printers were trying to match the original and they couldn't, and ended up with a sort of grayish reproduction."

Michael learned of the necessity for the highest-quality paper, which would hold intense inking from the presses yet remain even and smooth. And he discovered the value of running the printed pages through the presses yet again for a coat of varnish that would heighten luminosity. He watched Minor, original print in hand, standing over those presses as each sheet—four journal pages at a time—emerged, often rejecting and correcting two or three times. And in the process, Michael learned why the costs were so exorbitant for uncompromising quality.

The experience was life-altering because Michael's previous studies had been devoted to his own photography. His energies now turned to the possibility of continuing the magazine. "I said to Minor, 'I think we should keep this alive.' And he said, somewhat reluctantly, 'Go ahead if you want to. But you'd better go and see the accountant first.'"

Michael found the bookkeeper in an old, dilapidated building. "It was very depressing, very surreal, like a Kafka novel. He told me, 'Well, you don't have any money and you owe $25,000 to your subscribers.' So I went back to Minor and said, 'I know you don't want to do this. But I think if I could be a rodeo rider, if I could sell beads to the Indians, and if I could be an infantry officer, I suspect there's a chance I can do this.'" Minor then said he would help, but only in an advisory fashion. And at that moment he offered a piece of advice from his own experience: "Never apologize. For anything—not for what's in the magazine, not for being late. Apologize for nothing. It only makes matters worse!"

Michael was determined that his first publishing effort, in 1965, would be an expanded version of the Edward Weston issue that had been his inspiration. The Newhalls, primarily Nancy, encouraged his efforts to sustain *Aperture*, and she provided more extensive material from the *Daybooks*. The ensuing months were a frantic scramble for funds, for engravers and printers. To heighten the drama, Michael underwent knee surgery and, with Misty and Nancy helping, directed much of the work from an army hospital bed. Also, he had decided on a tremendous gamble: to print thirteen thousand copies—six times the normal print run—in hopes of selling the excess as a profitable book.

It was a disaster.

More than three decades later, Michael still cringed at the memory. "We couldn't afford the varnish, which gave it the luminosity. It was flat, with none of the quality of the earlier issue—or any previous *Aperture*. I had a fight with the printers, and I took the whole thing very, very personally. I felt very upset that I had let the public down. But I learned from the start what was right and what was wrong, what worked and what didn't. That lesson was essential to everything we did later."

Michael's knee turned out to be an unlikely stroke of good luck. The army deemed him unfit for active duty, and discharged him with a small disability pension—freeing his time for unfettered concentration upon the journal. Two more issues emerged in 1965, one of which included the first true Minor White photograph ever published in *Aperture*. For thirteen years, Minor had only published his own work as technical illustrations, virtually devoid of his considerable artistry.

The greatest assets, so often the case in *Aperture*'s early history, were the irrepressible Nancy and her power of networking. She made Michael known to an ever-widening group of influential and supportive individuals, pressed his cause, and touted his abilities. In particular, she persisted in urging him to meet one of photography's living masters from the Stieglitz era, Paul Strand. "I didn't understand why," Michael remembered. "I'd never actually seen a Strand print—almost no one had. At the time, I actually had him classified as a documentary photographer. I still can't believe that I felt that way!"

Their meeting would lead to a collaboration that would not only save *Aperture* at critical moments, but would also redefine its role in the history of photography.

(Parts III and IV of this essay will appear in Issue 169.)

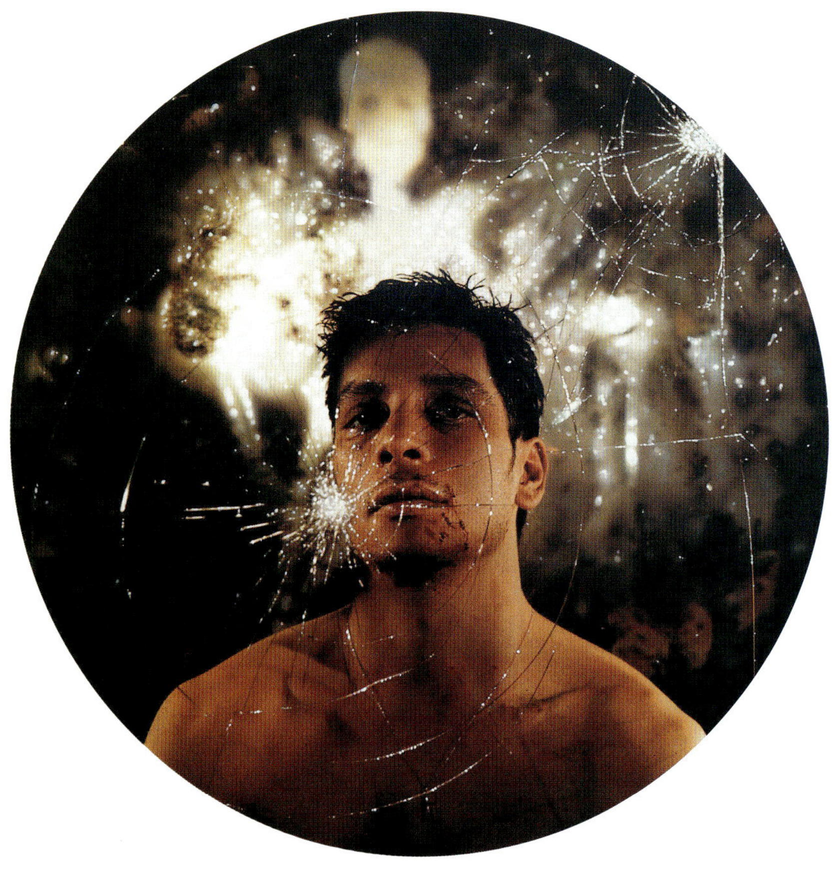

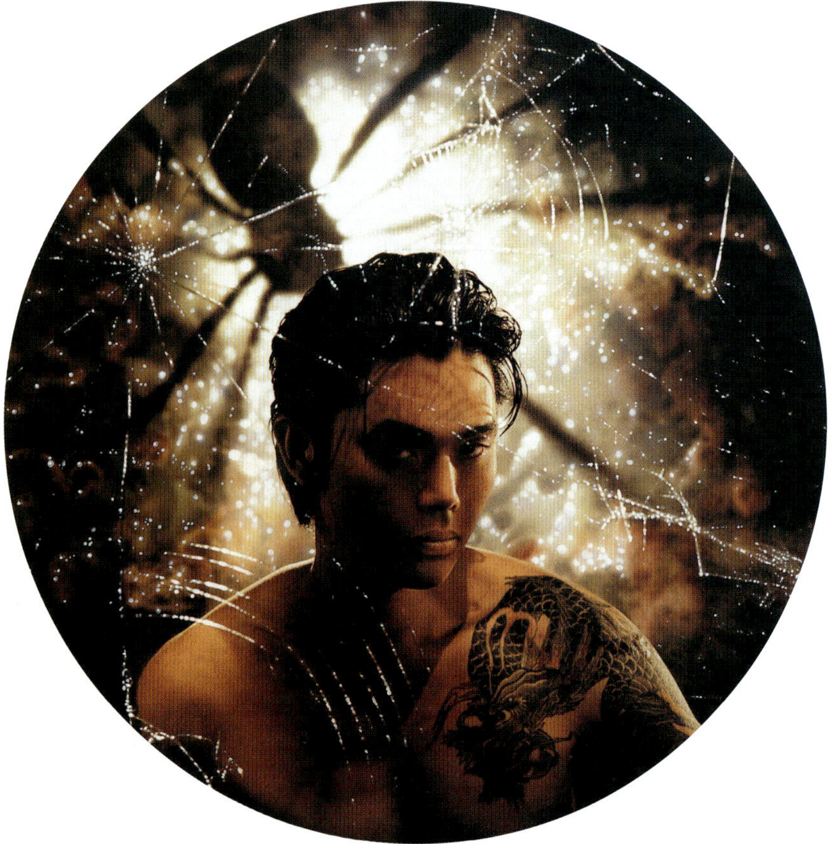

To the vast majority of people a photograph is an image of *something* within their direct experience: a more-or-less factual reality. It is difficult for them to realize that the photograph can be the *source* of experience, as well as the reflection of spiritual awareness of the world and of self. The painters have done little to dispel the impression of their superiority in the creative graphic fields; they point with scorn (and often correctly) to the shallow "storytelling" aspects of photography, and they also disapprove of photographers who attempt superficial "abstract" or "non-objective" effects within the limits of the photographic processes. To a large majority a photograph bears the same relationship to a fine painting as a contractor-designed house does to a fine architectural creation. This situation would be ridiculous were it not so tragic. The truth is that photography is limited only by the photographers!

—Ansel Adams, from "The Profession of Photography," *Aperture* vol. 1, no. 3, 1952

THIS PAGE: photographs by Pierre et Gilles.
TOP: *Fight—Ken*, 2001.
BOTTOM: *Fight—Osamu*, 2001.

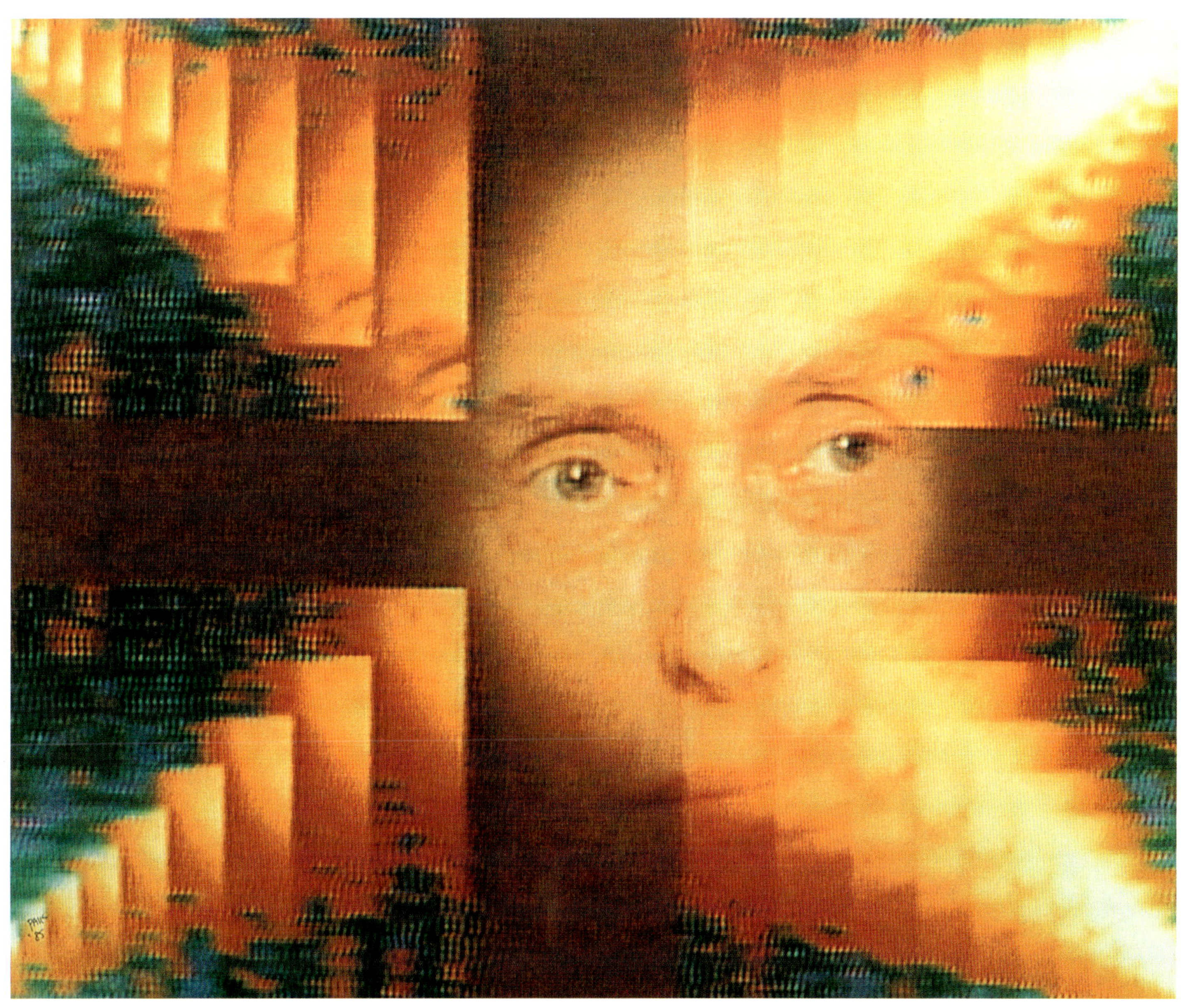

Nam June Paik, ***Julian Beck***, laser photograph, 1985; from *Aperture* 106, 1987.

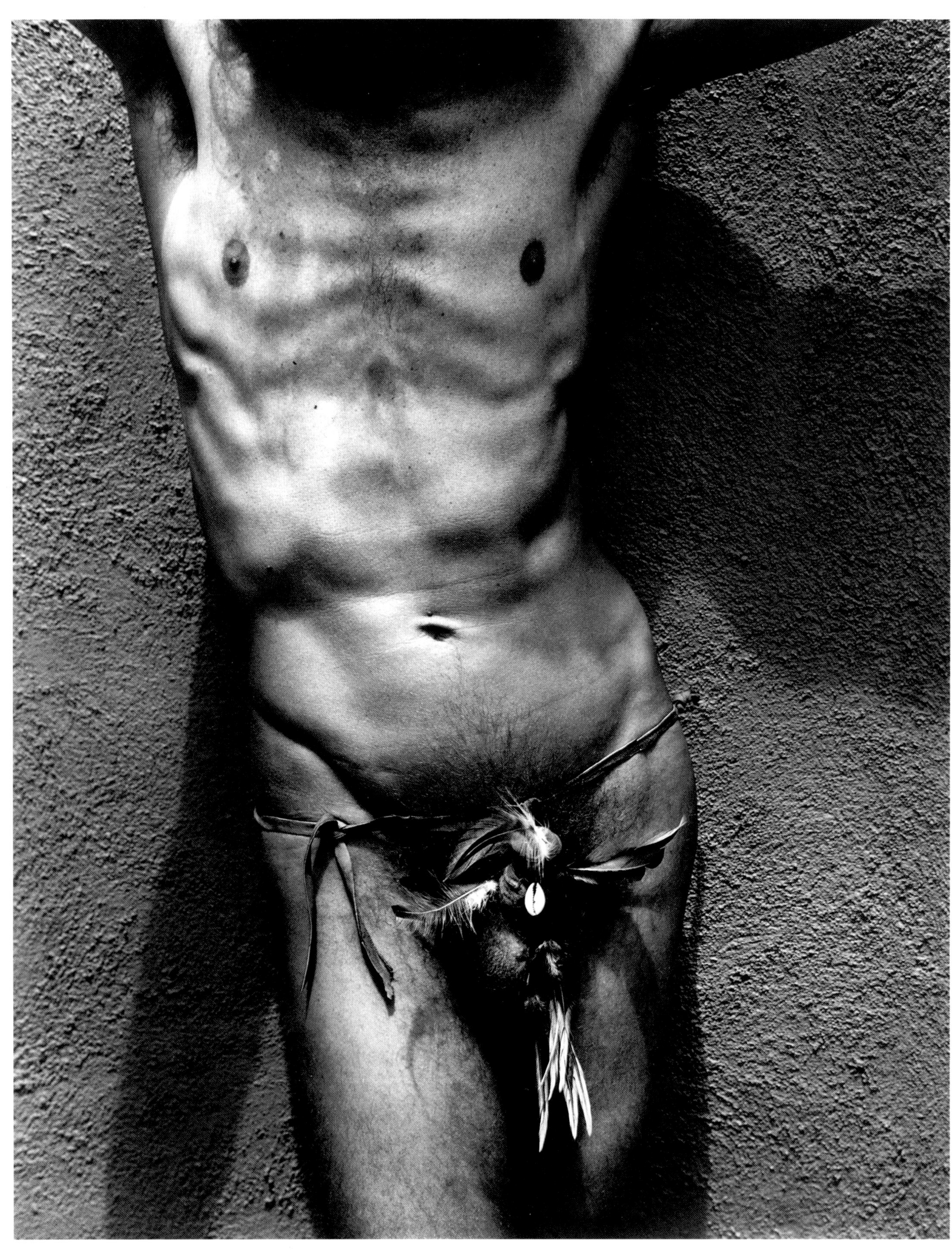

Walter Chappell, *Feather Torso Ceremonial*, 1967; from *Aperture* 79, 1977.

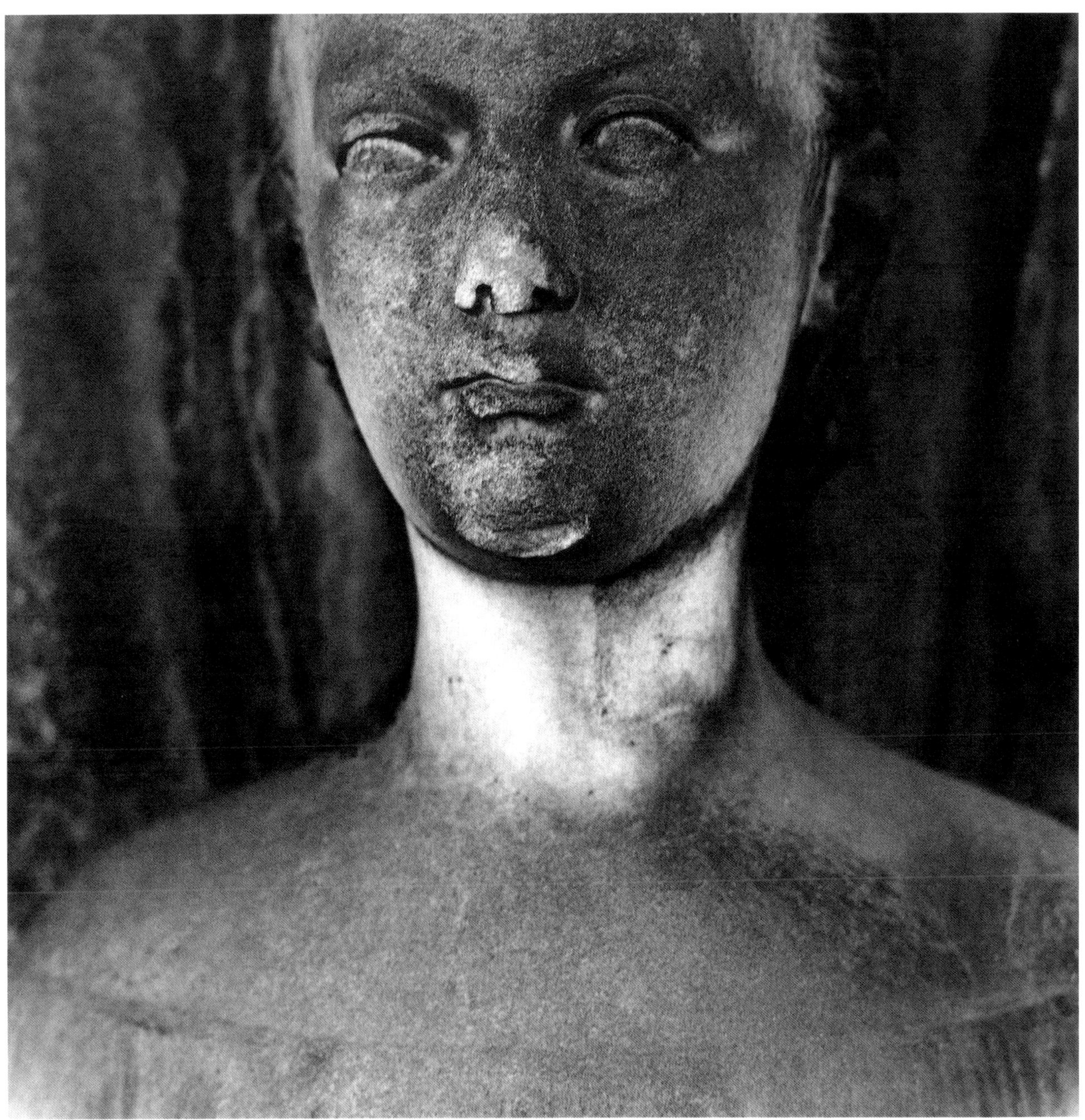

Ralph Eugene Meatyard, *Untitled*, n.d.; from *Aperture* vol. 7, no. 4, 1959.

How astounding is camera! With its unique ability to register continuous value or tone, camera can sanctify even the ugly and the dead, clarify the ordinary, and, in a moment, turn a hundred-and-eighty degrees to play iconoclast.

—Minor White, *Aperture* vol. 15, no. 3, 1970

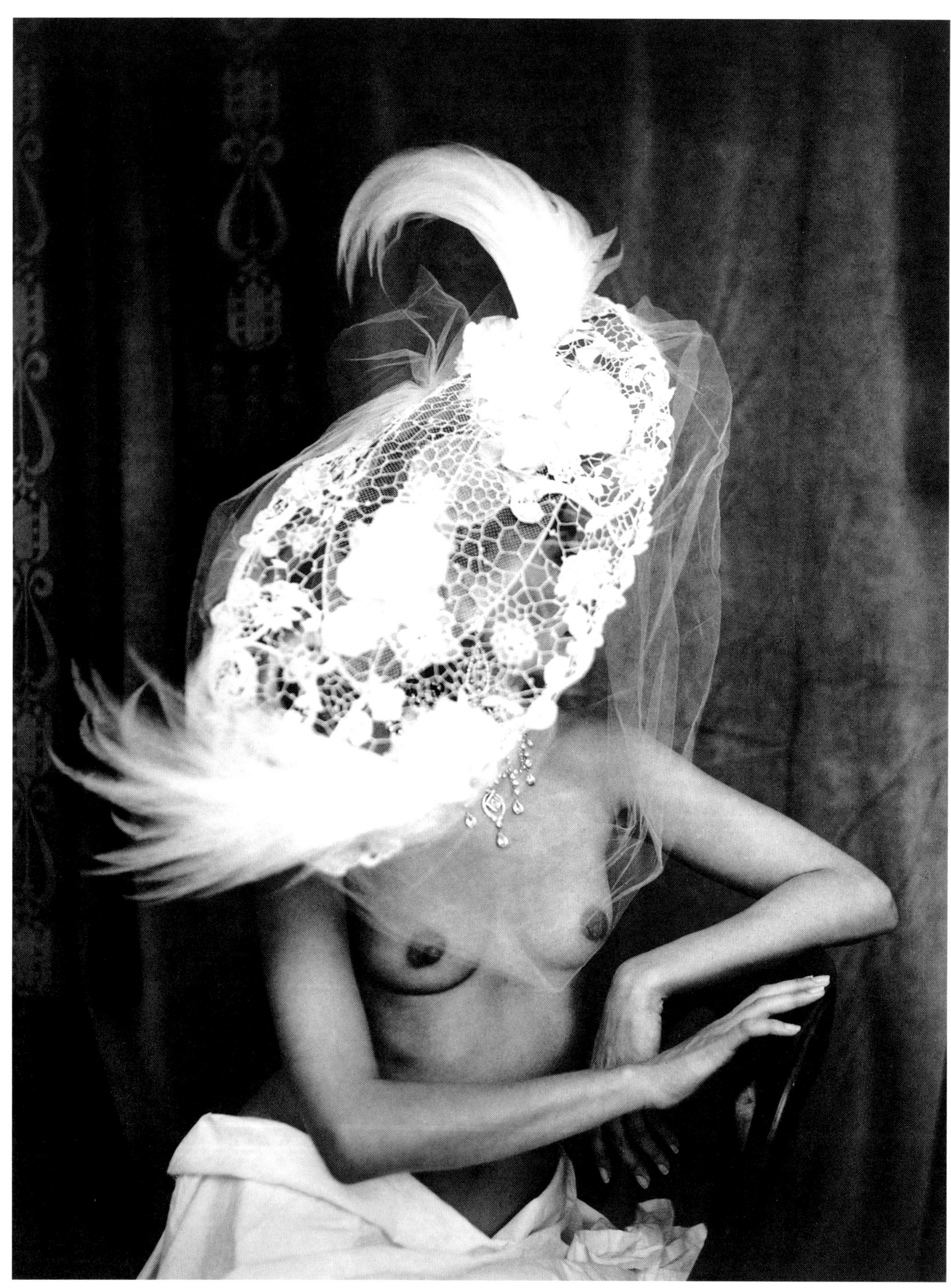

David McDermott and Peter McGough, ***Varying greatly in style, shape, and materials, Anh Duong, 1917*****, 2001.**

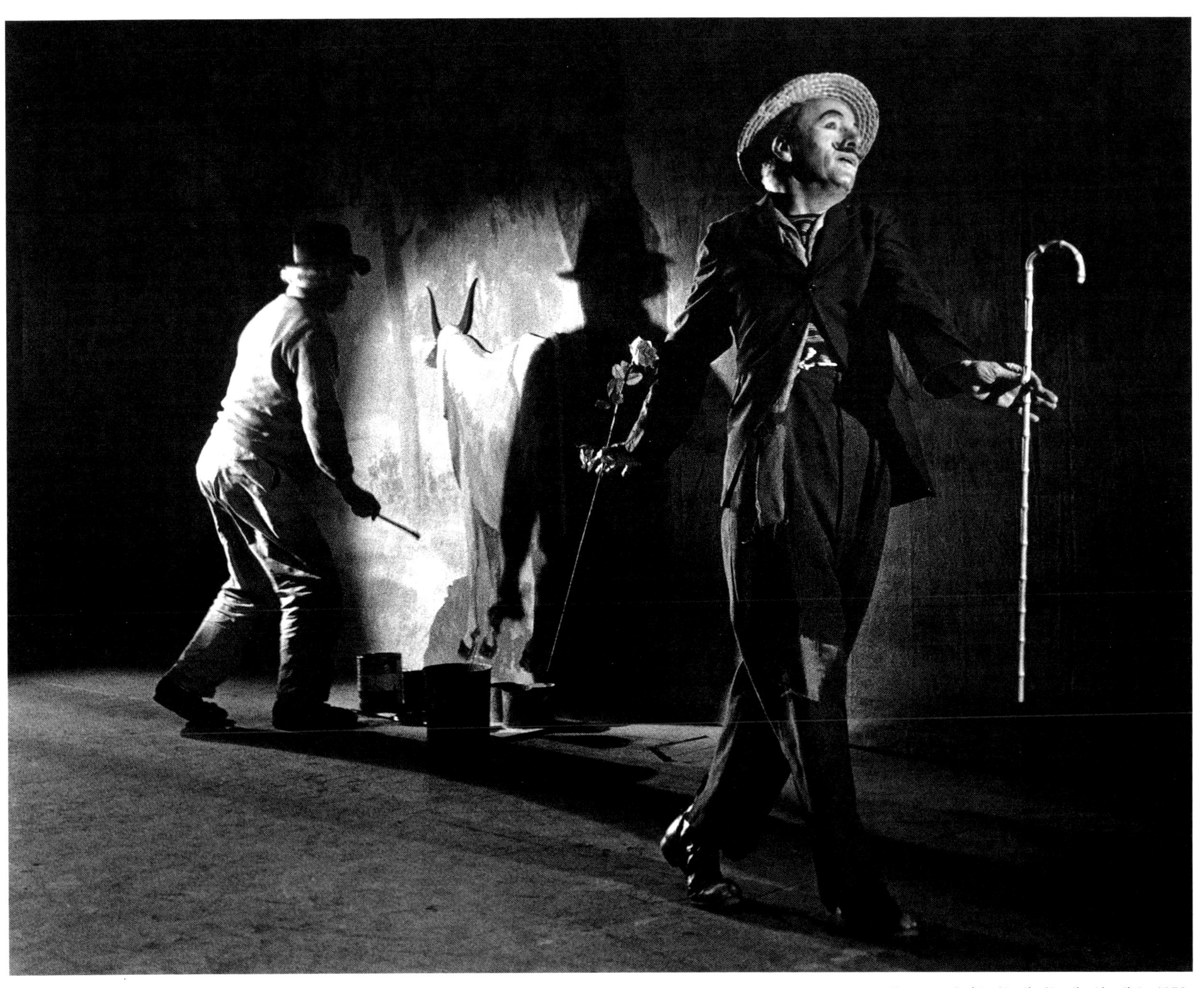

W. Eugene Smith, ***Charlie Chaplin, Limelight***, **1952;**
from *Aperture* vol. 14, nos. 3–4, 1969.

The photographer has the power and the talent to make his model come to life. In his creative state he works *with*, not *from* the model. In his creativity he *is*, and when he *is*, his model can *be*.

—Minor White, *Aperture* vol. 15, no. 3, 1970

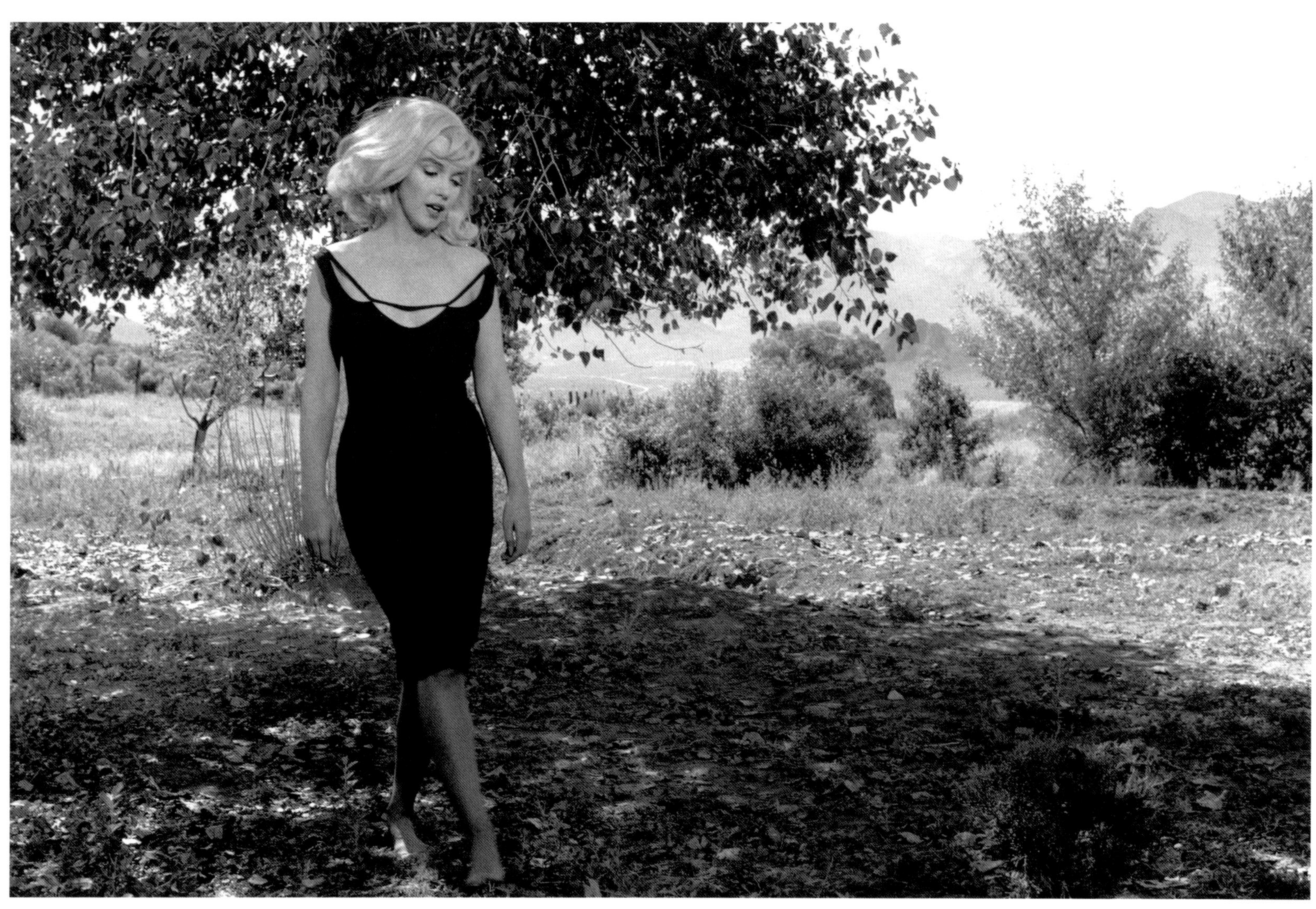

Inge Morath, *Marilyn Monroe,*
Reno, Nevada, 1960; from *Portraits: Photographs by Inge Morath*
(Aperture, 1986).

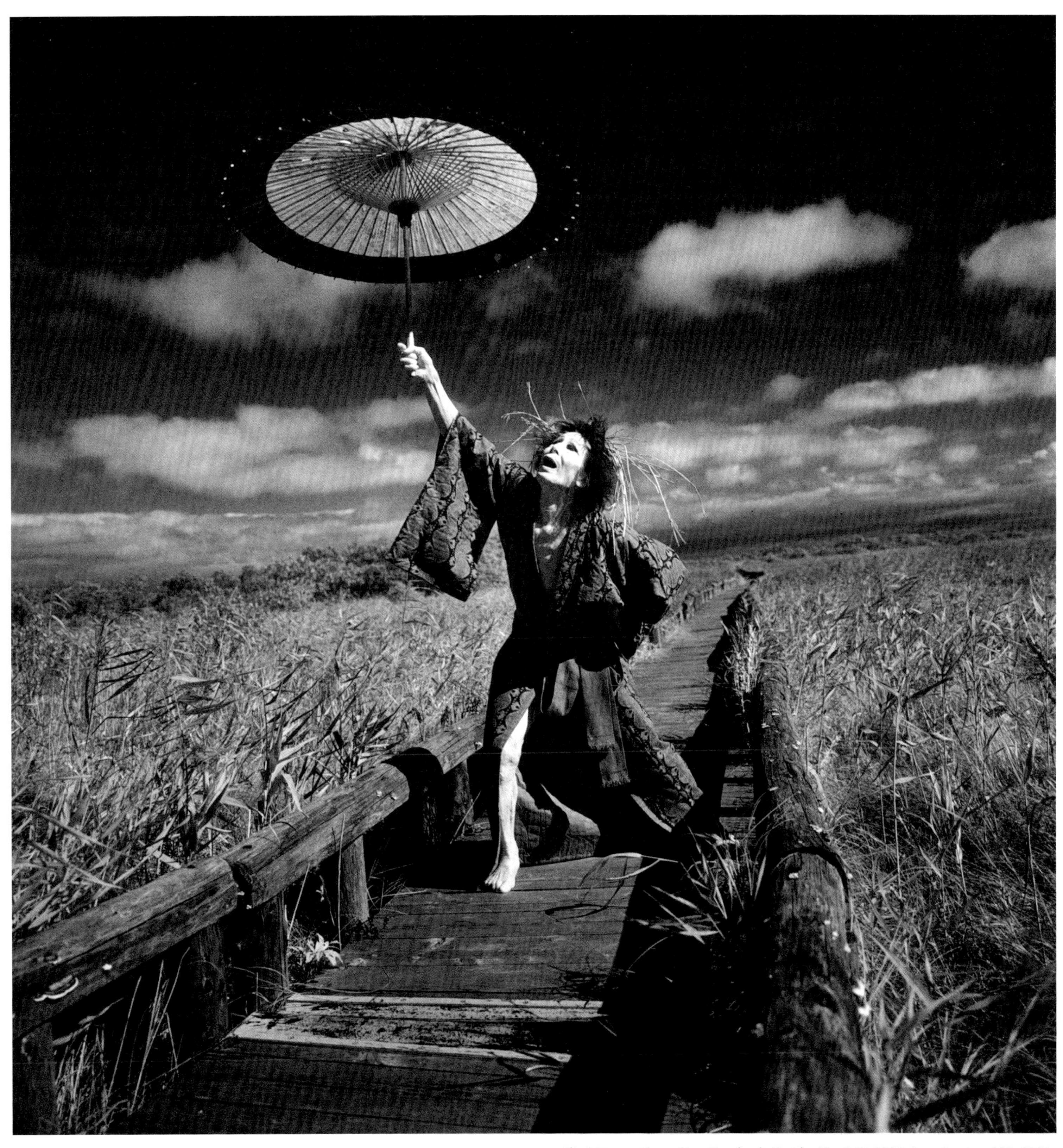

Eikoh Hosoe, *Kazuo Ohno Dancing in Kushiro Marsh IV*, 1994; from *Aperture* 165, 2001.

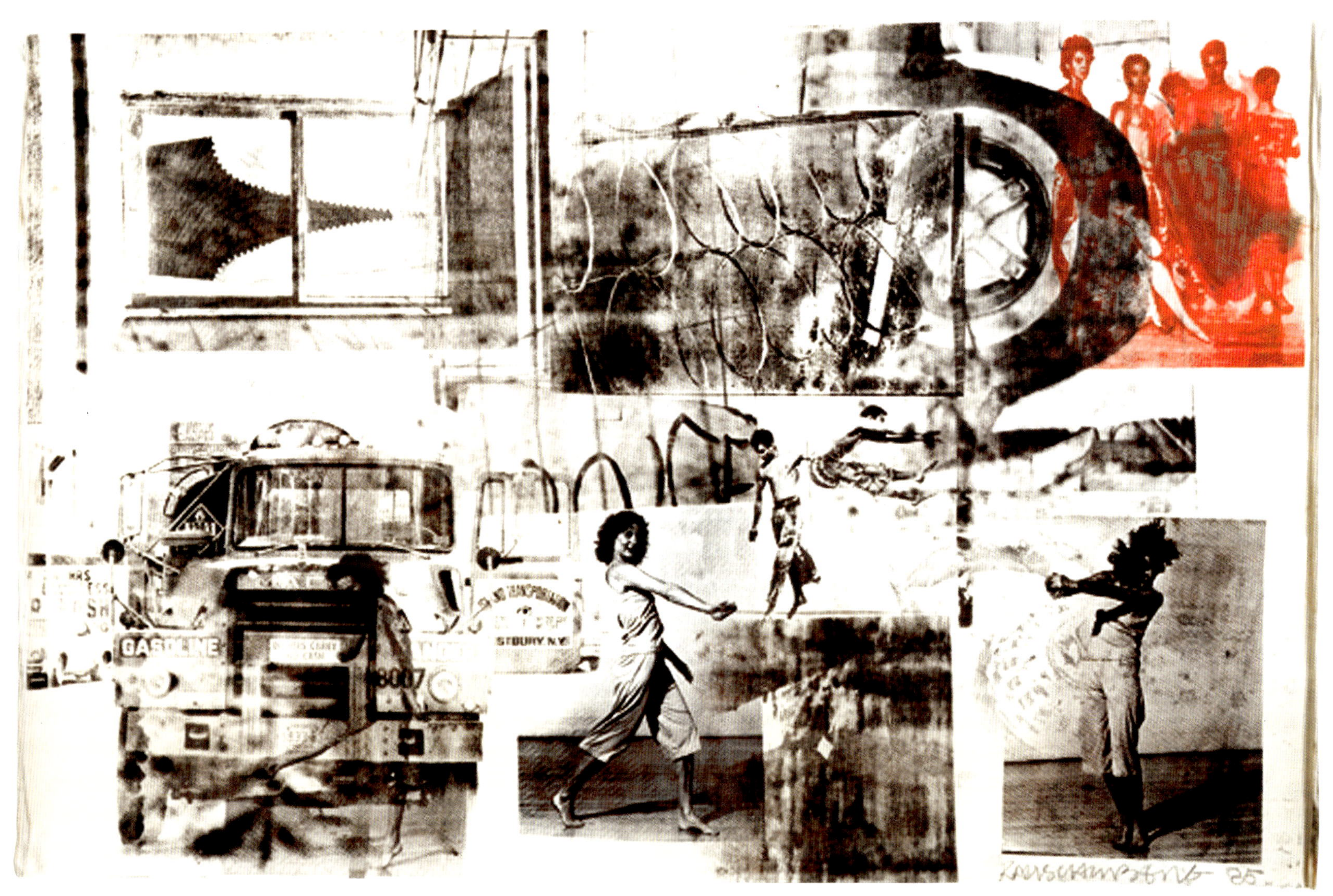

Robert Rauschenberg, *Untitled*, 1985; from *Aperture* 125, 1991.

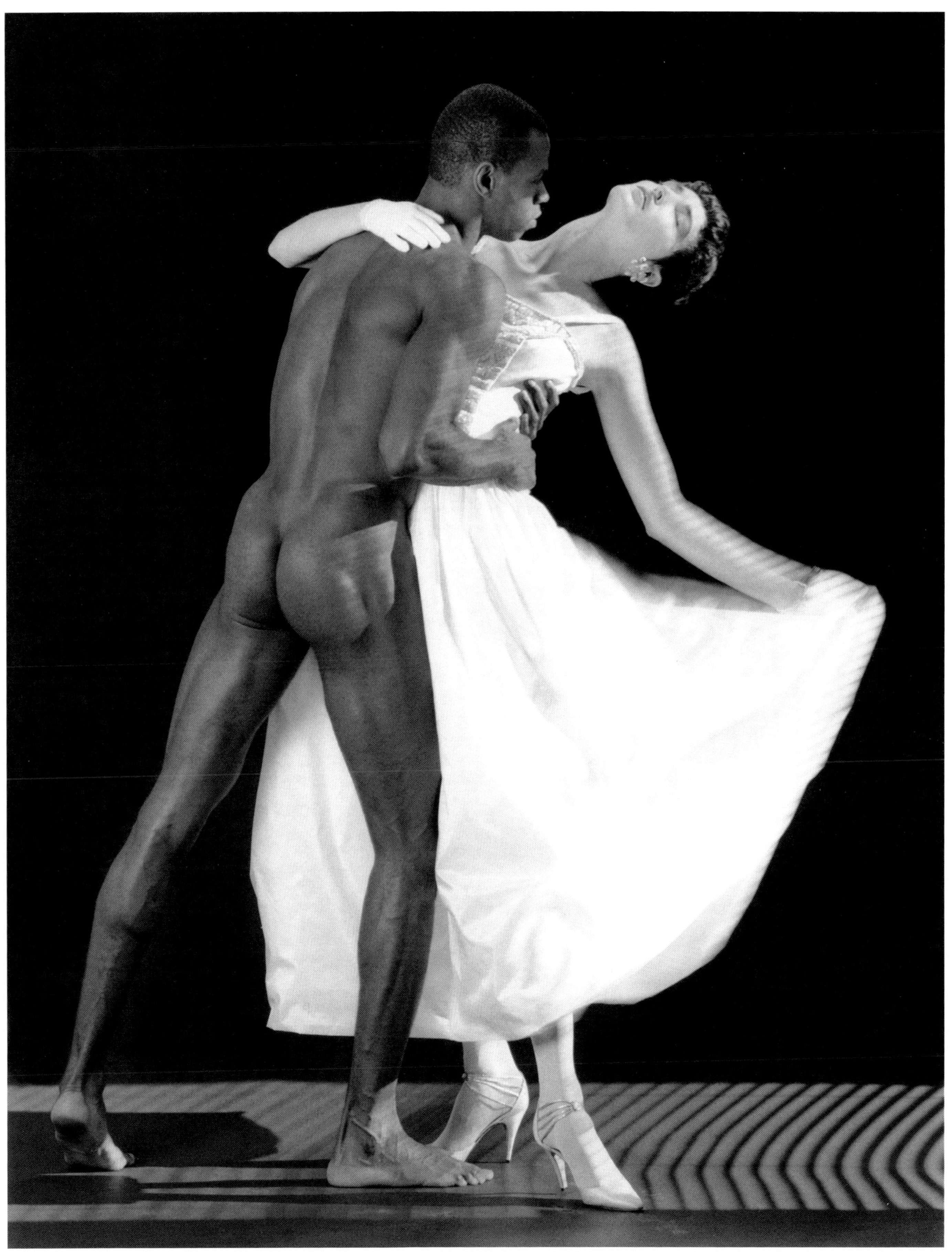

Robert Mapplethorpe, *Thomas and Dovanna*, 1986.

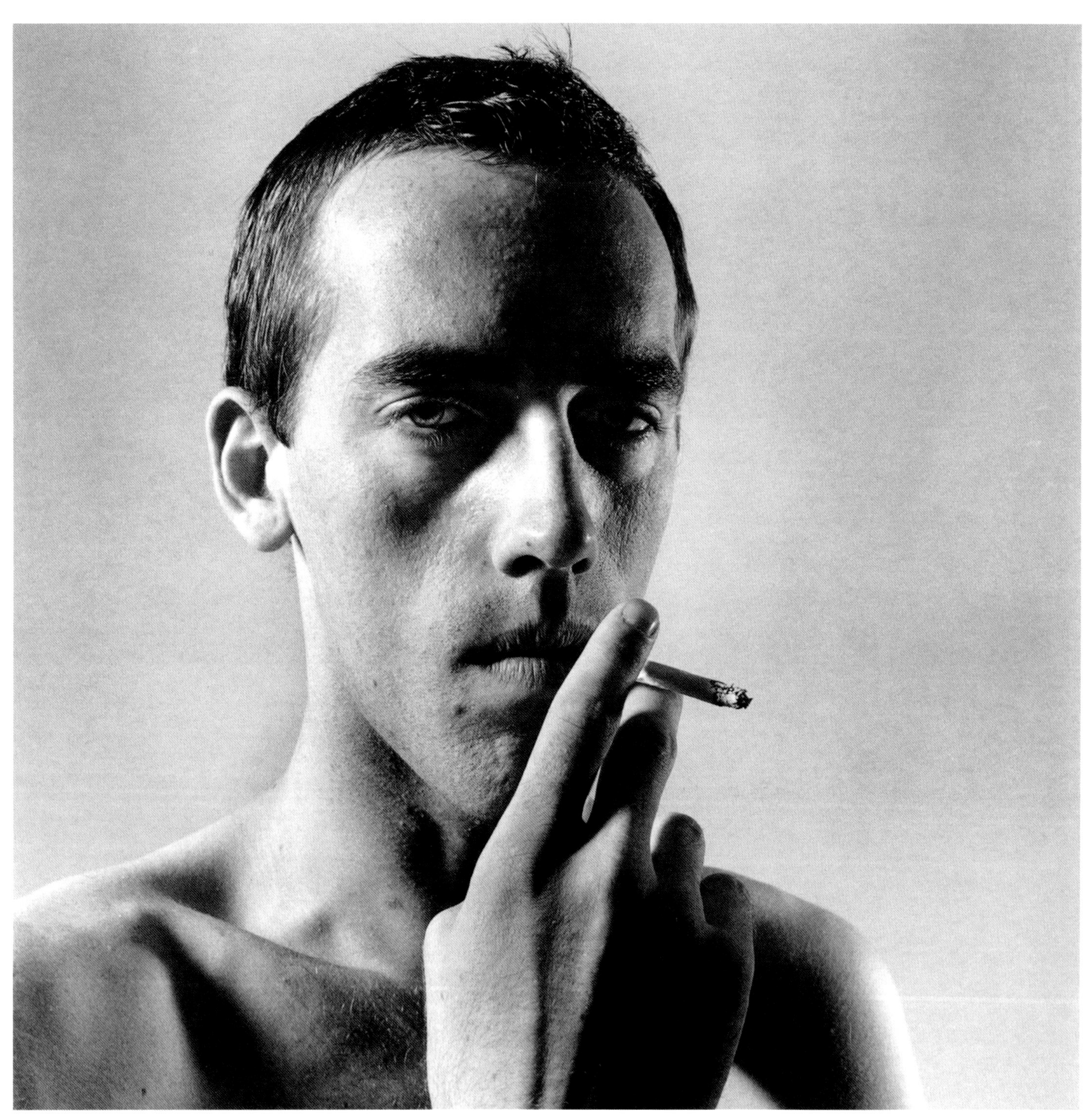

Peter Hujar, *Portrait of David Wojnarowicz*, 1981; from *Aperture* 114, 1989.

Photographers, when you get accosted by painters who, in their innocence, revive that tiresome old argument that Photography is *not* an art (which is true), reply that Painting is *not* an art. This last is also true.

Painting and photography, sculpture and photography, pottery and photography are only media, vehicles, pushmobiles, laundry chutes that get an intangible something from one unfindable part of one man to an unlocatable part of another person. And the ineffable something is not art because to name it implies that art is an object, or a thing, or a biscuit, or a building that can be moved about and grasped with the hands. As many have said *there is no art, only artists*. Every creative photographer has to find out for himself that it's the man behind the camera that is the artist, or not—wearisome as this may be to those who have gone through the process.

—Minor White, from "That Old Question Again,"
***Aperture* vol. 7, no. 1, 1959**

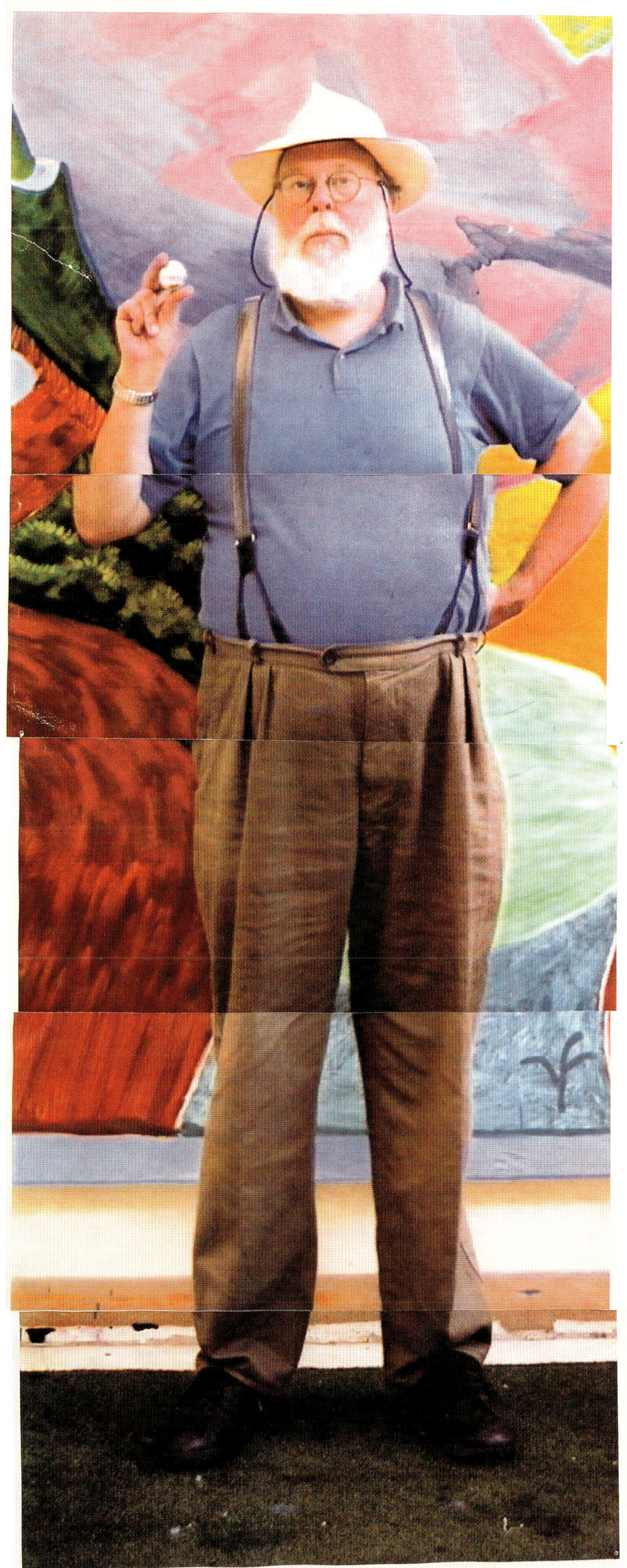

David Hockney,
***Henry Geldzahler #1*,**
September 5, 1990;
from *Aperture* 125, 1991.

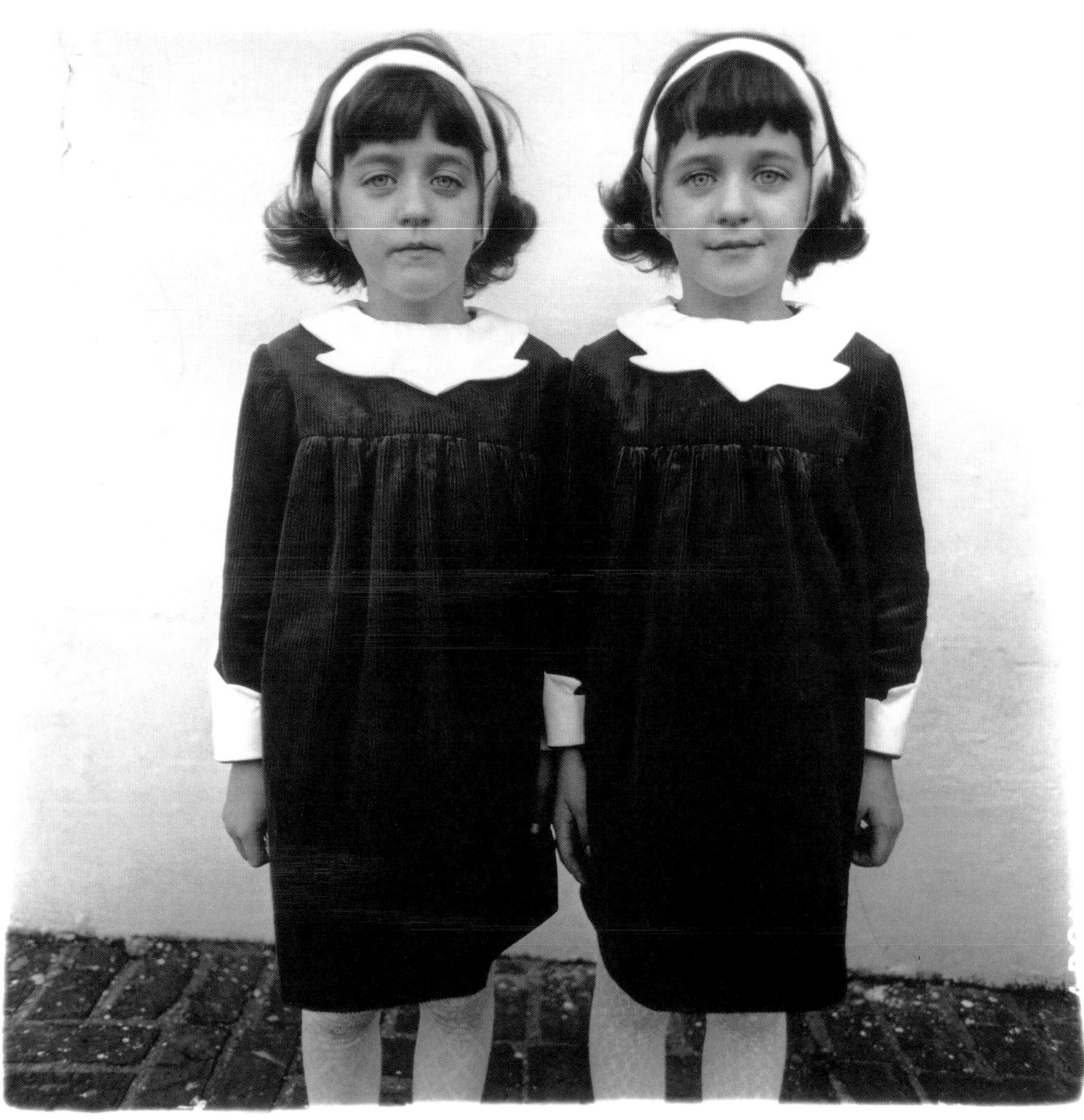

THESE PAGES: photographs by Diane Arbus. *Identical twins, Roselle, N.J.*, 1967; from *Diane Arbus: An Aperture Monograph* (Aperture, 1972).

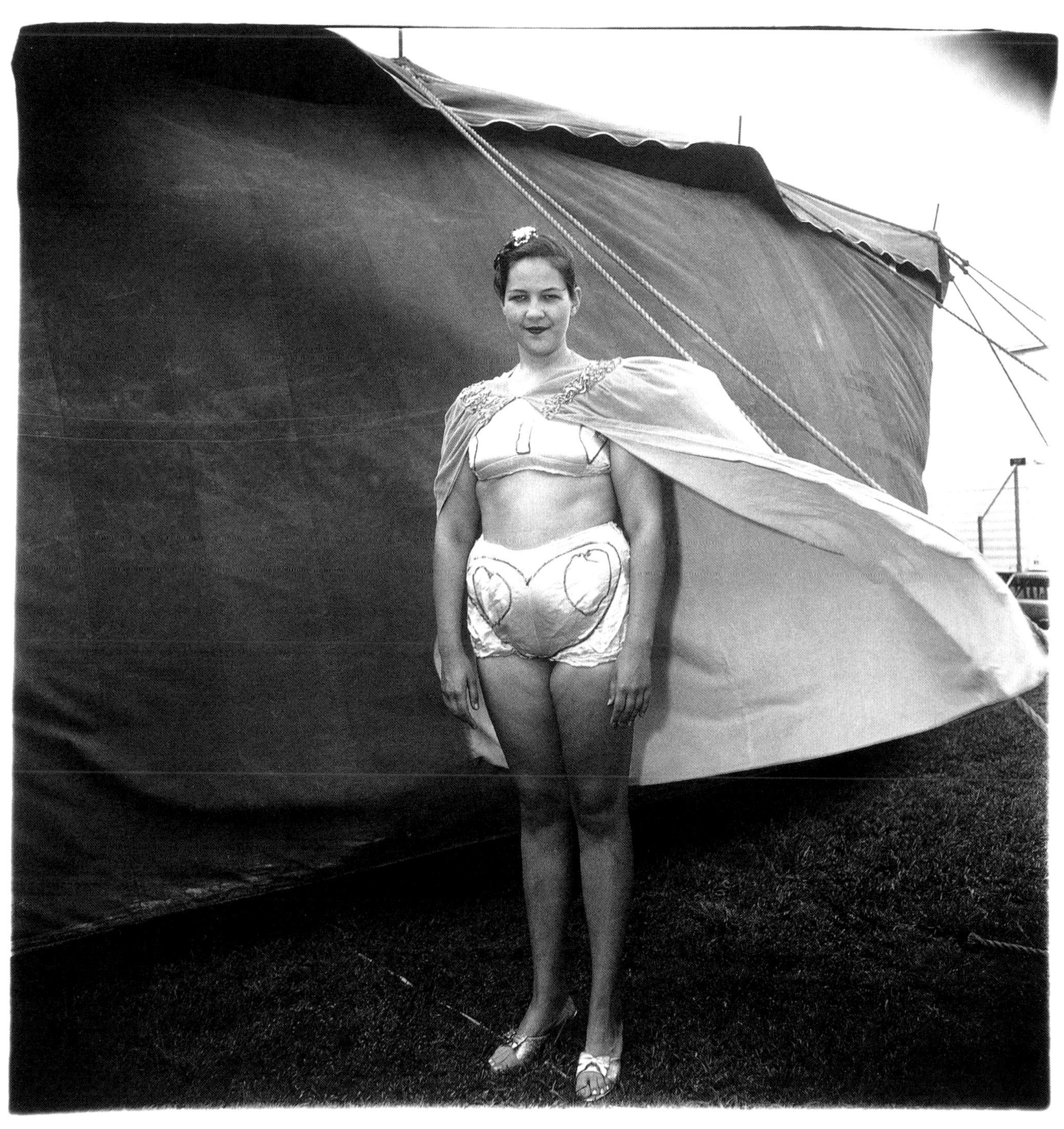

Girl in her circus costume, M.D., **1970; from**
Diane Arbus: An Aperture Monograph **(Aperture, 1972).**

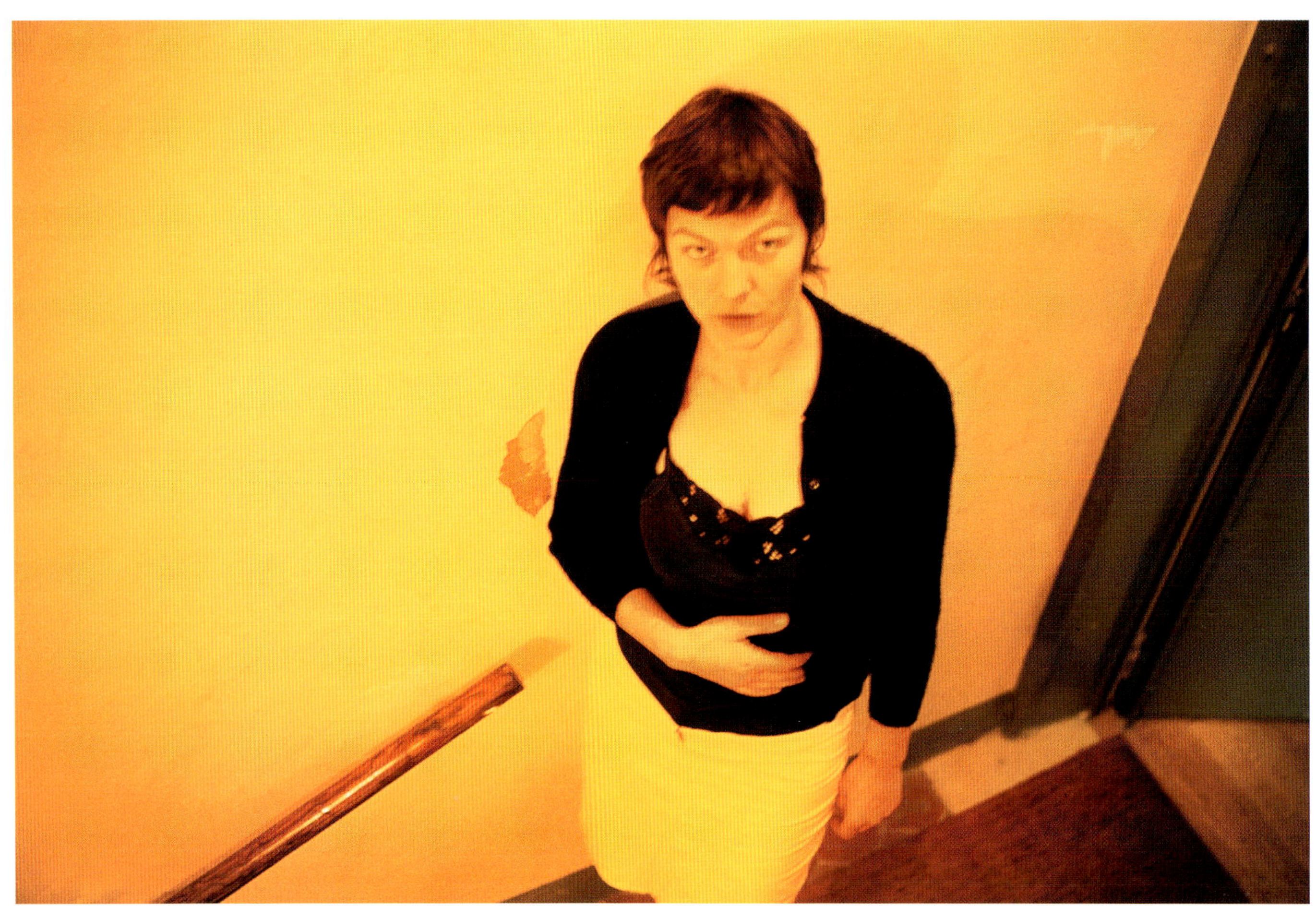

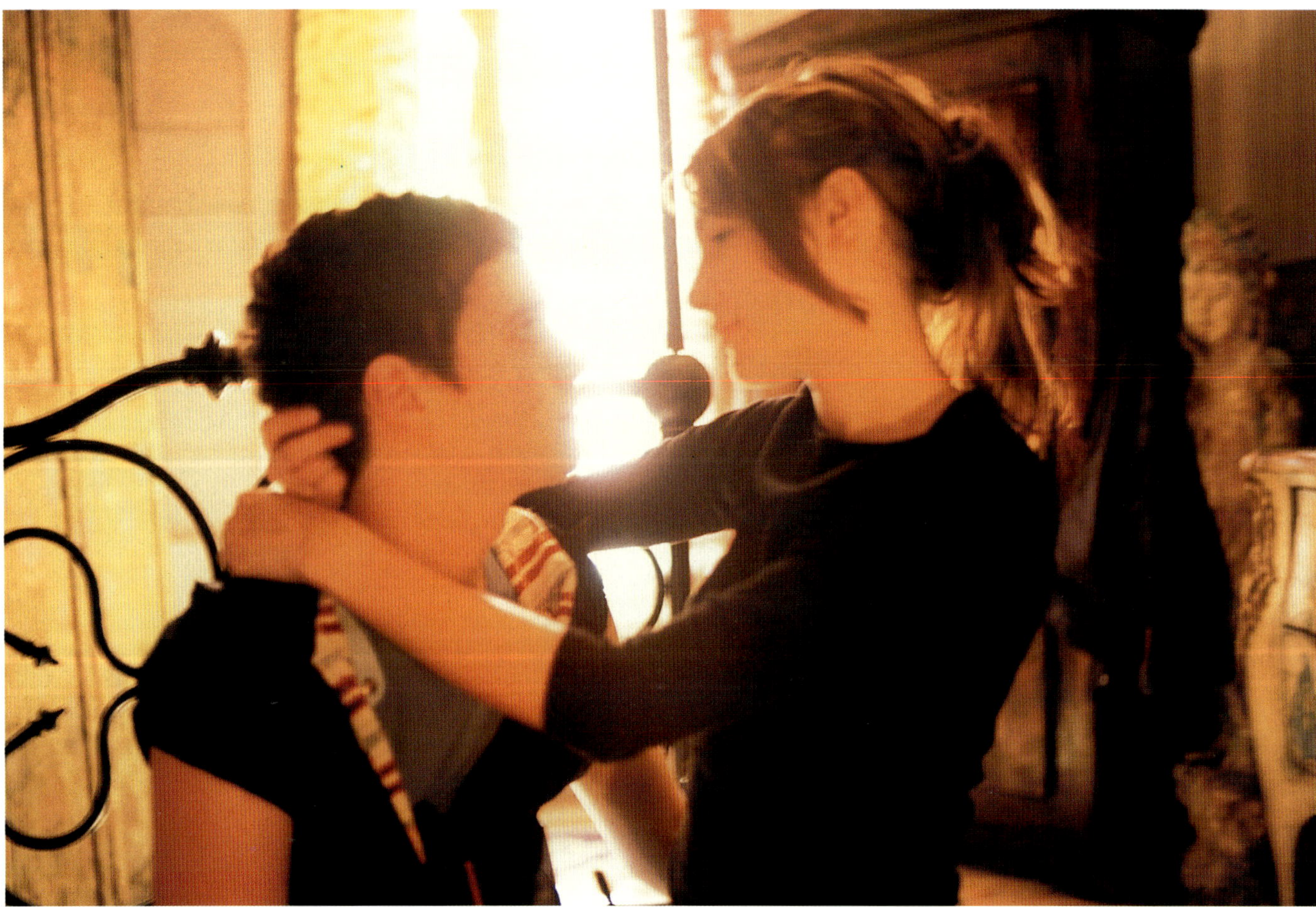

THESE PAGES: photographs by Nan Goldin.
TOP: Valerie on the stairs in yellow light, Paris, 2001. **BOTTOM:** Simon and Jessica, faces lit from behind, Paris, 2001.

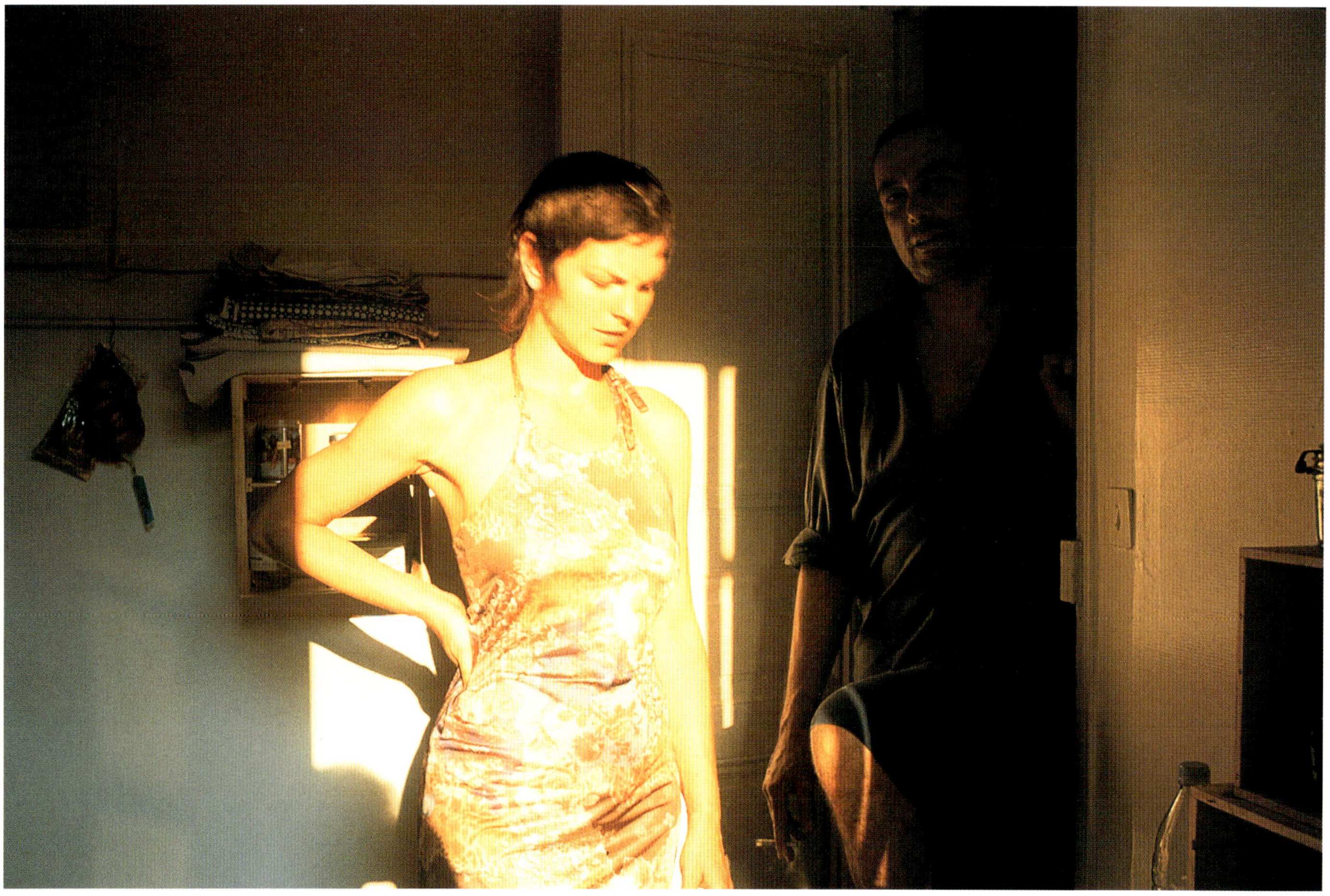

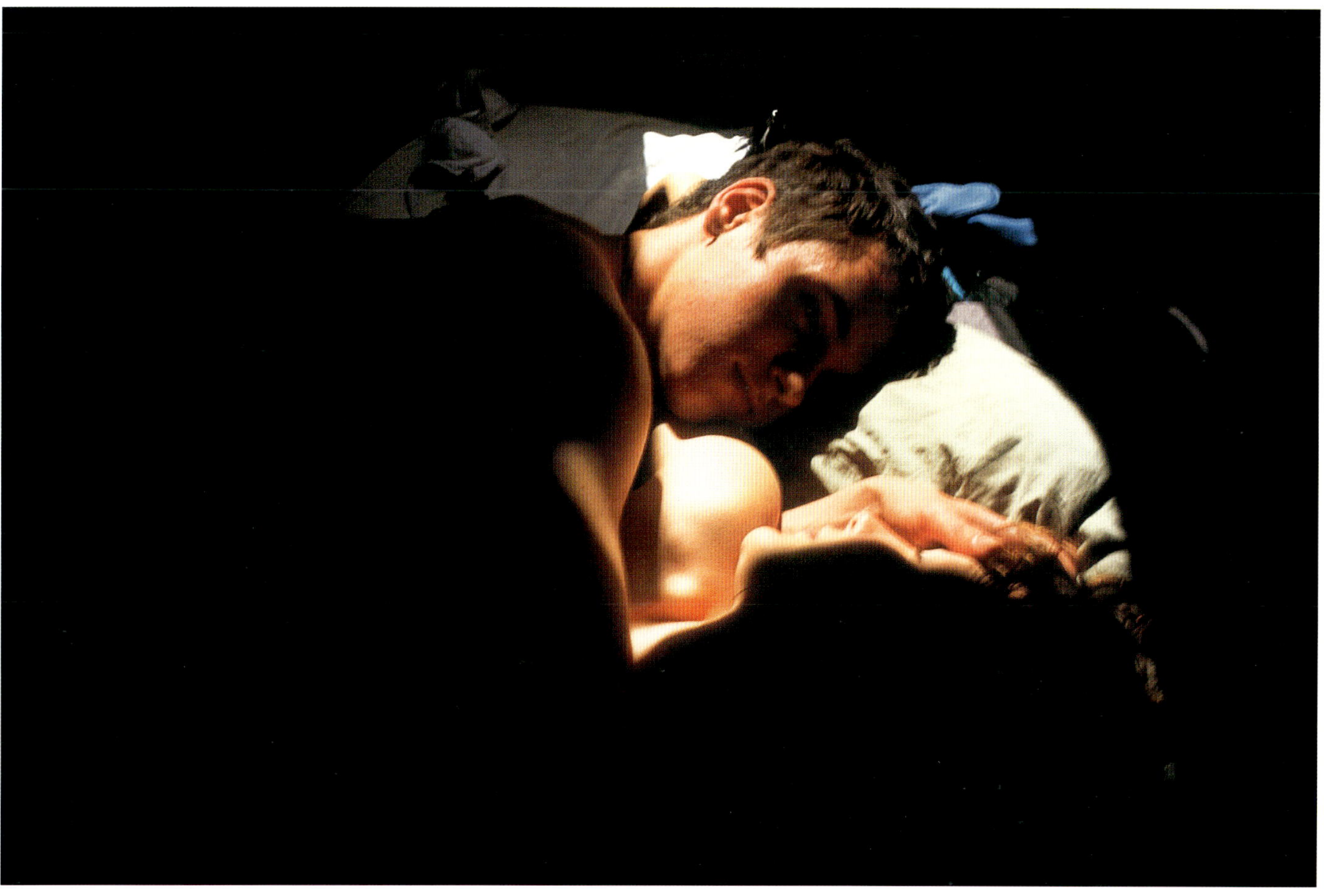

TOP: Valerie in light, Bruno in dark, kitchen, Paris, 2001. BOTTOM: Simon and Jessica looking at each other with faces lit, Paris, 2001.

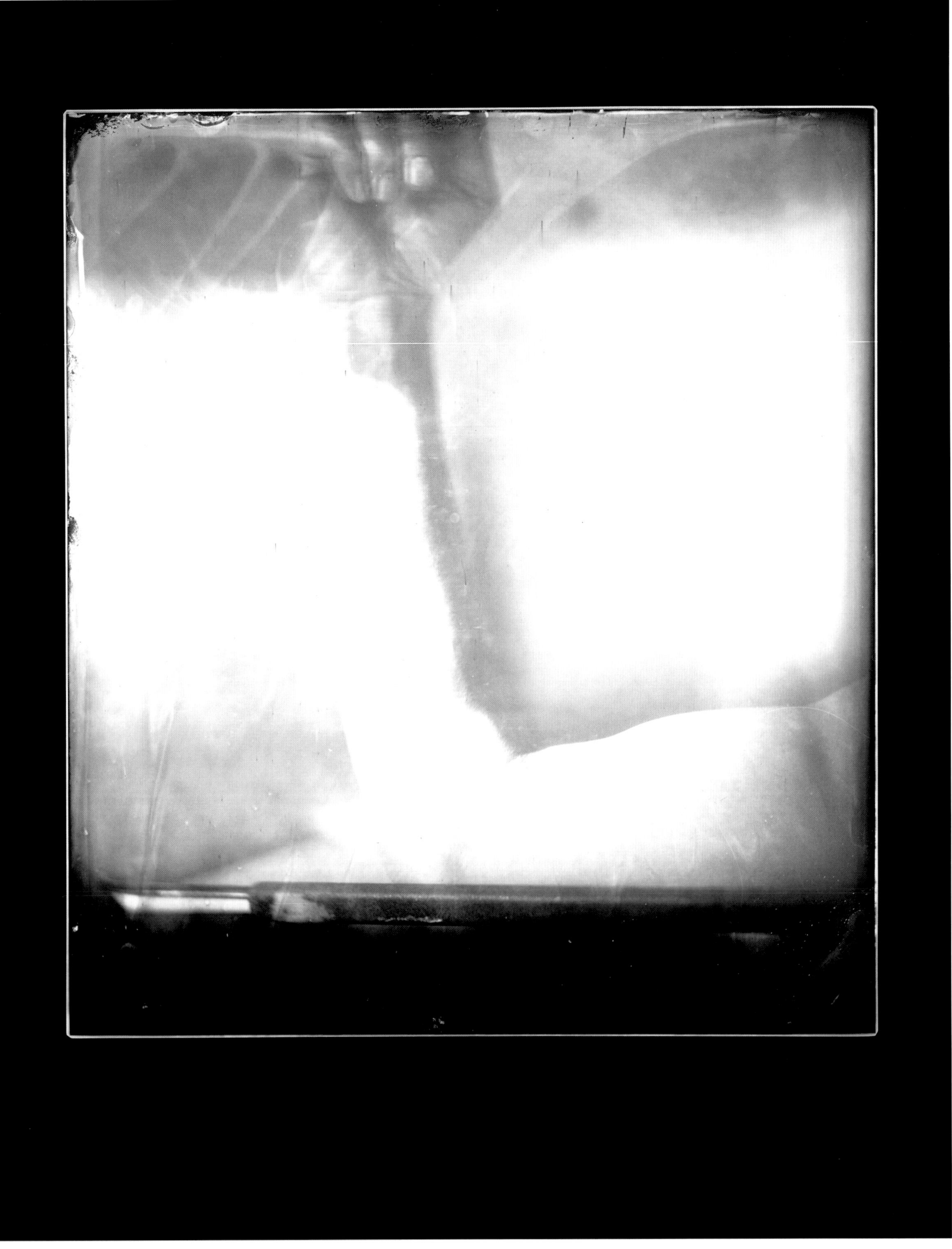

THESE PAGES: photographs by Sally Mann.
Untitled (Larry's Arm IV), 2002.

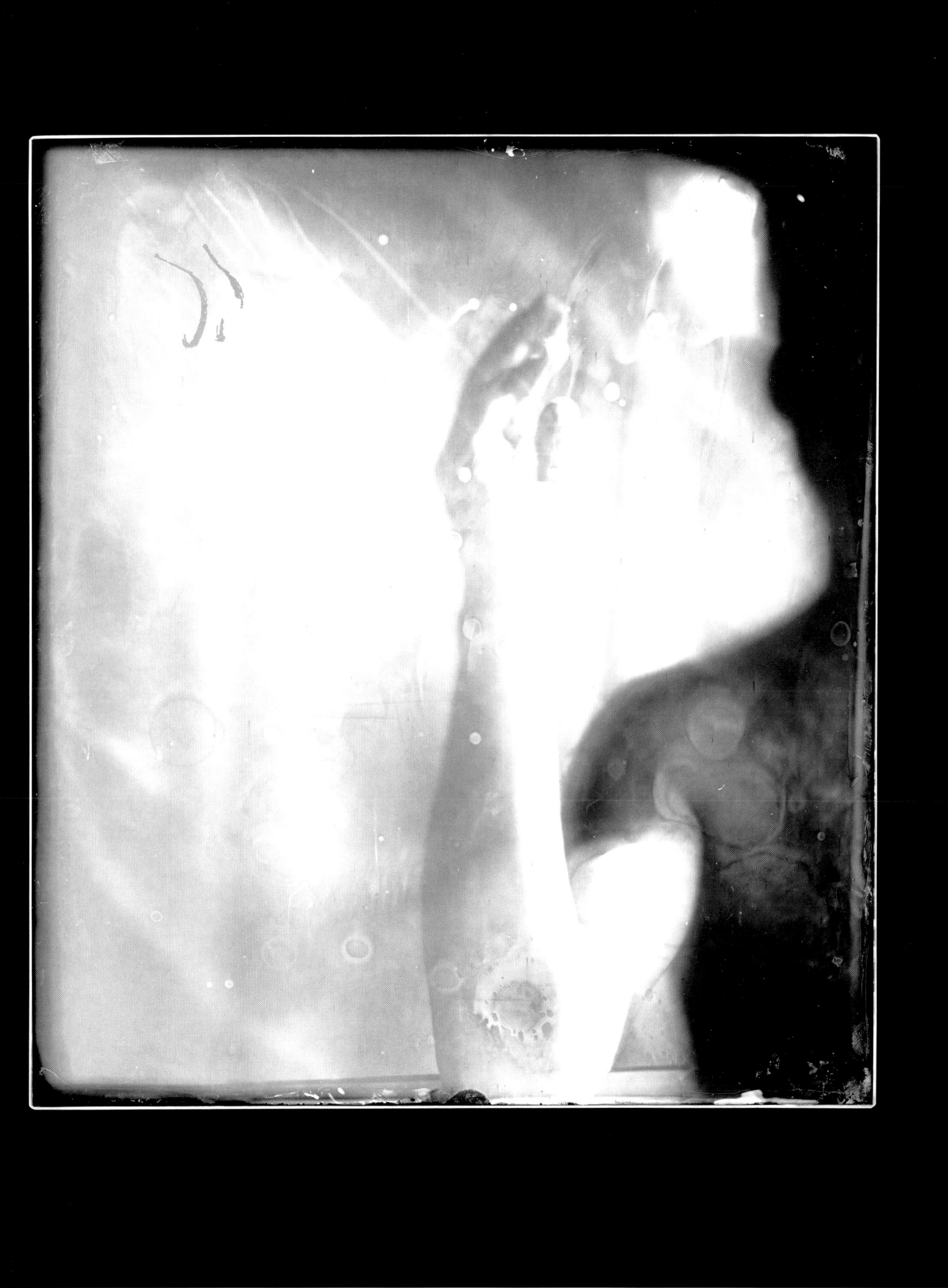

Untitled (Larry's Arm I), 2002.

Often it is in dreams that we communicate. . . . I am on a familiar street searching for a particular house. The moment I set foot in this street my heart beats wildly. Though I have never seen the street it is more familiar to me, more intimate, more significant, than any street I have known. It is the street by which I return to the past. Every house, every porch, every gate, every lawn, every stone, stick, twig or leaf speaks eloquently. The sense of recognition, compounded of myriad layers of memory, is so powerful that I am almost dissolved.

The street has no beginning nor end; it is a detached segment swimming in a fuzzy aura and complete in itself. A vibrant portion of the infinite whole. Though there is never any activity in this street it is not empty or deserted. Indeed, it is the most alive street I can think of. It is alive with memories, like an arcane grove which pullulates with its swarms of invisible hosts. I can't say that I *walk* down this street, nor can I say either that I *glide* through it. The street invests me.

—Henry Miller, from *Plexus, The Rosy Crucifixion, Book Two* (1965), *Aperture* 101, 1985

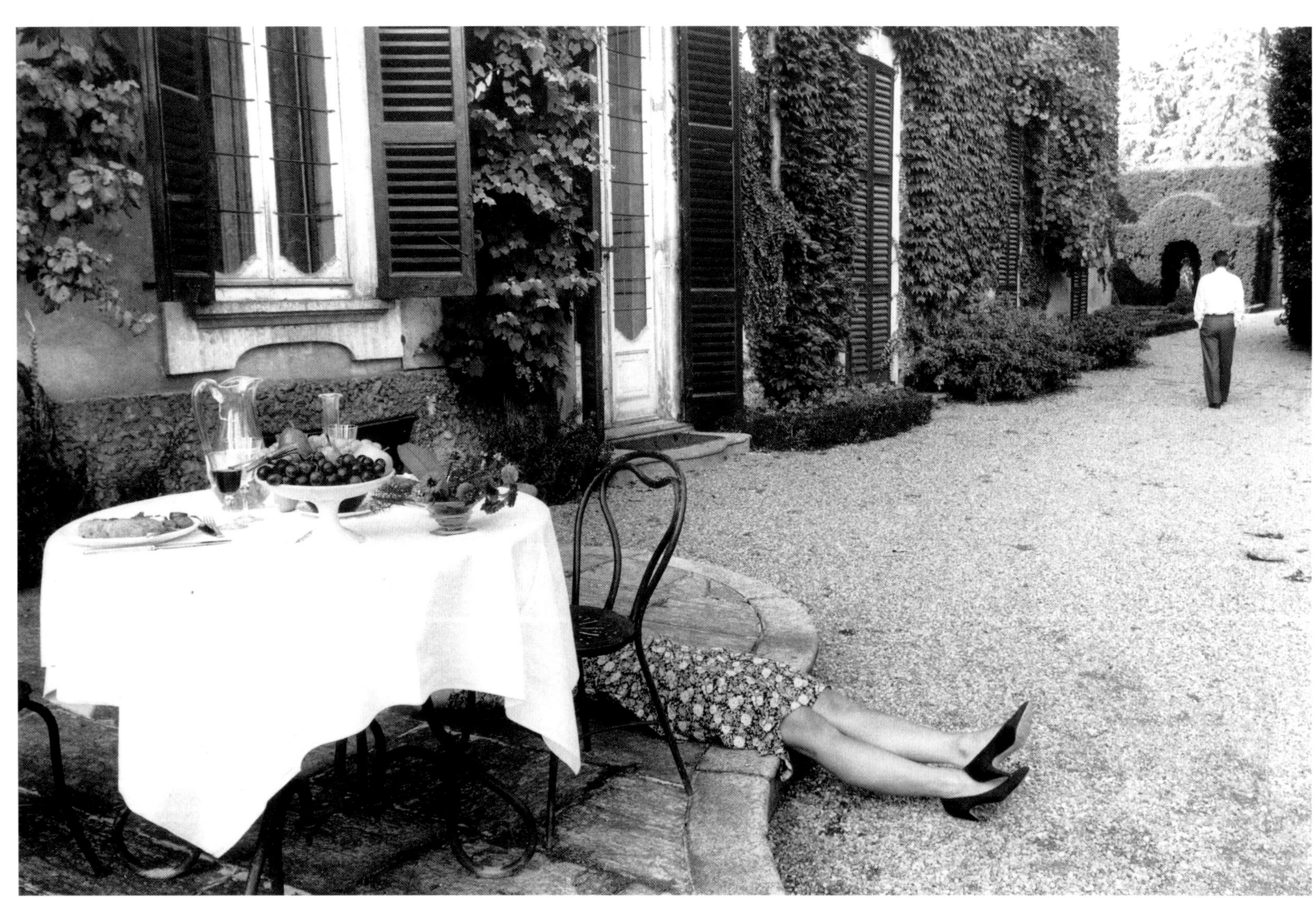

Gianni Berengo Gardin, *Milano, servizio fotografico, pausa di lavoro* (Milan, photographic service, work break), 1987; from *Aperture* 132, 1993.

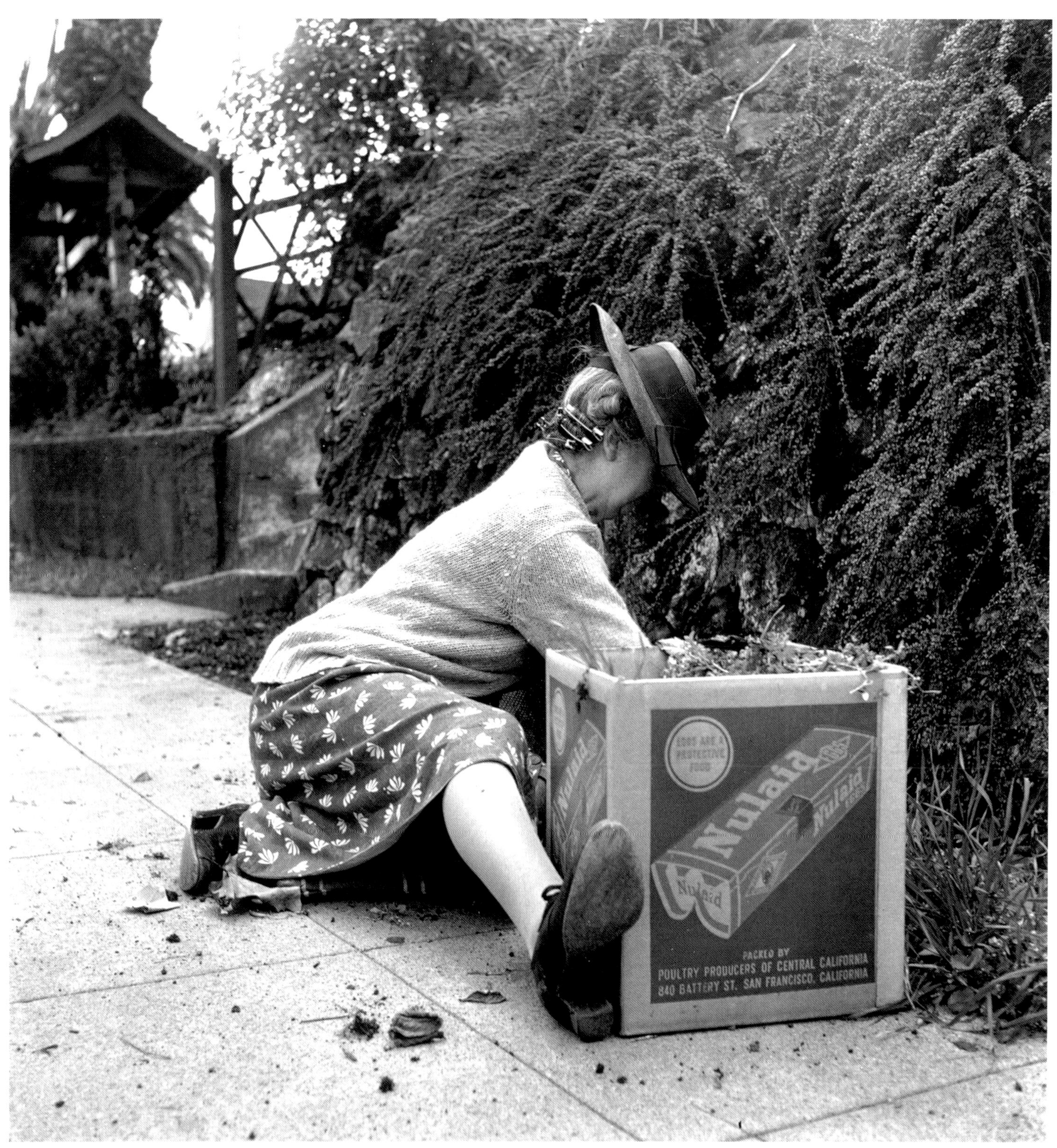

Dorothea Lange, *Spring in Berkeley*, 1951; from *Aperture* vol. 1, no. 2, 1952.

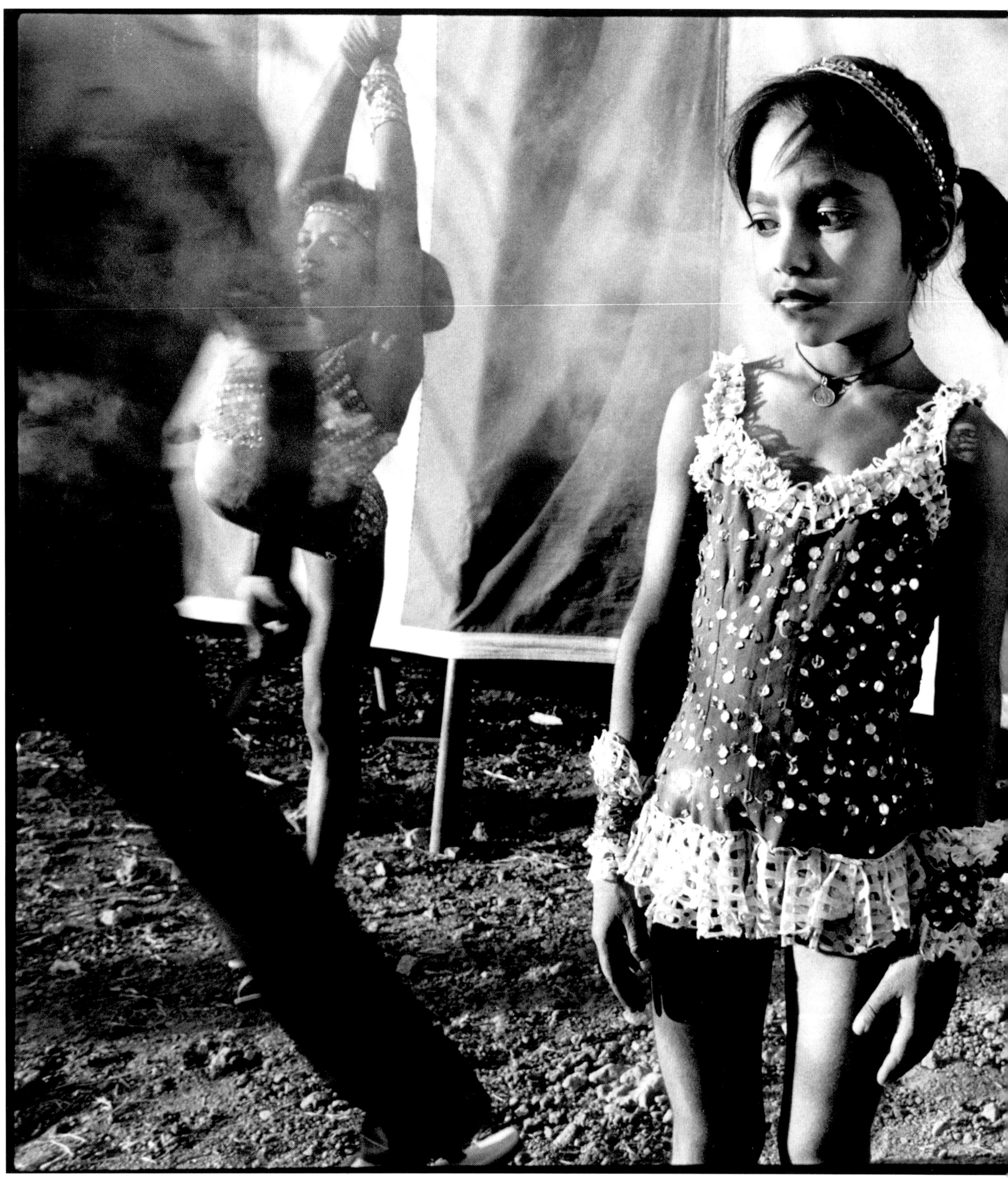

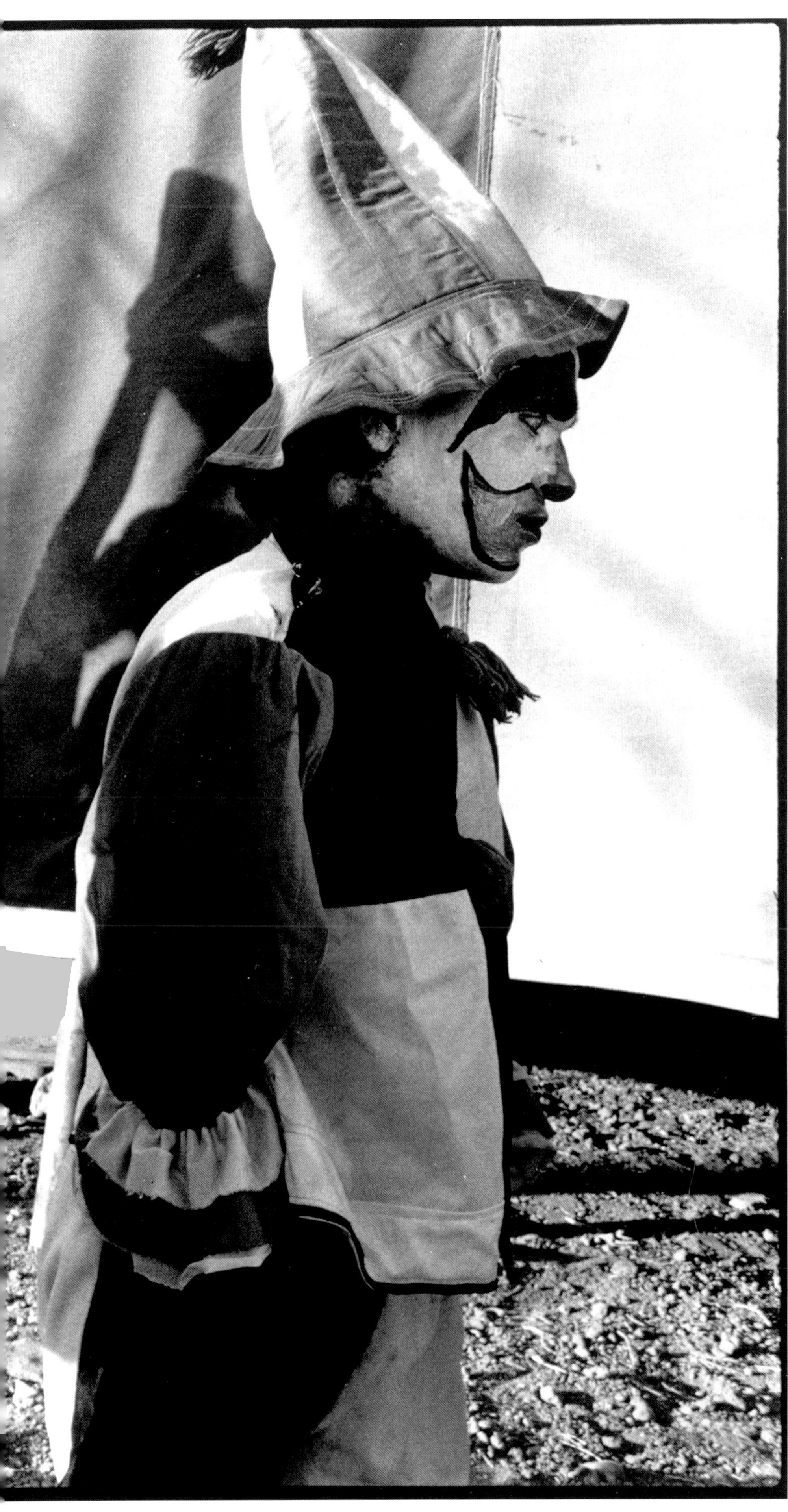

Mary Ellen Mark, *Pinky with Clown Man Passing on Left Side*, Royal Circus, India, 1990.

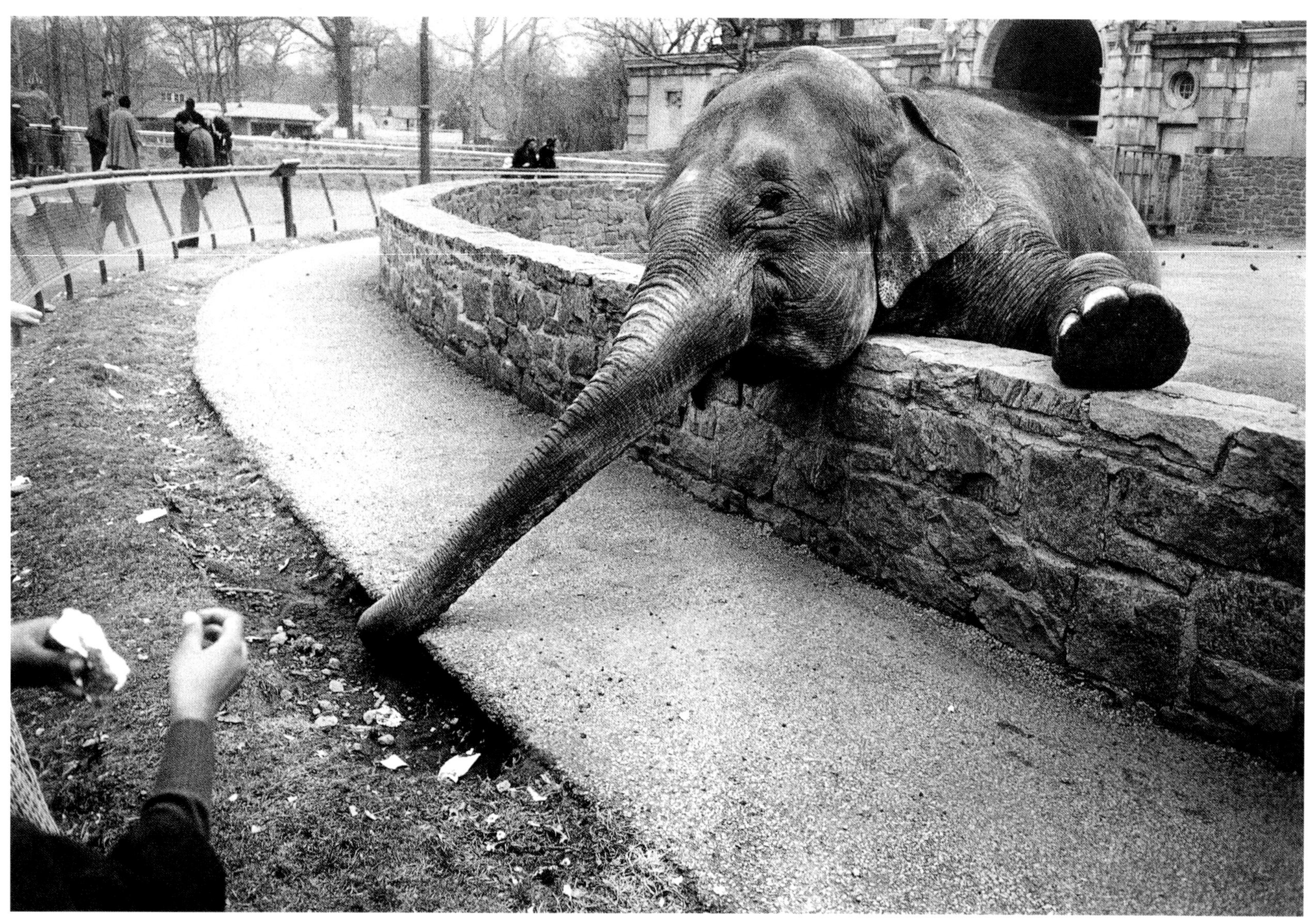

Garry Winogrand, *New York*, 1963; from *Aperture* 143, 1996.

I could take a cow and implant a camera in it and let it amble around in the city or in its own domain (I say a cow because a human being I would not trust). If the camera was programmed to go off at an indeterminate series of moments, the samplings would be fantastic.

We're not so damned inspired every day! If we rely on what we meet, some inspiration will arise. As an example, if I go into a grocery store . . . if I am smart I will take home what is best that day. I will not say that I want to

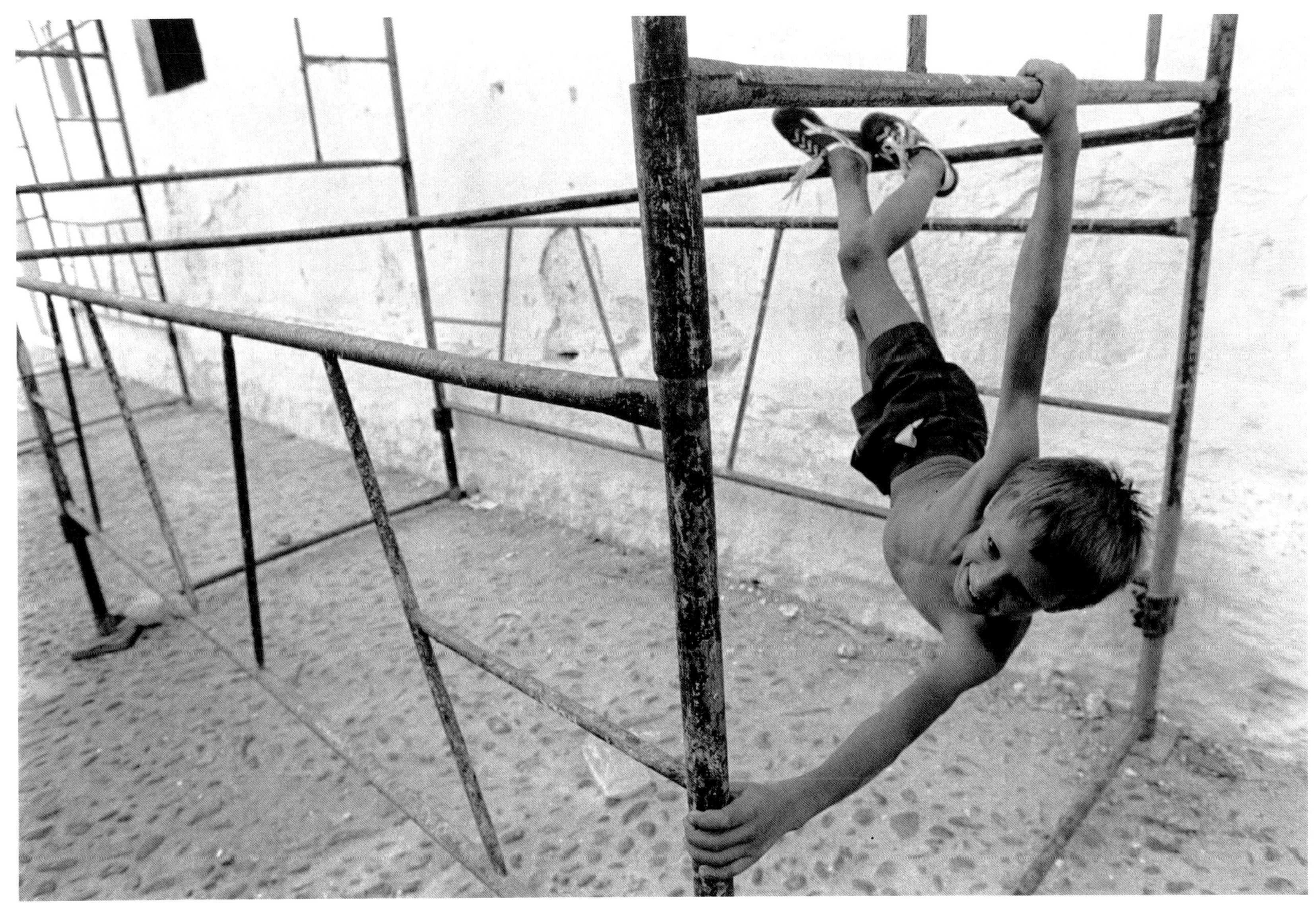

Ferdinando Scianna, *Carmona, Spain*, 1983; from *Aperture* 151, 1998.

buy apples today or that I want to buy oranges today. . . . I buy the best of what there is that day. If the beef looks good, I'm not going to buy lamb. . . .

The point of this is: if you work this way, if you live this way, if you just exist this way, you will find that by some strange coincidence (which I now know is not so strange), you will have brought together a number of things which make a magnificent meal. You consume this thing with champagne if you can afford it, and if not, you consume it just with enthusiasm.

—Frederick Sommer, from "An Extemporaneous Talk at the Art Institute of Chicago" (October 1970), *Aperture* vol. 16, no. 2, 1971

THE KENTUCKY KID

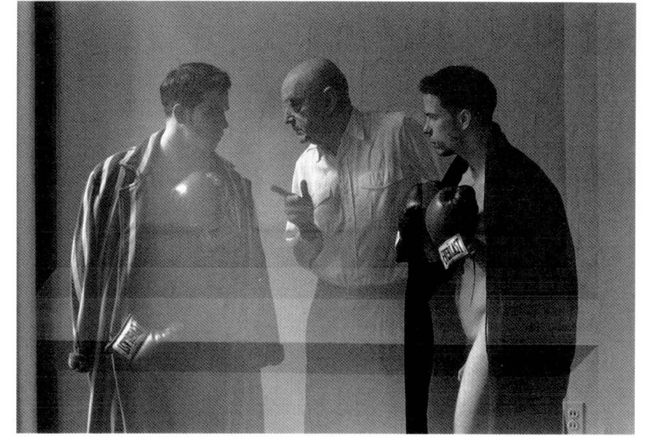

2

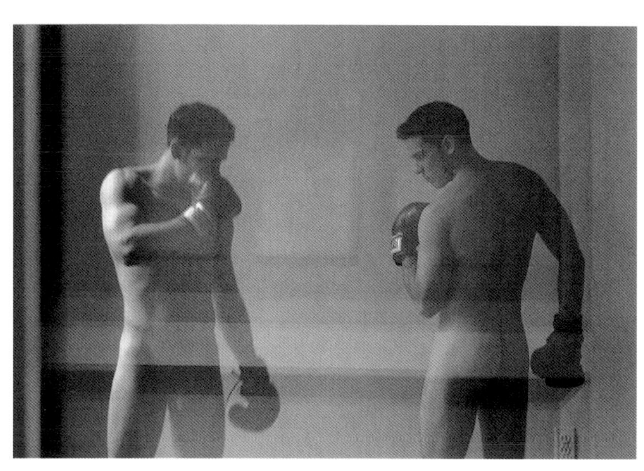

A. 3

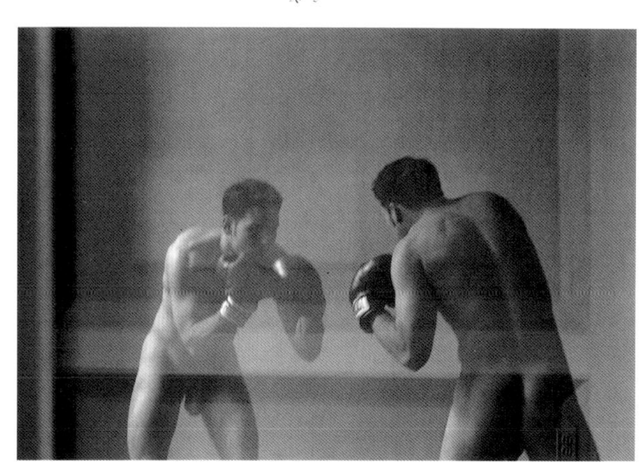

4

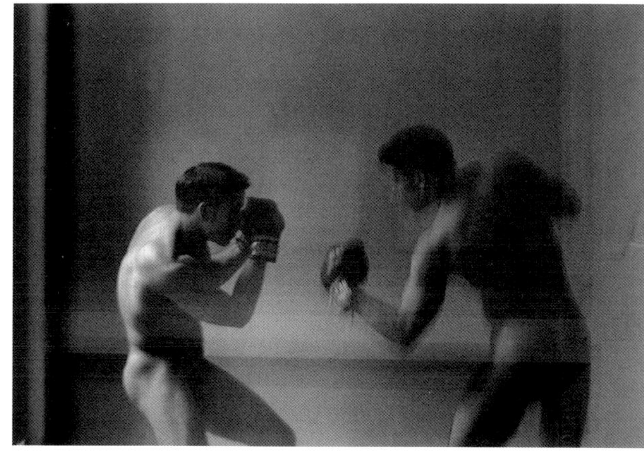

5

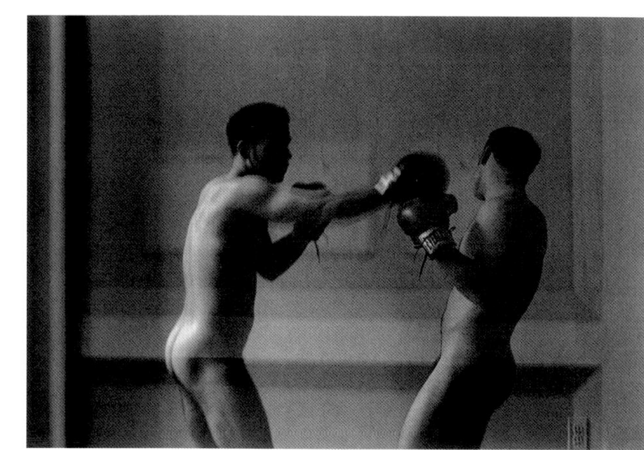

6

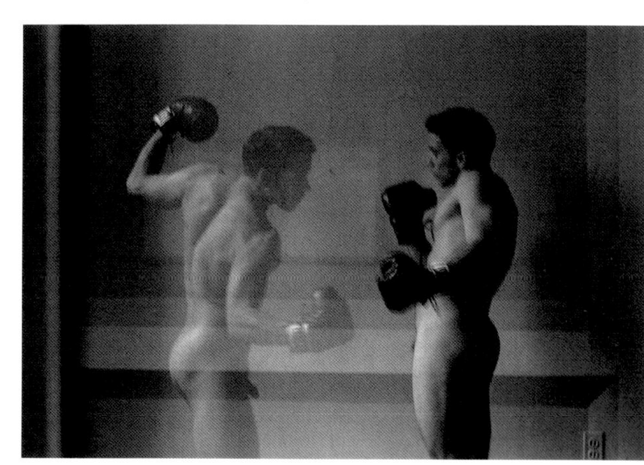

7

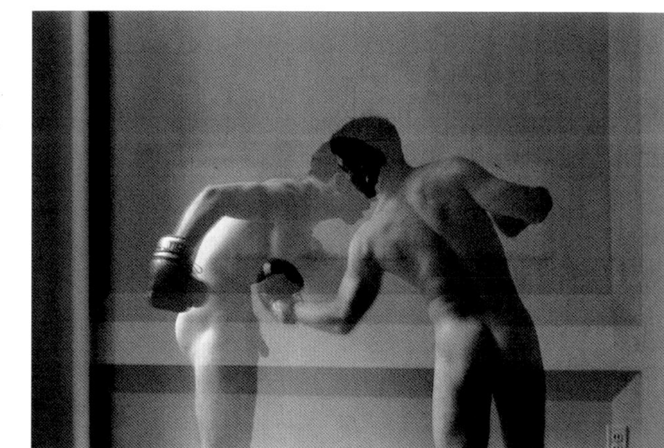

Perhaps the old literacy of words is dying and a new literacy of images is being born. Perhaps the printed page will disappear and even our records be kept in images and sounds. Perhaps the new photograph-writing—so new we have no word for it—is a transition form, and perhaps, instead, it is, in embryo and by virtue of principles now being discovered and applied, the form through which we shall speak to each other, in many succeeding phases of photography, for a thousand years or more.

We are not yet taught to read photographs as we read words. Only a few thousands, among our hundreds of millions, have trained themselves like photographers and editors to read a photograph in its multilayered significance. Yet more and more photographers have discovered that the power of the photograph springs from a deeper source than words—the same deep source as music. At birth we begin to discover that shapes, sounds, lights, and textures have meaning. Long before we learn to talk, sounds and images form the world we live in. All our lives, that world is more immediate than words and difficult to articulate. Photography, reflecting those images with uncanny accuracy, evokes their associations and our instant conviction. The art of the photographer lies in using those connotations, as a poet uses the connotations of words and a musician the tonal connotations of sounds.

—Nancy Newhall, from "The Caption: The Mutual Relation of Words/Photographs," ***Aperture*** **vol. 1, no. 1, 1952**

8

9

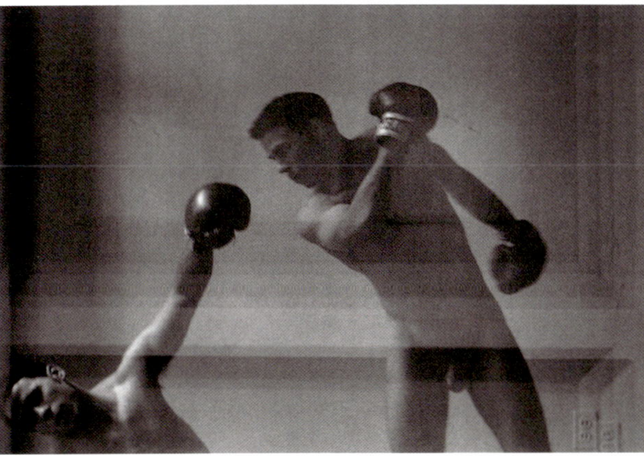

10

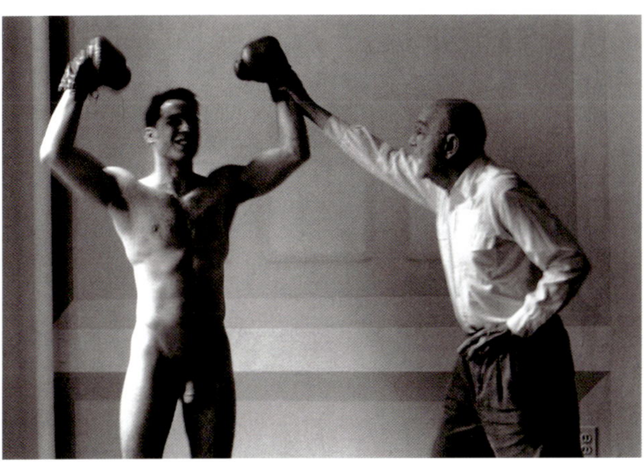

Duane Michals,
The Kentucky Kid 1–10**, 2001.**

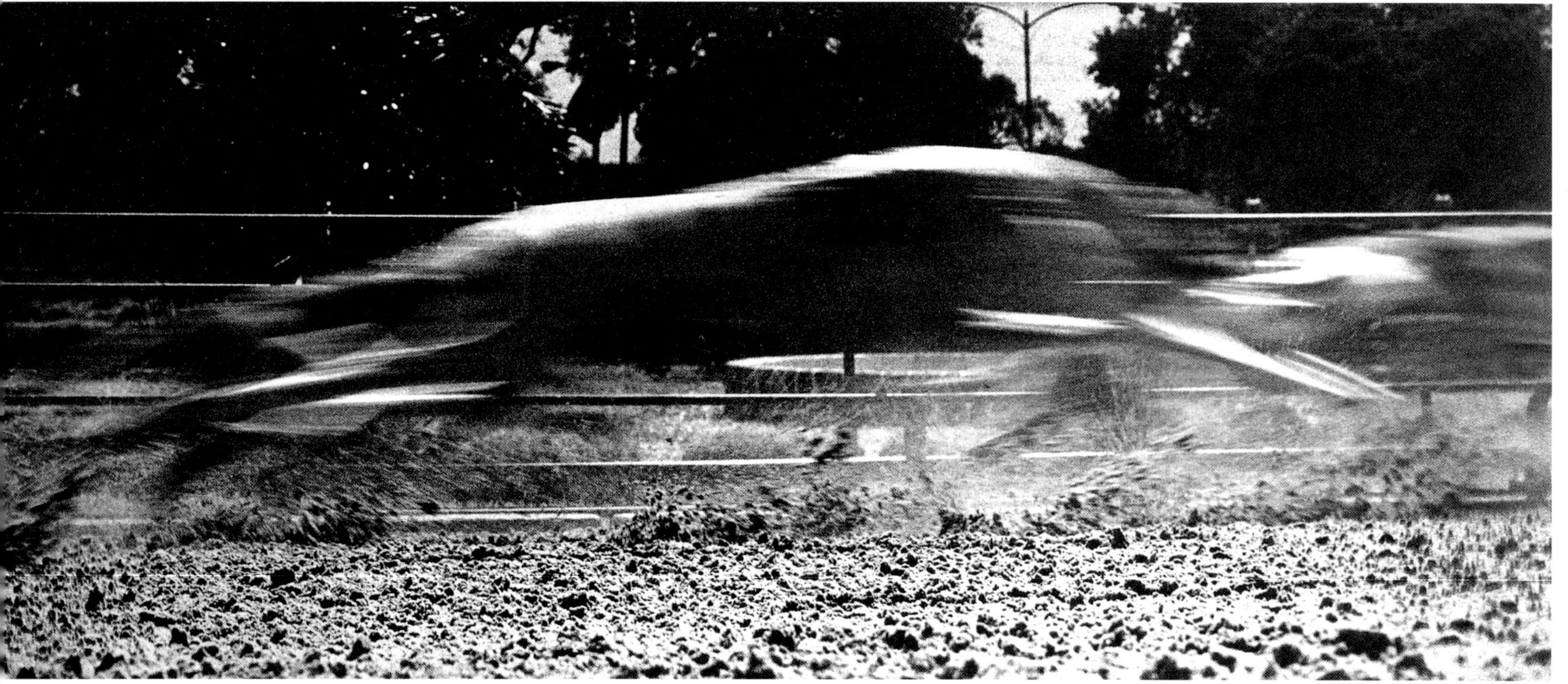

Graciela Iturbide, *Galgo* (Greyhound), Hernan de Soto's, Tampa, Florida, 1996.

The camera is a means of expression with virtues and limitations of its own; the photograph which looks like a drawing, etching or painting, is not a real photograph. The peculiar virtue of photography, and at the same time, in the hands of a purely mechanical operator, its severest limitation, is its power of revealing all textures and revealing all details.

The art of photography is to be sought precisely at this point: it lies in using this technical perfection in such a way that every element shall hold its place and every detail contribute to the expression of the theme. Just as in other arts there is no room here for the non-essential. Inasmuch as the lens does not in the same way as the pencil lend itself to the elimination of elements, the problem is so to render every element that it becomes essential; and, inasmuch as in the last analysis there are no distinctions in Nature of significant and insignificant, the pursuit of this ideal is theoretically justified. A search for and approach to this end distinguishes the work of Alfred Stieglitz. It must not be supposed that the adoption of a particular equipment (such as lenses of critical focus or particular color screens) can by itself achieve the desired result; here, as elsewhere, it is the man behind the tool, and not the tool, that counts.

—Coomaraswamy, *Aperture* vol. 16, no. 3, 1972

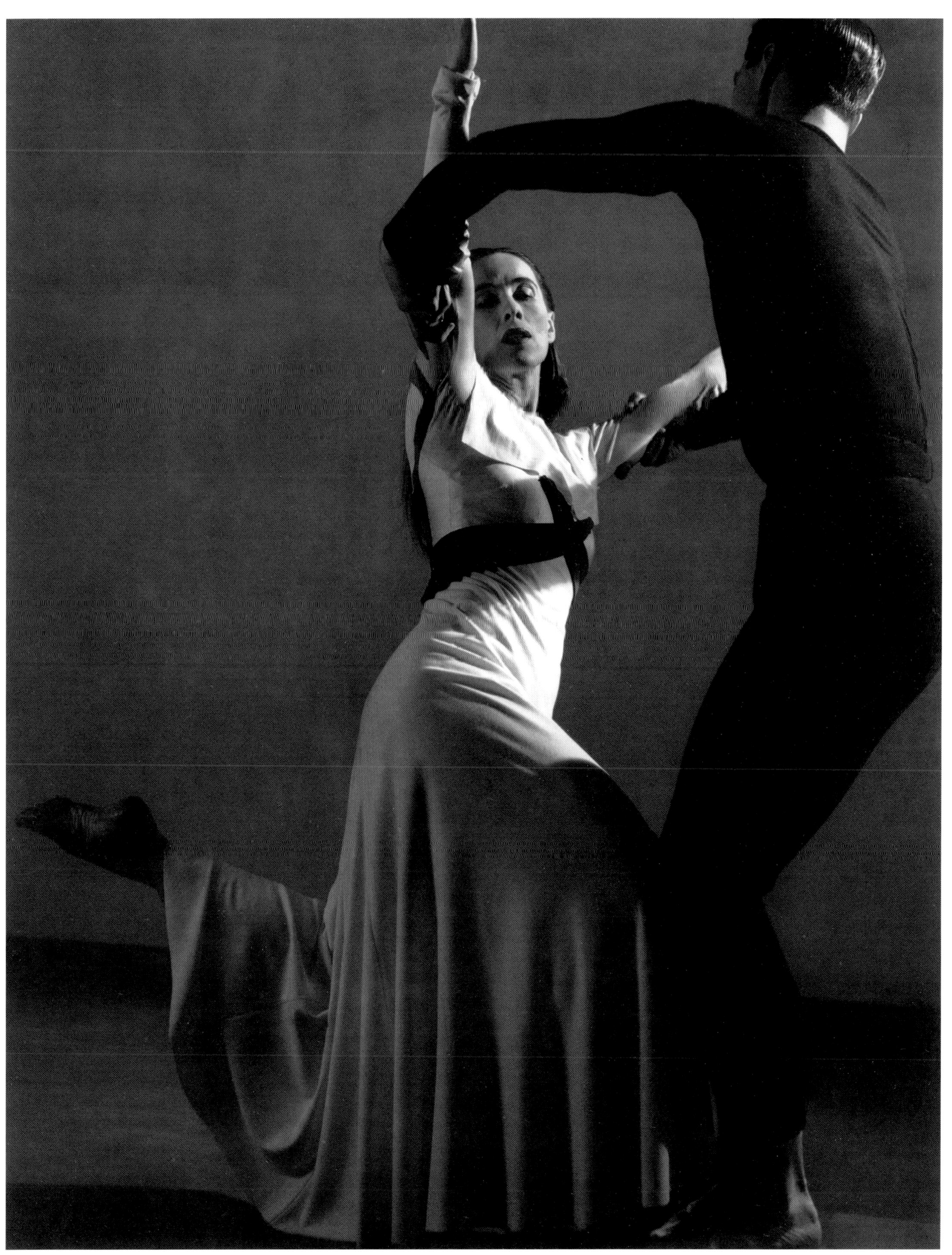

Barbara Morgan, *Martha Graham—American Document—Puritan Love Duet (with Erick Hawkins)*, 1938.

Aperture Foundation, Inc. publishes *Aperture* at 20 East 23rd Street, New York, NY 10010.

Call 866-457-4603 to subscribe

Visit the Aperture website at www.aperture.org

e-mail letters to the editor at magazine@aperture.org

TEXT CREDITS

Unless otherwise indicated, all excerpted texts are from issues of *Aperture* magazine and are copyright © Aperture Foundation, Inc.

Page VI, Founders' statement, reprinted courtesy the Minor White Archive, Princeton University, copyright © 1952 by Minor White, renewed by The Trustees of Princeton University, all rights reserved; p. 12, excerpt by Minor White, reprinted from the *PSA Journal* vol. 29, no. 7, copyright © 1963 Photographic Society of America; p. 15, excerpt by Barbara Morgan, reprinted courtesy the Minor White Archive, Princeton University, copyright © 1953 by Minor White, renewed by The Trustees of Princeton University, all rights reserved; p. 40 excerpt by Beaumont Newhall, reprinted courtesy the Minor White Archive, Princeton University, copyright © 1956 by Minor White, renewed by The Trustees of Princeton University, all rights reserved; p. 52, excerpt by Ansel Adams, reprinted courtesy the Minor White Archive, Princeton University, copyright © 1952 by Minor White, renewed by The Trustees of Princeton University, all rights reserved; p. 63, excerpt by Minor White, reprinted courtesy the Minor White Archive, Princeton University, copyright © 1959 by Minor White, renewed by The Trustees of Princeton University, all rights reserved; p. 70, excerpt by Henry Miller, from *Plexus, The Rosy Crucifixion, Book Two,* New York: Grove Press, 1965; p. 77, excerpt by Nancy Newhall, reprinted courtesy the Minor White Archive, Princeton University, copyright © 1952 by Minor White, renewed by The Trustees of Princeton University, all rights reserved; p. 78, excerpt by Coomaraswamy, courtesy Yale Collection of American Literature, Beinecke Rare Book and Manuscript Library, Yale University.

IMAGE CREDITS

All photographs are courtesy and copyright © the artist unless otherwise indicated.

Page 9, photograph by Walter Chappell, courtesy Walter Chappell Estate, all rights reserved; p. 13, photograph by Minor White, reproduction courtesy the Minor White Archive, Princeton University, copyright © 1982 by The Trustees of Princeton University, all rights reserved; p. 14, photographs by Lynn Davis, courtesy Edwynn Houk Gallery, New York; p. 15, photograph by Ansel Adams, courtesy Ansel Adams Archive, Center for Creative Photography, copyright © Trustees of the Ansel Adams Publishing Rights Trust; p. 16, photograph by Charles Sheeler, courtesy Gilman Paper Company Collection; pp. 18–19, photograph by Thomas Struth, courtesy the artist and Marian Goodman Gallery; pp. 22–23, photographs by Bruce Davidson, courtesy and copyright © Bruce Davidson/Magnum Photos, Inc.; pp. 24–25, photographs by Sebastião Salgado, courtesy Amazonas Images; p. 26, photograph by Chris Steele-Perkins, courtesy Magnum Photos, Inc.; p. 27, photograph by Raghubir Singh, copyright © 1974 Raghubir Singh; p. 28, photograph by Henri Cartier-Bresson, courtesy Magnum Photos, Inc.; p. 29 (bottom), photograph by Alex Webb, courtesy Magnum Photos, Inc.; p. 30, photographs by Raghu Rai, courtesy Magnum Photos, Inc.; p. 33, photograph by Tina Modotti, courtesy Throckmorton Fine Art, New York; p. 34 (bottom), photograph by Larry Towell, courtesy Magnum Photos, Inc.; p. 35, painting by Gerhard Richter, courtesy Marian Goodman Gallery; p. 36, photograph by W. Eugene Smith, courtesy Collection Center for Creative Photography, The University of Arizona, Tuscon, copyright © The Heirs of W. Eugene Smith, courtesy Black Star, Inc., New York; p. 38, photograph by Brian Weil, courtesy Collection Center for Creative Photography, The University of Arizona, copyright © 2001 Brian Weil Estate; p. 39, photograph by Lee Miller, courtesy and copyright © Lee Miller Archives; pp. 40–41, photographs by Don McCullin, courtesy Contact Press Images; p. 49, photograph by Jonathan Saadah, courtesy the collection of Arlette and Gus Kayafas; p. 52, photographs by Pierre et Gilles, courtesy Galerie Jérôme de Noirmont, Paris; p. 53, photograph by Nam June Paik, courtesy the artist and Holly Solomon Gallery; p. 54, photograph by Walter Chappell, courtesy Walter Chappell Estate, all rights reserved; p. 55, photograph by Ralph Eugene Meatyard, courtesy Fraenkel Gallery, San Francisco, copyright © Estate of Ralph Eugene Meatyard; p. 56, photograph by David McDermott and Peter McGough, courtesy Galerie Jérôme de Noirmont, Paris; p. 57, photograph by W. Eugene Smith, courtesy Collection Center for Creative Photography, The University of Arizona, Tuscon, copyright © The Heirs of W. Eugene Smith, courtesy Black Star, Inc., New York; p. 58, photograph by Inge Morath, courtesy Magnum Photos, Inc.; p. 60, work by Robert Rauschenberg, courtesy the artist and Untitled Press, Inc; p. 61, photograph by Robert Mapplethorpe, courtesy the Robert Mapplethorpe Foundation, Inc., copyright © Estate of Robert Mapplethorpe; p. 62, photograph by Peter Hujar, courtesy Matthew Marks Gallery, copyright © Estate of Peter Hujar; pp. 64–65, photographs by Diane Arbus, courtesy Robert Miller Gallery, New York, copyright © Estate of Diane Arbus, 1971; pp. 68–69, photographs by Sally Mann, courtesy the artist and Edwynn Houk Gallery, New York; p. 70, photograph by Gianni Berengo Gardin, courtesy and copyright © Gianni Berengo Gardin—Contrasto/Matrix; p. 71, photograph by Dorothea Lange, courtesy and copyright © the Dorothea Lange Collection, Oakland Museum of California, City of Oakland. Gift of Paul S. Taylor; p. 74, photograph by Garry Winogrand, courtesy Fraenkel Gallery, San Francisco and Collection Center for Creative Photography, The University of Arizona, Tuscon, copyright © Estate of Garry Winogrand; p. 75, photograph by Ferdinando Scianna, courtesy and copyright © Magnum Distributions/Magnum Photos; p. 79, photograph by Barbara Morgan, courtesy and copyright © Barbara Morgan Archive.

All spreads from issues of *Aperture* are copyright © Aperture Foundation, Inc., except the following: page 4 (top), *Aperture* vol. 1, no. 1, 1952, pages 4–5, reproduction courtesy the Minor White Archive, Princeton University, copyright © 1952 by Minor White, renewed by The Trustees of Princeton University, all rights reserved; p. 7 (top), *Aperture* vol. 2, no. 4, 1953, pp. 30–31, reproduction courtesy the Minor White Archive, Princeton University, copyright © 1953 by Minor White, renewed by The Trustees of Princeton University, all rights reserved; p. 10, *Aperture* vol. 3, no. 4, 1955, pp. 20–21, reproduction courtesy the Minor White Archive, Princeton University, copyright © 1955 by Minor White, renewed by The Trustees of Princeton University, all rights reserved; p. 44 (top), *Aperture* vol. 1, no. 4, 1953, pp. 28–29, reproduction courtesy the Minor White Archive, Princeton University, copyright © 1953 by Minor White, renewed by The Trustees of Princeton University, all rights reserved; p. 47, *Aperture* vol. 6, no. 1, 1958, pp. 40–41, reproduction courtesy the Minor White Archive, Princeton University, copyright © 1958 by Minor White, renewed by The Trustees of Princeton University, all rights reserved.

Aperture: #168, Fall 2002 **TO SUBSCRIBE**: *Aperture* (ISSN 0003-6420) is published quarterly, in spring, summer, fall, and winter, at 20 East 23rd Street, New York, NY 10010. A one-year subscription (four issues) is $40 and a two-year subscription (eight issues) is $66. A subscription for four issues outside the United States is $60. Single copies may be purchased at $18.50 for most issues. Periodicals postage is paid at New York and additional offices. Postmaster: Send address changes to *Aperture*, P.O. Box 3000, Denville, NJ 07834. Address queries regarding subscriptions, renewals, or gifts to: *Aperture* Subscription Service, 1-866-457-4603. For U.K. subscriptions, contact Falsten Partnership at subscriptions@falsten.com or call (020) 88062301. Call (800) 221-3148 for information regarding newsstand distribution or to find out the nearest location where *Aperture* is sold.

Library of Congress Catalog Card No.: 58-30845. Printed by Sing Cheong Co., Ltd., Hong Kong. Duotone separations by Martin Senn. Color separations by Bright Arts (H.K.), Ltd., China.

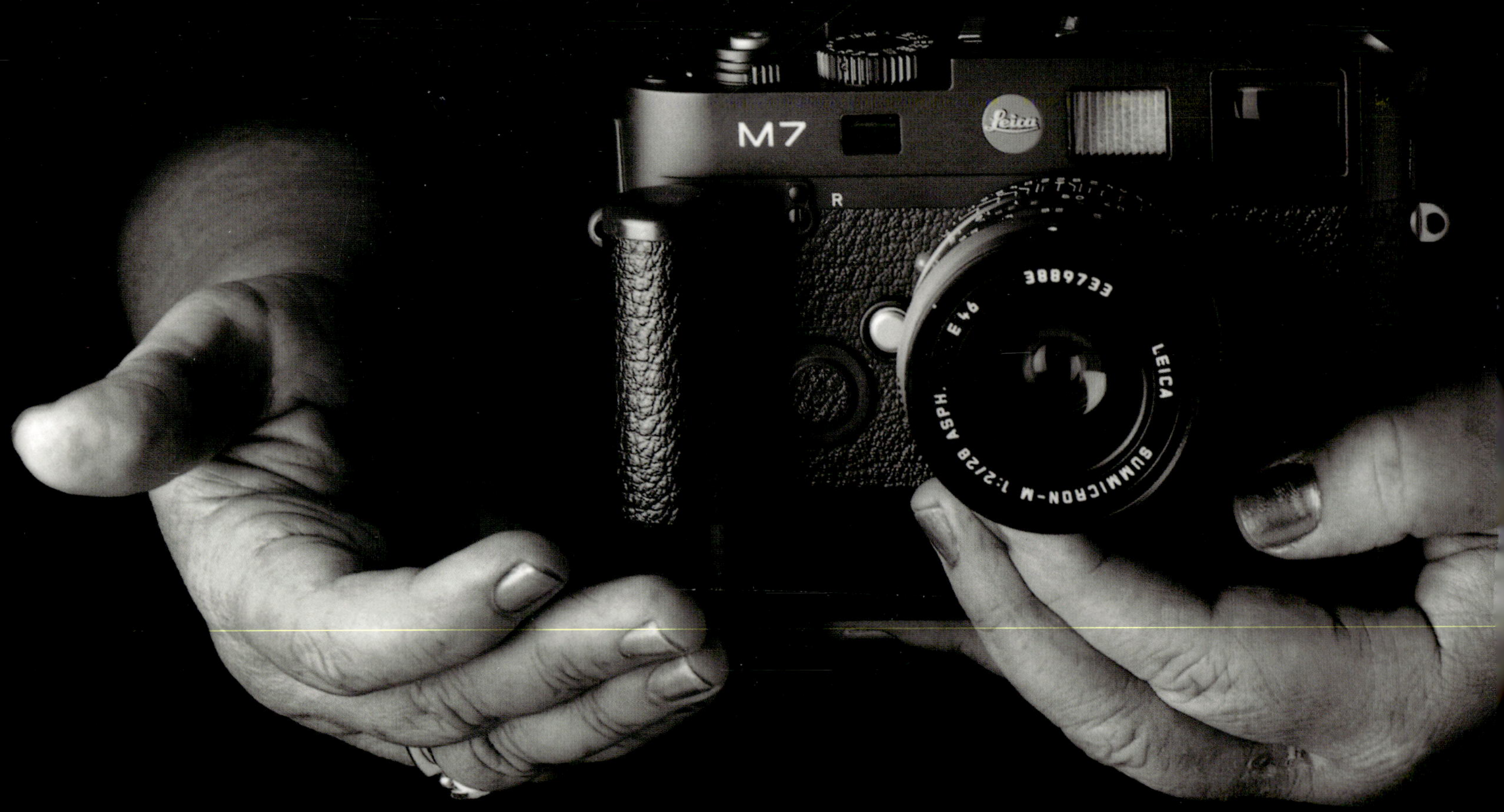